GHOST TOWNS
OF
THE SOUTHWEST

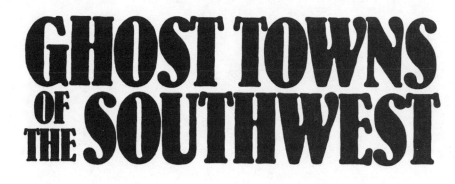

GHOST TOWNS OF THE SOUTHWEST

By Lambert Florin

PROMONTORY
PRESS

Published in 1992 by

Promontory Press
A division of LDAP, Inc.
386 Park Avenue South
New York, NY 10016

Promontory Press is a registered trademark of LDAP, Inc.
Published by arrangement with Darwin Publications
Abridged from Ghost Towns of the West

Library of Congress Catalog Card Number: 86-63844
ISBN: 0-88394-066-3

Printed in The United States of America

CONTENTS

WHAT IS A GHOST TOWN?

One of several dictionary definitions of "ghost" is "a shadowy semblance of its former self." We have elected to prefer this somewhat ambiguous phrase, because it accurately describes many towns on the borderline of being dead or alive. Most of the towns described and pictured in this book are "dead" ghosts, but some still have life, though nothing to compare with the lusty vigor they enjoyed in their heyday.

Some even have a future, and the shadowy remnants of a fascinating past are being sacrificed on the altar of a new strike, possibly of a newer metal such as Molybdenum. An example of this is Kokomo, Colorado. Here is a town full of interesting relics of Colorado's early mining days with a corner full of new buildings and developments.

Some have never really died but are much smaller than before, with a population sufficient to keep up a post office, a store or two and an eating place (and, of course, a tavern). Examples a r e Skamokawa, Washington; Shaniko, Oregon and Gem, Idaho. Many others still have a community spirit and hopes for a brighter future, perhaps more brilliant than the past.

Some are even crowded with people. The saloons are "revived," some buildings "restored" and in general are inflated with a sort of artificial respiration. Examples are Virginia City, Nevada and the town with the same name in Montana. These are well worth while, easily accessible and full of diversion, but they lack the charm of the deserted or nearly deserted places, for some, at least.

Our ideal is a town completely abandoned by all business and permanent residents, and many of the subjects included fall into this category.

GHOST TOWN ETIQUETTE

Such souvenirs as are found in the brush by the side of the road are legitimately carried home. Parts of buildings still standing, or furniture in them, we don't include in the souvenir category, however. The old towns are melting away too fast as it is.

One of the towns in our book, Shaniko, Oregon was written up in a local newspaper this year, and about the same time was a subject for a T. V. program. The results to the town were drastic. One of the tiny group of remaining inhabitants wrote to the newspaper as follows—"Today, your cameraman would find something new added to the panorama he viewed a few weeks ago," reads the letter. "The inhabitants have been forced to tack up 'No trespassing' signs, in order to preserve a bit of privacy and rights as property owners. Why? Because the public is carrying Shaniko away, piece by piece. . . . Among us are several who have had belongings of varied value, both sentimental and intrinsic, taken from their property, and the schoolhouse and surroundings have been devastated by souvenir-seekers. In short, our privacy has been invaded and we are irked to say the least . . ."

ARIZONA
GHOST TOWNS

BUMBLE BEE, ARIZONA

The prospectors were evidently more impressed with bumble bees than with Mr. Snyder for they changed the name of the settlement from Snyder's Station to Bumble Bee. Or it is possible they stumbled into bumble bee nests or as another story has it, they found Indians "as thick as bumble bees".

When W. W. Snyder settled in the valley there was plenty of water in the creek the year around with lots of lush pasture for his horses and cattle. There was also a crude road that penetrated the wild, "Indian infested" land. The term was Snyder's and the other whites', for of course the Indians were marauders for trying to drive the invaders from the Indian lands. And they were making some success of it when a small detachment of U.S. soldiers was sent into the valley to protect Snyder and other ranchers and prospectors to the good soil and water.

A stage line soon began irregular service and Snyder built a small hostelry and stable to accommodate travelers. The stop was known as Snyder's Station for many years. When gold was discovered in the adjacent Bradshaw Mountains, prospectors were soon dipping their pans in the creek.

Most gold discoveries were not made at Bumble Bee itself but in neighboring camps such as those along Turkey Creek — Golden Turkey, Cleator, Gloriana, the enormously rich Tip Top above Gillette, the Silver Prince, Black Warrior, Cougar, New Jersey and many more famous mines along the southwestern fringes of the Bradshaws. The Peck was outstanding. The first ten tons from that mine were sold to Prescott merchants for $10,000, so an old Prescott newspaper stated. Since the stage road to these areas led through Bumble Bee, the town shared a little of the prosperity.

Bumble Bee had gold of its own but the deposits were so rich a man could get no more than a little section the size of a blanket — hence a "blanket claim". From even this small area he might make $100 a day, for a few days. Some of the gravel beds large enough and lasting long enough to acquire names and an illusory fame were Chinese Bar, Portuguese Bar and the Dead Man. Even these were practically exhausted by the early 1900s and remained dormant until depression years when desperate men combed the sands for a few flakes of gold.

All through the years the town has tried to stay "by the side of the road", moving to follow survey realignments three times. At last it was by-passed so far by the Black Canyon highway it could not follow, now remains complacent on a good graveled side road.

PRESENT TOWN OF BUMBLE BEE was offered for sale in eastern newspapers, was purchased lock, stock and barrel by magazine publisher Charles E. Penn and wife Helen, who have restored it to original form.

DISTILLED FROM BLOOD AND COURAGE

Calabasas, Arizona

Oh yes, the old timer agreed, the Apaches were cruel, ruthless, bold and bloodthirsty. But he knew of one case where 200 of them were bitten by white men's bullets and none ever lived to retaliate. Well, there was proof of that too. Don Frederico Hulseman showed Peter Bady a string of what looked to him like dried apple slices, about three feet long. "Ears, my friend," said Don Frederico, "cut from those dead Apaches. See the gold and beaded earrings?"

In this part of southern Arizona and many areas of the southwest travelers take note of curious, spreading vines, each plant usually covering roughly about ten feet in diameter. Early in the season there will be many blossoms scattered along the vines, replaced in late summer by globular fruits about grapefruit size. When dry they are hollow except for seeds that rattle on shaking, leaves and other succulent parts disappearing to leave the hardshelled globes, now pale straw colored, conspicuous on the vines.

These are the wild form of Cucurbita Pepo, an inedible form of pumpkin. They grow in abundance in southern Arizona. Early Spanish explorers found the vines growing everywhere and in the Indians' field of corn, cultivated pumpkins. They called the village Calabasas, either for the little inedible gourds or table pumpkins. The native vines proved far more enduring and still flourish at the townsite long bare of almost any trace of busy life.

For several years following 1691 Father Kino spent most of his time traveling between his mis-

LONELY REMNANT of adobe building, likely last surviving trace of Calabasas with its dark, bloody history. Searching for old town best directions available led author to spot on banks of dry Santa Cruz River where large field of cotton flourished in full bloom. Spanish speaking Mexican workers disclaimed ever having heard of town but said this patch of cotton was called "Calabasas field." Beating thorny mesquite brush revealed this broken relic.

sion at San Xavier del Bac and the head mission at Dolores, Sonora. As a matter of convenience he later established a second mission at Guevavi (sometimes Guebabi). With a priest station here the Indian village of Calabasas became a more readily accessible *visita*.

In 1767 the Spanish government expelled all Jesuit priests from the new world including the area around Calabasas. By 1827 all Spanish, whether priests or ranch owners were expelled by the now dominant Mexican authorities, leaving missions and *visitas* fully vulnerable to murderous Apaches. Calabasas was reduced to little more than a tiny village, a few Mexicans working a gold mine nearby.

In 1842 the square leagues of land comprising Tumacacori, Calabasas and Guevavi were combined into one huge grant which, two years later, the state of Sonora sold to one Francisco Aguilar for $500. A coincidence that Aguilar was the brother-in-law of Manuel Gandra, Governor of Sonora?

During the next decade Gov. Gandra built and fortified a large hacienda at Calabasas, the most attractive site along the generously flowing Santa Cruz River. He stocked it with huge herds of cattle, horses and sheep, the watching Apaches holding back until the rancho was complete, then moving in for the kill. Driving off all stock for butchering and burning, they slaughtered some Mexicans and put the rest to flight. An American dragoon passing by in 1854 stopped there and later wrote, "... at the rancho de las Calabasas are the ruins of an old church with the altar still standing and the bell hanging in the belfry. The road from Tucson lay in the valley of the Santa Cruz as far as this ranch which is occupied by two Germans. A third brother has been killed by the Indians and all their cattle and horses have been stolen by the savages. The two brothers kept an awful old 'bachelor hall'."

Plenty of water for irrigation on good soil brought Indians and Mexicans back to occupy Calabasas during what proved to be only a short lull between Apache raids. Late in 1854 engineer Peter Bady, surveying the 32nd parallel for a rail line, was camped on the Sonoita when he was informed by two Mexicans recently escaped from Apache warriors that their captors were planning to attack Calabasas again and this time kill everybody. Bady took ten men and headed for the

town, meeting on the way sixty Mexican dragoons and forty Apache *mansos* (tamed or domesticated Apaches) who joined his party. Reaching the ranch, now headed by Don Frederico Hulseman, Bady made known the impending danger and instructed Hulseman to his plan, retreating with his forces to heavy brush cover a few hundred yards from the ranch.

About mid-day the watching Hulseman spotted advancing Apaches and blew a high-pitched call on the cavalry bugle as prearranged. Bady and men responded at once, mounting and charging directly into the center of the two hundred Apaches. He later reported, "No cry of mercy was given and no mercy shown." Most of the invaders were killed outright by the Mexican dragoons, the wounded finished off by the mansos, leaving not one survivor. Not long after the slaughter Bady received a dinner invitation from Don Frederico. "Before we eat," the host said, "let me show you something." What Bady saw in the courtyard was the three-foot string of dried Apache ears.

Some protection was being extended by U.S. troops, the territory having become part of the United States the year before. In 1861 the soldiers were removed to fight in the Civil War and the town of the pumpkins was again left to the mercy of the Apaches. In 1864 peripatetic reporter J. Ross Browne wrote to his magazine, Harper's, that he

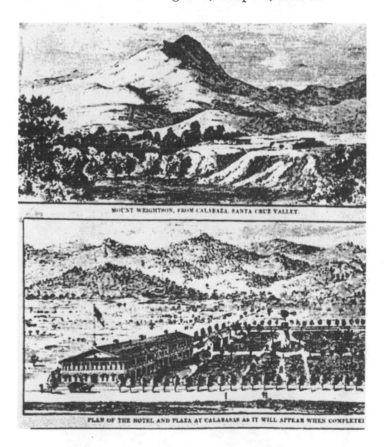

MOUNT WRIGHTSON, FROM CALABAZA, SANTA CRUZ VALLEY.

PLAN OF THE HOTEL AND PLAZA AT CALABASAS AS IT WILL APPEAR WHEN COMPLETED

DRAWINGS are part of promotional spread appearing in New York **Daily Graphic,** Oct. 18, 1878. Variation in caption spelling of Calabasas persists to present day. Form using letter "z" is original Castilian spelling first applied to village. Later Mexican spelling uses "s".

had visited the valley, a place of rich soil, ample irrigation and surrounded by mines of copper and gold. "It might be made profitable in the hands of some enterprising American . . . at present, however, military protection in the country is worthless owing to the incursion of the Apaches." He recounted the well known story of Mrs. Page, daughter of early settler "Old Man" Pennington, of how she was captured, tortured and thrown into a gulch for dead, and how after several days of near unconsciousness she managed to crawl to a point where she was seen and rescued.

By 1878 nearby Tucson was in the throes of a boom, fast building up with stores and saloons for travelers arriving at the Old Pueblo. At this time two men from San Francisco chose Calabasas as a delightful place for a luxury hotel. They were John H. Curry, ex-judge, and Charles P. Sykes, newspaper publisher, both visionaries. They went to ex-Gov. Gandra and brother-in-law Aguilar and from them purchased the site for about $6,000.

In late 1878 Tucson papers noted there was much activity at the old town, that the whole area was being surveyed and a hotel building started. Col. Sykes was quoted as saying his hotel would be two-storied and made of brick being fired in the vicinity as the stables and corral would also be. G. W. Atkinson, the best brick man in San Francisco had been hired to oversee the project. Sykes sent out glittering brochures and worked up much enthusiasm for his new hotel. On the negative side the Tombstone *Epitaph* sneered at what it called "Pumpkinville," fully expecting Sykes to

have heavy ocean going vessels plying the Santa Cruz right to the town, unloading world merchandise at its teeming docks.

Yet in spite of these and other spoofing attitudes with dire warnings that the Apaches would stop the building, the hotel was finished. In October of 1882 Sykes arranged for a large delegation from Tucson to come to Calabasas for the grand opening, hiring the Tucson Brass Band to serenade the party all the way. The group left Tucson at 5 a.m. and finally arrived in Calabasas dog-tired in the evening, the account adding, "as only water was available to drink along the way."

Col. Sykes welcomed the party with open arms and uncorked bottles. He fed the delegates roasts of mutton, chicken, beef and game, including wild turkey, quail, plover and British snipe. After supper the party observed floors covered with Brussels carpet, solid black walnut furniture in every room. Plied with more spirits the party danced until midnight. Sightseeing the next day, all returned to Tucson singing praise for Sykes' hotel, "the best between San Francisco and Denver."

Not long after the successful grand opening the colonel began to miss some of his cattle and after several more depredations the losses were traced to the Apaches. One night they were so bold as to enter the brick corral and drag away a pair of blooded black carriage horses. Probably unable to ride them the savages killed the blacks not far from the hotel. Next they kidnaped three members of the Peck family in the area and brutally murdered them. In spite of all this Col. Sykes carried on, filling his registers with the names of some of the most prominent people in the country.

But the end of the dream was coming up sharply. In 1894 the Court of Private Land Claims voided all Spanish land grants along the border. The action wiped out Boston syndicates operating mines leased from Col. Sykes, townsite of Calabasas and hotel. Sykes died on a trip to New York City, his widow living in a room in the hotel until her death in 1910 and the heirs made their homes in houses near it, using some rooms for hay storage after the mother passed away. In 1927 fire broke out in the stored fodder and the entire building burned to the ground, bricks and other unburnables hauled away by Indians and ranchers. Calabasas, distilled from blood and courage, is today almost invisible.

PUZZLING ARRANGEMENT of wooden posts few feet from adobe ruin at edge of Calabasas cotton field. Framed is what appears to be same peak called Mount Wrightson in old sketch. Named for Prof. W. Wrightson, early historian, peak often called Old Baldy now, is highest in Santa Cruz County. One of author's few clues in locating Calabasas was lining up peak as in old drawing of town.

CHARLESTON, ARIZONA

It was Red Dog in Alfred Henry Lewis' fiction, historians called it "a place of bloody violence", to Nell Murbarger it was Devil's Den and Muriel Sibell Wolle said: "If the corpse had a gun on him and the fatal shot came from the front, you didn't look for the killer."

All this and much more was Charleston which was connected to Mexico by the San Pedro River and to Tombstone by a constant stream of ore wagons. The ten-mile stretch of the river supplied the water, which Tombstone did not have, to mill the rich gold ore and for like purpose accounted also for the other adobe-built towns along the river — Millville and Contention City.

Perhaps the first white man to build a shelter here was Frederick Brunkow, a German scientist who left his native land under a cloud and wound up in Arizona doing odd jobs. But the School of Mines at Freiburg, Saxony, prepared him for a job with the Sonora Exploring and Mining Co. and he was valuable in locating several rich silver veins. About 1858 Brunkow found one of his own but his efforts ended with death at the hands of his own peons.

In 1879 Richard Gird and Ed Schieffelin formed the Tombstone Mining and Milling Co. with the help of Gov. Safford. Schieffelin was familiar with the Brunkow location and its advantages as a mill site, having worked for a time in those diggings. Gird agreed with him and a ten-stamp mill was built on the east bank of the San Pedro, water reaching it via a wooden flume from a dam constructed a mile south. Milling activity centered here to be called Millville, the town growing up across the stream known as Charleston.

Strictly a company town, Charleston was solidly constructed of the prevailing adobe material, some buildings with wooden floors and plastered walls.

CHARLESTON is in complete ruin, remnants of once thriving town hard to find. Buildings like these, of stone instead of common adobe have endured in part. Area once supported good stand of pasture grass, now grows drought-enduring scraggly stand of thorny mesquite with spines that often draw blood from too careless ghost town explorer. If and when projected Charleston Dam is completed, San Pedro River's trickle will be converted to vast lake inundating site of Charleston.

MOST IMPOSING RUINS of Charleston-Millville complex are those of Richard Gird's "Big House", standing conspicuously on rise above San Pedro River. Rock foundation may have aided drainage, helping preserve ruins beyond life of others.

Hardly had the town been officially laid out in the winter of 1878-9 when it began its career as headquarters for bandits, horse thieves, murderers — at least in the public fancy, nourished by many writers of fact and fiction, notably called Red Dog in Alfred Henry Lewis' stories in an Eastern newspaper. Any number of reputable historians refer to Charleston as a place of bloody violence. Alma Ready said the town literally lived and died to the sound of gunfire and quoting Muriel Sibell Wolle in THE BONANZA TRAIL: "No one seemed disturbed when dead men lay in the street. If the corpse had a gun on him and the fatal shot had come from the front you didn't look for the killer. Guns made the law and men had to react in a split second." James G. Wolf who arrived in Charleston in 1883 wrote: "There were four saloons going twenty-four hours a day. All kinds of gambling houses operated continuously. There were lots of naughty girls living close to the saloons. . . When paydays occurred at Fort Huachuca many of the soldiers came to Charleston to drink. . . . . ."

Nell Murbarger says in her GHOSTS OF THE ADOBE WALLS: "Here, if we could believe even half

that has been written about the place, was a second Bodie, an embryo Dodge City, a short-lived Devil's Den where dead men littered the streets and gunsmoke drifted over the land like smog."

The other side of the coin is presented by Mrs. Mary Wood who with her husband moved to the town in 1880. The Murbarger book quotes a Tombstone EPITAPH interview with her in 1929 when she said: "If you came to Charleston looking for trouble there were plenty of citizens who would have supplied you with any amount of it . . . but the honest, law abiding citizen went his way with little if any greater hazards than he faces today in any large city". It may be that Mrs. Wood was unaware of some illicit activities in her community, or as Miss Murbarger suggests, the town came nearer its image of toughness as it grew older. There is one singular fact, according to Mrs. Wood, that while $1,380,336 worth of bullion was shipped out from the mill in one year's time, "not a dollar of it was ever molested by highwaymen."

The two noisy stamp mills ran day and night except when a breakdown occurred, even on Sundays. Eastern backers of the operation heard about

8

this desecration of the Sabbath and protested to Dick Gird and manager Wood. They were invited to come to Millville and watch the results of a trial layoff over Sunday. They came, and on Sunday they watched with horror as miners indulged in all-day sprees in the town's saloons. And on Monday they watched the bleary-eyed miners stagger back to work, noted the difficulties of reactivating the cooled-down equipment and left town, convinced the men should be busy every day. How many of Charleston's carousers took advantage of one unique feature is not known but Alma Ready in an ARIZONA HIGHWAYS article writes of the rare luxury of drinks "on the rocks", the town being the proud possessor of one of the first ice machines in Arizona Territory, even supplying the commodity to Tombstone.

In its busiest period Charleston had four general mercantile stores, meat market, drug store, with two restaurants and two laundries operated by Chinese. Mrs. Hughes' Boarding House, Eagle and Royal Hotels served citizens and transients as did saloons, estimated as five to thirteen. Regular visits to these drink emporiums by such notables as the McLowery bunch, Clanton gang and Johnny Ringo did not contribute to law and order.

The town had no jail and Constable James Burnett apparently paid himself. Just when a drunk was rowdy enough to arrest is not known but when a public nuisance was collared, Burnett held him at the point of a sawed-off shotgun, tried, convicted and fined him on the spot, pocketing the proceeds.

As for the usual lynchings with stories of twitching bodies dangling from trees and derricks, it seems Charleston only came close to one. A disgruntled employee at the Gird mill, Johnny-Behind-The-Deuce whipped out his gun and shot chief engineer Henry Schneider fatally. Rumblings of a lynching were stymied by removing him to Tombstone and later to Tucson where he broke jail and vanished.

There was a school in Charleston and legend has it that pupils were accustomed to carrying guns like papa did. While supposedly studying the temptation was great to wing a buzzard flying by the window or pin a fly to the wall. But one Professor Wetherspoon had stricter ideas than his prede-

YUCCAS GROW at Pick-Em-Up stage stop, appropriately marked by ancient trunk. Tiny mining community between Tombstone and Charleston was stop only if stage passengers stood beside road to flag down drivers who were instructed to "Pick 'em up".

cessors. He installed a shelf in the cloakroom and ordered all boys to park their six-guns there.

Another tale concerns the largest bordello. School children would wander to the place after school to look in the windows at whatever was going on. When several of the girls announced at home they had decided what to be when they grew up, owners of the house were ordered to move it. The new location was near Fort Huachuca. Christmas came often for the soldiers.

Whether Charleston or neighboring Tombstone should rightly be termed the toughest town in Arizona Territory may be debated for years to come. Contender Charleston offers at least one well-authenticated incident for its side — the murder of young M. R. Peel.

Across the river stood the immense adobe structures of the Tombstone Mining and Milling Co. including offices and residences facing the river, one room containing a safe built of brick. One evening in 1882 the popular company engineer — Peel — was sitting in the office talking with three friends when two masked men threw open the door. Both intruders raised their rifles and fired point blank at Peel, one slug entering his body, the other bury-

ing itself in the adobe wall. Still without a word, the two murderers fled to their horses held by a third man and disappeared in the darkness. Peel's funeral was held in Tombstone with burial in its famous Boot Hill.

The killing seems to be explained only as a boner in a badly planned payroll robbery attempt. One of the gunmen, identified as William Grounds, was shot and killed the following day while "resisting arrest". The other, Zwing Hunt, though wounded, lived to be placed in the Tombstone jail, later recovering and escaping.

Charleston, spawned with Tombstone, died with Tombstone. When Tombstone's already declining mines began filling with water in the '80s, production of ore slowed to a standstill, leaving little excuse for Charleston to linger on. On top of that, the smaller town's once highly profitable underground trade with Mexico was now cut off by the border town of Nogales.

But it was a caprice of nature that wrecked Charleston — a major earthquake occurring May 3, 1887. Thirty minutes of continued shocks reduced the adobe buildings to rubble and the town was never rebuilt. Its birth as a company town had been sudden, its destruction complete in one half hour.

THIS ROOM in Tombstone Mining and Milling Co. buildings housed company safe, constructed of fire brick and closed by substantial iron door. Door has long since vanished but location of safe is shown here, marked by bricks differing from larger unfired adobe ones.

CHLORIDE, ARIZONA

Here is a town whose classification is dubious because it has changed its status from living to dead and back again several times. Right now it is in-between, with plenty of the old for interest and with a certain amount of respiration not too noticeable.

In this last category is the little, newish building not more sizable than many a living room. It fronts on the main street and bears the proud sign "Chloride City Library." The movie house, on the other hand, shows a view of sagebrush and cacti through the boxoffice. And so it goes with Chloride. One of its ups was a good turquoise mine, owned by Tiffany of New York. One of its downs was the calamity, common to all silver towns, of the collapse in silver values.

Just when a big silver boom had pumped the veins of Chloride full of blood, the deflation period set in. This began in 1884, and when it ended by the demonitization of silver in 1893, Chloride's collapse was complete, at least as of then.

RELIC OF LATER BOOM was movie house. Through once ornate entrance one now sees a framed view of sagebrush and abandoned shacks.

CLEATOR, ARIZONA

The story of Cleator, the town, is the story of Cleator, the man. It was his enterprise that built it and his right to sell it. You could have bought it in 1947 and it is there today to see.

James Patrick Cleator was born June 12, 1870, in Dhoon, Machold Parrish, on the Isle of Man in the Irish Sea. He went to school for a time but later admitted he "knew it all" when he reached the sixth grade. At 12 he went to sea as a cabin boy on the fishing boats and at 15 he was in the crews of grimy coal boats plying the coast from Newcastle to London. After working in a Thames River shipyard for several months he signed on, at 16, as able seaman on a ship hauling iron from Spain.

In 1887 young Cleator was a hand on the clipper ship *Arthur Stone* making a voyage around the Horn to Chile, loading nitrates there for San Francisco and flour there for Ireland. Now he was 19 and Jimmie knew the salty sea was not for him but the New World was. As a passenger he took ship to Halifax, train to Winnipeg and worked his way by odd jobs to San Francisco.

There was gold talk in the air and the erstwhile sailor turned to prospecting, finding a gold claim in California in 1898 and selling it for $10,000. Then he headed for Mexico, Chihuahua Province where he found nothing interesting and prospected various sections of Arizona. Attracted to British

OVER ALL VIEW OF CLEATOR—Town is placed in desert country at foot of pine-clad Bradshaws. Highest peak, Mount Wasson, over 8,000 feet, is in background. In center is original store and saloon. Left, nearer foreground, is stone schoolhouse built in WPA days. Original two-room schoolhouse is now home and rock shop of Phil and Audrey Reasoner. Desert growth is abundant, **Opuntia**, known as prickly pear, seen in clumps everywhere. Plant in left foreground is **Yucca**, bearing spikes of beautiful white flowers resembling lilies to which it is related. Author's camper is accidently left in photo.

ONE OF MANY STONE CABINS in hills behind Cleator. Primitive structure is typical of many shelters built of available material before lumber came in. Spiky plant in foreground is **Agave**, each leaf normally armed with stout, extremely sharp spike. Some have been trimmed off as plant has encroached on trail, wounding passers by.

Columbia he found the placers along the rivers long exhausted, so returned to the country he liked best, Arizona. Cleator found the Bradshaw Mountains to his liking and remained among them the rest of his life.

In 1902 a railroad was being built from Mayer to the area near the summit of Mount Wasson in the pine-covered Bradshaws where the fabulous Crowned King mine was being exploited. In the foothills the railroad passed the big Golden Turkey mine named for the many wild turkeys in the state. At the point of convenient access to this mine the rail line established loading platforms called Tur-

key Siding. A considerable crew of men was required to handle freight from and equipment to the Golden Turkey and several other mines along Turkey Creek. Some of the men were stationed there permanently, shacks and bunkhouses being built for them. One "Lev" Nellis set up a saloon and added a store beside it.

On New Year's Day, 1905, James Patrick Cleator walked into the saloon, had a drink and struck up conversation with Nellis. The two men found much in common and before the day was over formed a partnership, Cleator buying half-ownership. Lev had always wanted to raise cattle,

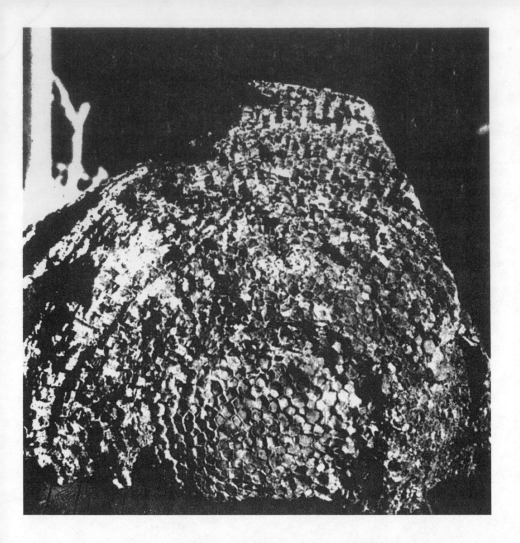

STRANGE "ROCK" is owned by Phil and Audrey Reasoner of Cleator. Object seems to be petrified hornet's nest which it strongly resembles in size, form, even color. Phil Reasoner mined in most of shafts and tunnels of New Mexico and Arizona, was forced to retire from effects of long continued breathing of dust from broken and crushed ore. He and wife now run interesting rock shop in Cleator.

had been too busy with the merchandising but now, with amiable and well-liked Cleator to run the store and saloon, he could turn most of his attention to the small herd he already owned.

In ten years both branches of the business had flourished to the point that both partners decided to separate, each taking over his favorite operation. By this time the settlement had grown to need a post office. Although known as Turkey Siding, the word "turkey" was in common use in the area, a new post office at Turkey Creek not far away. Cleator applied for a post office at his store and authorities gave it his name.

With the mines going well, Cleator also prospered as a supply base for them and its principal citizen took advantage of the situation to include real estate in his business. He built a number of small houses, renting and selling them. In all of them he installed the newfangled element—electricity—and piped in clear spring water. Cleator is in the desert but close to the high Bradshaws where rainfall is abundant.

At 77, James Cleator made a decision. He had been married years before to Pearl Hunt, the couple having a son and daughter. Now he would retire. Accordingly he advertised his town for sale, lock, stock and barrel, in the ARIZONA REPUBLIC. Other newspapers over the country caught the romance of the town for sale idea, repeating the ad with stories of the colorful life of James Patrick Cleator. A flood of letters came in, sometimes as many as fifty a day, but few of the curious wanted to buy a town and no sale was consummated. One newspaper reporter asked what he would like to do if he found a buyer. "I'd fix up an auto rig," Cleator answered, "and see the country."

The ruddy old gentleman died at 85 without fulfilling this wish. His widow, who also reached 85 in January of 1964, still lives in the town her husband built, retaining a keen memory for names, dates and events.

14

CONTENTION CITY, ARIZONA

"What is it?" asked the grizzled miner from Tombstone when the waitress in a Contention City cafe set a glass in front of him, informing him it was water. "Oh, that," said the miner. "I've heerd. Even tuk a bath in it onct. Say, miss — will you put it in a bottle or sumpin so I can show it to the boys down home."

Water was scarce enough in Tombstone for ore milling purposes and Contention City was one of the most northerly of the several towns established along a ten-mile stretch of the San Pedro River to process the Tombstone ores and took its name from the big mine owned by partners Ed Schieffelin and Richard Gird. Arizona Pioneer Historical Society records explain the use of the name "Contention":

"Hank Williams was one of the thousands of prospectors who flocked to Tombstone when the word got around that Ed Schieffelin had struck it rich. His camp was close to that of Schieffelin and partner Dick Gird. One of his mules got away and in trailing it he noticed that the animal's halter chains were scraping the dirt off of rich ore. He immediately staked a claim, the location of which was hotly contested by Gird. Williams could not have been very positive about his rights in the dispute; he was persuaded to sell out to Schieffelin and Gird. They developed the claim in question, naming the mine Contention."

As soon as the mill site was established just above the San Pedro on the east bank the town site was bought early in September, 1879 by D. T. Smith and John McDermott. By the middle of the month the partners had surveyed the town, within a week were selling lots and up jumped a hotel, saloon, restaurant, laundry and a hodge podge of shanties. The mill on the bluff, 170 feet long with a depth of 142 feet, was being built and three more expected.

In a year or two the place grew to be a solid city, most buildings of adobe, the available material. By that time there were more businesses with a rash of saloons. The most imposing structure facing the "waterfront" was a railroad station, Contention having achieved the proud distinction of being the railhead for the New Mexico, Arizona and Sonora Railroad. While the line was building, contractors and crews had their headquarters in the town and if there was any danger of Dull Care showing up, the boys kept it safely out in the desert.

When William Henry Bishop visited Contention City in 1882, he wrote of the experience in his book MEXICO AND HER LOST PROVINCES. The section concerning the milling town is reprinted in ARIZONA GUIDE: "We changed horses and lunched at Contention City. One naturally expected a certain amount of belligerency in such a place, but none appeared on the surface during our stay. There were

WHAT BUILDING? While rather extensive, ruins give little or no clue as to nature or purpose of building. Low angle of sunlight brings out surface texture of unfired adobe bricks.

RUINS OF Contention Mining and Milling Co., described as having extended 170 feet along side of rocky cliff. Diligent, thorn-harassed search reveals many remains of wood beams, stamp pistons, rusting tools, cables.

plenty of saloons, the Dew Drop and the Headlight among others, and at the door of one of them a Spanish senorita smoked a cigarette and showed her white teeth.

"Contention City is the seat of the stamp mills for crushing ore which is brought to Tombstone. The latter place is without sufficient water power. The stamps are heavy beams which drop on the mineral on the mortar and pestle plan, with a continuous roar, by night as well as by day. 'That's the music I like to hear', said our driver gathering up his reins. 'There ain't no band ekils it' "

Today Contention is a silent place except at night when coyotes croon their spine-tingling wails,

sounds very different from that of crashing stamps. An unmarked dirt road approaches a small turning area on the west bank of the San Pedro. Peering from the mesquite brush lining the river banks, the ghost town hunter can sight the remnants of the railroad depot on the other side. One swims the stream, wades or jumps over it, depending on the season, crosses several sand bars — and there is what is left of the town. No building remains intact, the depot only partly preserved. Many adobe ruins are encountered and many mesquite thorns. The mill ruins lay back against the bluff, only foundations and rotting beams remaining.

If the weather is wet the advice is to stay away, this reporter learning the lesson the hard way. It is impossible to get traction on slippery adobe and while wheels are spinning, the sticky stuff piles up on fenders and undercarriage. And several dips in the road fill rapidly with any fall of water.

CROWN KING, ARIZONA

Just how was an army officer going to take time to work a gold claim? Maybe somebody smarter than he was had an easy answer but prospector A. F. Place, now an officer stationed at Fort Whipple, couldn't see one. The claim on the slopes of Mount Wasson in Arizona's Bradshaw Mountains did not offer too much but Place had to work it to keep it.

With some diligence he found an idle prospector, provided him with shovels, drilling and blasting tools and against his better judgment, paid him in advance. The man started for the claim through Tiger Camp, later Bradshaw City, and spotted a saloon where the doors seemed always to swing in. So he delegated his assignment and tools to two bull whackers and proceeded to relax.

The pair set to work on the claim and soon got down to hard rock. "Well, I guess it's about time you shot a hole," said one. The other looked blank. "Hell, I though you were the dynamite expert. I couldn't drill a hole let alone load it."

Falling back on the shovels they put in time on one spot and another. Toward evening they gathered up a few pieces of rock and walked back to the Tiger saloon where they found the prospector thoroughly mellow. "Nothing but these here pirates", the bull whackers reported." Jumping out of the fog, the prospector whooped: "Pyrites, hell — that's gold!" Such was the first discovery in the district and others would be richer.

Newspapers of that day gave such news full play and one of Prescott's flung banner lines across its pages, February 6, 1899: "The Richest Strike In The History Of Arizona!" and almost as heavy headlines followed: "Ore that runs $180,000 to the ton." Another mine in the Bradshaws was covered in the next line, only a little less black: "The Riches of The Peck Pale Before The Wealth In The Crowned King Mine!"

This splatter of ink stemmed from a letter written by Lester Jackson of the nearby War Eagle mine, just north of the Crowned King property. Jackson had descended the shaft to the 500-foot level, taken a "grab sample" and the assay had re-vealed the fabulous values. The newspaper article quieted down to continue: "Mr. Jackson states that the sample was taken from a 10-inch chute of ore. He does not state the extent of the chute. Much excitement prevails all through the Bradshaws over the strike which is the greatest bona fide find in the history of Western quartz mining."

The paper's glowing reports failed to state the difficulty encountered with much of Crowned King ore. From the very first mills had trouble extracting the gold which assays showed was there. The first samplings of ore sent down by burro to the mills by the river proved so obdurate that run-of-the-mine ore was refused, mills accepting only less refractory material. Since burro-back transportation was expensive and slow, much ore was cast aside on the dumps. Later a railroad angled down the mountain as steeply as possible to where the wheels lost traction, then went through a series of switchbacks with the little train reversing itself on every hairpin turn.

By this time ore was being taken out at deeper levels and was improving in quality. Yet much of it

PHIL ANDREWS REVISITS MILL and assay office where he worked thirty-five years ago, was never able to recover gold values in ore discarded long ago as refractory. Scene is in Bradshaw Mountains named for David Bradshaw, pioneer who came to area from California where as member of Bear Flag party he was instrumental in capturing Sonoma, California, in 1846. Bradshaws at these higher levels are covered with dense timber, mostly pine.

ANDERSON'S SALOON, wild rendezvous of miners and prospectors in uninhibited early days of Crown King. Downstairs had large dance floor with bar at right, upper floor having central hallway with rooms for dance hall girls. Saloon had tamed down in days of town's rebirth when attempts were made to recover gold in dumps, but to Phil Andrews and other young, single men saloon was "off limits."

was still being thrown aside as too hard to mill. From time to time mining experts would cast covetous eyes at Crowned King ore but even as more modern methods of recovery came into use a big proportion was rejected either at mine or mill. While usage was shortening its name to Crown King piles of "good ore" remained on the dumps and became a legend into modern times. These were the times of Phil Andrews.

Having just graduated from college with a degree in chemistry, Stanley Phillips Andrews was ready for a career. One of his closest friends in San Diego in 1928 was Arthur Kipp, whose father was a mining engineer and friend of the senior Stanley Phillips Andrews. Young Phil was approached by Foster Kipp to take the job of laboratory technician and assistant in the assay office at the Crown King mine. The properties had been closed and abandoned for many years but the dumps of valuable ores were still tempting and Kipp thought he had figured out ways and means of converting them into money. He had backers ready to invest in a quarter million dollar mill at the site, another quarter mil-

lion in equipment and men to work over the old dumps. Previous assays of it ranged from $520 to $540 a ton and now it was estimated there were two and a half million dollars in the dump which could be worked profitably.

Of course the road was a hazard. Years before the railroad had been taken out and an automobile road built over the grade which had some comparatively gentle curves but the same precarious hairpin turns where the switchbacks had been. But it was the old trestles that raised the back hair. Planks were laid on these, barely wide enough for tires of cars which were Model Ts and later Model As. The spindly trestles that spanned deep canyons were but one car width, one of them having a sharp curve in the center, a driver honking his horn vigorously before venturing onto the span. All materials for the

CORNER OF DANCE HALL, Anderson's Saloon. Pancho Villa "got his start" as woodchopper at Crown King mine. When winter snows were deep and wood inaccessible, inveterate poker player Villa sought this cozy spot near stove.

new mill had to be hauled over these death-defying spans.

When Phil Andrews arrived for work he found about fifty people in the reactivated town. He had dinner at the fixed-up mess hall and bunked with several other young fellows in a small frame and sheet metal shack dubbed the "Y.M.C.A." The rest of the crew were all married.

Although actual assay work was new to him the process was familiar and he soon mastered the art of "bucking down" a batch of hard ore on the block, to "quarter" it again and again with a frame with two metal dividers to obtain a "quantitative analysis" by saving one quarter in each operation and discarding the rest. The weight of the sample saved was carefully compared with that of the shining silver and gold "button" which resulted from roasting the powdered ore, giving the values per ton. Silver and gold could be separated for exact measuring.

Life after work was somewhat dull except for Saturday nights in the town where Phil and the other single fellows found a preponderance of girls, as most boys old enough to leave home were at jobs in Phoenix or away at school. There was a weekly dance in the old schoolhouse that attracted the local young people and ranchers from "below" who drove twenty miles or more even over the hair-raising trestles. The school desks would be moved against the wall, floor dusted with wax and Victrola started. There would be "Two Black Crows" and "Yes, We Have No Bananas" until things got going then waltzes and fox trots until the small hours — a family affair rather than a wild west or mining camp dance, everybody having a good time without too much drinking. It could be a man thought he needed a clear head for driving on a road that included two planks on a spidery trestle over a deep canyon.

But things were not going well at the mill. Although Phil Andrews' assays continued to show the same good values, "we just weren't recovering," he says. "The values weren't going into the tailings either and we never did find out why the gold didn't show in the concentrates." The absentee backers be-

gan to think something was wrong and made a series of changes. Foster Kipp was discharged, Tomlinson had a chance to try his method and when nothing came of this, Earl Cranz was made manager and he tried his method which also failed. At this point the entire crew was let out and the operation ended.

Later other companies, or perhaps the same one, tried to extract Crown King's stubborn gold. One possibly had some success, as evidenced by a considerable pile of tailings, but at least three-fourths of the dump remains intact. When the WPB stopped gold mining in 1942 all further attempts at conversion were also stopped. Crown King today is occupied sparsely by a new non-mining group of summer visitors. The mountain refuge is a pleasant spot being about seven thousand feet high, cool in summer and shaded by whispering pines.

STAIRS USED BY MALE CUSTOMERS of girls in Anderson's Saloon. No girls now — hardly any stairs.

19

COPPER IN APACHELAND

Dos Cabezas, Arizona

The old town of Dos Cabezas lies sleeping in an easy hollow between two low mountain ranges. Conspicuous on the summit of one and directly above the near-deserted camp are the twin granite knobs that give the town and range the name, Dos Cabezas, Spanish for "Two Heads." Hardy Spanish explorers named it as they did many noticeable landmarks in the early 1500s when they scoured the southwest seeking the fabled Seven Cities of Cibola.

Later Mexicans forced the native Chiricahua Apaches from the area and after the end of the war with Mexico and acquisition through the Gadsden Purchase, the country was opened up to white settlers. The first party to camp at Dos Cabezas Spring was composed of soldiers under command of the Capt. Richard Stoddard Elwell who became a Confederate officer of some note. He found the spring of good water directly on the emigrant trail, originally an Indian trail, and camped there before the Gadsden Act was ratified. Later he returned to establish the first stage station in the area, a building erected close to Elwell's Spring of gushing water. Some of the tired emigrants stopped at this sign of civilization and refused to go on.

They were easy prey for the Apaches who pillaged and plundered in a reign of terror that whites seemed as unable to repel as Mexicans had earlier. At the end of eighteen months, sixteen stages and drivers failed to get to the Spring, almost certainly having fallen victims to the savages. The burned remains of one stage was located nearby, the nude body of one man bearing more than a hundred inch-deep burns made by fire brands. The station then closed down. Several others attempted to operate it, Jim Birch being one who held off the Indians until 1858. Then came John Butterfield who made stage coach history. Precious metals were being worked near Cabezas and in 1858 he located his new stage stop a quarter mile from the old spring site, nearer the nucleus of what was rapidly becoming a town.

By this time Dos Cabezas was a center for prospectors, some of them just passing through, others finding traces of metal in the nearby hills. Several small mines were operating and "home made" mills established. With Elwell's Spring no longer adequate for the increased population and too far from the new "city center", a well was dug which proved to be a large success, the water table showing at shallow depths. Every family had a handy supply of water in the back yard, each well equipped with a hand windlass and wooden bucket at the end of a rope.

About 1906 a man known only as "Old Man Mitchell" ran across a rich vein of copper just north of town near the foot of the range. The simple prospector had neither strength nor money to develop his claim, but talk about it reached another man who though also lacking money, had initiative. T. N. McCauley bought the property and then searched out wealthy, influential men who organized the Mascot Copper Company, Inc.

The new company installed the most modern equipment at the mine and built a modern complex near it to house officials and personnel. Dormitories for store employees flanked a movie house, grade school, cafeteria, store, dairy and numerous other facilities. A generator supplied electricity. All structures utilized the easily obtainable adobe and were plastered neatly white. Mexican laborers did the work being familiar with adobe construction. Although development of housing had gone on at top speed, adobe took time and all manner of tents and shacks went up to temporary use of mine and office workers and their families.

For twenty years the Mascot was big news in mining journals. The company built a smelter that cost many thousands, a new powerhouse about a million. Irked at having to haul copper to the nearest railhead at Wilcox, Mascot built its own railroad to that point.

For a time the town had its own post office. Its biggest business was sorting out the daily mail orders with money and checks for stock, and mailing out gilt-edged certificates. Then this stopped abruptly for shortly after the big powerhouse was finished miners came up to daylight with bad news. The rich lode of copper had come to an end. Experts were sent into the mine to survey the situation and they could find no metal, so at a time when prosperity and optimism were at their heights, copper mining at Dos Cabezas was something in the past.

More than 300 employees were told there would be no more checks and to leave town if they

DOS CABEZAS STORE was spared general destruction for unexplained reason when town died as important mining center. Large company dance hall, center of joy unconfined for 20 years, remains as shell at left. Each house in town had own well, this old one with concrete curbing. Shaft now serves as daytime home for large horned owl who sleeps on rocky ledge, shows strong resentment at being disturbed by snapping bill.

could. Those owning the little frame houses sold them for pittances. Wrecking balls were swung against all permanent-type buildings including offices, dormitories and the showplace powerhouse. Dos Cabezas became an instant ghost town.

Several families still make the town of two heads their home, living there in the hope that some day another copper vein may be uncovered or having nowhere else to go. Nell Merwin is one who likes the town and clings stubbornly to her old home, one of the oldest houses still standing, a museum of relics and artifacts of old Dos Cabezas. She likes people, the town that was and takes pride in entertaining random visitors interested in the history of the one time copper metropolis. She provided most of this story of Dos Cabezas.

ADOBE STRUCTURE reputed to be Butterfield Stage Station, built in 1858. It was erected as overnight stop for Argonauts heading for California gold fields. John Butterfield chose location nearer center of town than near Elwell's Spring where community started. First building there was long used as family residence. After some years residents fled house in terror, saying ghosts chased them away. Another family moved in with same results. The whiteclad spirits were reported hovering near and making unearthly noises. At last historic building was razed, a sacrifice to superstition. This second stage station will soon crumble away, stone foundation prolonging survival.

EHRENBERG, ARIZONA

Whiskey, loose women, pigs and the law were all mixed up in Tom Hamilton's life. He served some of the whiskey over the bar and drank about the same amount to keep it from spoiling. Loose women were no problem as long as he could get enough customers for them. But his pigs caused the judge no end of trouble — and he was the judge.

Hamilton ran a combination store, saloon and brothel in Ehrenberg, a brawling frontier town in the late '60s and through the '70s. The drab cluster of adobe buildings was not a mining town but served as a supply center for the placer activity along the Colorado River's east shore.

As a bartender, Hamilton set up the bottles and glasses, pawed in the money and gold dust and took three fingers himself when anybody wanted to pay for it. And if there were fights and shootings, he was no man to stop the boys from having a little fun. Somebody was bound to be thrown in the calaboose and who would he face in the court in the morning? Tom Hamilton, justice of the peace.

That is, if and providing the j.p. was sober enough to face anybody. If not, he was regaining his strength in bed and further derelict in another duty — looking after his pigs. The porkers had no respect for the flimsy fence around the sty and were not inclined to lead their lives in quiet desperation. They wandered. And most of the time into stores to root around in the leather, lamp wicks and lard and cause general consternation. They also invaded pri-

vate kitchens and found no welcome greetings from the women trying to get a pot of beans in the oven.

Complaints became so numerous the judge decided he would have to do something but nothing as drastic as staying sober to look after his swine. He simply commandeered a raft, took the pigs across the Colorado and turned them loose. They had to be content rooting around in the willows, until the happy day they discovered a prospector's camp and reduced the food supply to a shambles. The prospector evened things up by shooting one of the vandals and hanging the butchered carcass to a convenient tree branch.

But these goings on were witnessed by one of the Indians in the j.p.'s employ and he reported them to Hamilton. Already unsteady, the owner of the pigs downed a couple more, groped for his gun, crossed the river and found the guilty pig shooter still in camp and very indignant. "This is California," he protested to Hamilton with a show of bravado. "Your jurisdiction is good only in Arizona and you can't force me to cross the river." The judge responded that his gun said he could and he did.

The hearing was held in the saloon immediately. Tom Hamilton lubricated his throat and made a speech to the effect that the prospector was now in Arizona where he was subject to the law laid down by Ehrenberg's justice of the peace. He had stolen and killed a pig belonging to the said jurist and the crime had been witnessed. Nobody could say he had

ALMOST COMPLETE ANONYMITY is lot of pioneers buried in old Ehrenberg cemetery. The good markers of wood have long since weathered away, as many carried off by souvenir hunters, those remaining showing little or no legend, as board at left. Sometimes cacti, such as cholla, right center, afford a sort of temporary monument. One grave is said to have been marked: "J.C. 1867", with brand of the man's horse and year he died of gunplay in street.

not had a fair trial so the penalty was fair — to Hamilton. "I fine you $50 for stealing and $50 for the hog."

In New Mexico Territory in January, 1862, Captain Pauline (born Paulino) Weaver discovered some flakes of gold in a wash called by the Mexicans Arroyo Del Tinaja. The location was roughly halfway between what would later be Ehrenberg and Quartzsite, some 140 miles north of Yuma (then Arizona City) on the Colorado. Weaver is said to have secreted the gold in a goose quill pen for safekeeping but the legend does not explain how he happened to have such an object in his possession as he was illiterate. The yellow granules were taken to Yuma where their glint created a sensation and started a full-scale gold rush.

Jose Maria Redondo was in the vanguard. He found a nugget, called by the Mexicans *chispa*, weighing two ounces. When he spread the news in Yuma a second exodus depopulated the town even more. Then in February Juan Ferra discovered a *chispa* of nearly three pounds.

Now the news spread to the coast and the cities of Los Angeles and San Francisco began to feel the impact with so many hopefuls leaving for the gold fields on the Colorado. But now came an obstacle almost unique in gold rush history — the blazing heat. The climate had been most pleasant in January but by July the hordes of would-be miners arriving from the cool coast found temperatures rising to 120 degrees, with suffocating humidity from the river and its vegetation. There were many heat prostrations and some deaths, particularly among women and children.

Many were discouraged, many returned to the coast, replaced by hardy Mexicans from Sonora. Then a nugget was displayed in the window of a California jeweler, C. Ducommun. The glittering curiosity weighed almost four pounds. This reversed the traffic flow and soon there were so many travelers arriving at the riverbank that enterprising William Bradshaw established a ferry and reaped a harvest comparable to those in the placers where hardly a man made less than $100 a day, some $1,000.

Soon a town came into being as a center for supplies and liquid refreshment — Laguna de la Paz, shortened to La Paz. Olivia, Mineral City and Ehrenberg sprang up nearby, only the latter reaching any size. Laguna de la Paz or "Lake of Peace" was bordered by a quiet backwater of the Colorado when founded, yet the valley became a menace, anything but peaceful, when the floods came roaring down. Olivia was named for "Ollie" Oatman, one of two sisters who were taken into brutal captivity by Apaches near Gila Bend in 1851 when their parents were killed and brother badly beaten. The other sister, Mary Ann, died while held by the

Indians but Olivia was released in 1856 and joined her brother who by then had recovered in Yuma. Mineral City was hopefully named when good deposits of gold ore were panned in the nearby wash, booming for a short time and dying as the metal petered out.

Ehrenberg lived longer. Herman Ehrenberg, mining engineer and hero of the Texas Independence War, was a famous figure in early Arizona history, having prospected almost all the state. Right after the Gadsden Purchase he and another well known Arizona pioneer, Charles D. Poston, spent some of 1854 and 1855 looking over the hills above Tubac. Ehrenberg gradually worked his way northwest toward the placers along the gullies and washes.

"Mike" Goldwater, grandfather of the present senator, had a business in La Paz. It flourished with the town but when mud deposits cut it from the river about 1869 the place began to falter and Goldwater established a new store six or seven miles down the Colorado where a number of adobe houses had been erected around an army post installed ten years earlier. He named the new town for his long-time friend Ehrenberg who had been murdered at Dos Palmas.

Until 1877 when the railroad reached and passed beyond Yuma, the store of J. Goldwater & Bro. was supplied mainly by river boats plying the Colorado, returning downstream with many pounds of placer gold for the San Francisco mint. The light boats went down to Puerto Ysabel at the mouth of the river, their cargo shifted to ocean-going vessels for the voyage down the Gulf of California and north to San Francisco. Several of the river boats were owned by Capt. Isaac Polhamus under the name of the Colorado Steam Navigation Co. He and the Goldwater brothers were cronies, for although Polhamus lived in Yuma, he was often in Ehrenberg with one of his steamers.

The town was so well supplied with saloons it could spare one. When forced out of business for lack of patronage, the building was put into use as a school house, the town's first. In April, 1872, bright-eyed Mary Elizabeth Post came from San Diego by stagecoach to Yuma where she waited ten days for the flat-bottomed boat to take her to Ehrenberg as its first teacher. Barely settled in the raw, dusty frontier town, Mary Elizabeth was confronted by fifteen bashful, dark-eyed Mexican children, none of whom could speak a word of English — and she no word of Spanish. She was rescued by the kindly owner of the store next door who took over as interpreter. In addition to formal lessons, pupils and teacher sat outside in the evenings with lights out so as not to attract insects and did exercises in language and poetry.

Living was rugged in Ehrenberg. All water had to be hauled from the muddy Colorado and settled in tanks. Four inches of dust lay in the street and building lumber was imported at great cost, the only local trees being scrubby willows and cottonwoods. Construction was almost entirely adobe and sun-dried bricks whose thickness gave some protection from the hot sun. Insects were obnoxious, especially the stinging, biting types and non-biting black flies that swarmed in black clouds over all food. Part of the plague was due to garbage decomposing at the edge of town in the intense heat and there were always burro and cattle droppings.

Yet as long as gold was harvested nearby and as long as river traffic was important, Ehrenberg continued to thrive. But the $7 million in gold panned out of the arroyos was all there was. When the railroad was completed past Yuma the river boats lost their lifeline and stayed tied to the wharves. Olivia and Mineral City succumbed, leaving almost no trace.

OLD PHOTO OF LA PAZ taken at turn of century shows long abandoned river port as ghost town. Buildings were adobe, only material available. Town was originally called Laguna de la Paz, situated on backwater lagoon of Colorado River. Harbor proved liability, filling with sand when river became raging torrent in unusually high water from melting snows in Rockies. Isolation from vital river traffic proved fatal to port.

Ehrenberg has almost vanished too. Until a very few years ago there were numerous adobe ruins standing forlornly near the river to give some semblance of shape to the once busy port. Then came a trailer park and the historic remains were leveled to the ground, except for one pitiful corner remnant still visible from the road. The cemetery is somewhat more permanent although most markers have vanished and the legends on the few remaining ones are illegible.

La Paz is even more nebulous. It gave up the county seat to Yuma in 1870 and quickly faded out. A few mounds of adobe remain at the edge of the Colorado River Indian Reservation six miles above Ehrenberg, almost impossible to find in the brush and sand.

WAGON HAS STOOD near cemetery many years, protracted weathering making pattern of wood grain.

FAIRBANK, ARIZONA

Fairbank, on the Santa Cruz River and between Contention City and Tombstone, was a supply center for both and way station for drivers hauling ore from mines at Tombstone to the mills at Contention. It was also an important point on the railroad from Guaymas, Mexico and Benson and a stage terminal for mail and express. Generally supposed to be a corruption of "faro bank," the name of the town more likely honors Chicago merchant K. N. Fairbank who had many mining interests in the area. Early Spanish missionaries reported an Indian village named Santa Cruz on the site in 1700. Even today heavy rains will sometimes expose such artifacts as arrowheads and pottery shards.

The river is subject to sudden flash floods, storms on the headwaters in old Mexico will sometimes swell the usually meager flow to a torrent sweeping all before it. One of these floods occurred in September 1890 and the damage was all the more terrifying because it hit in the night when everyone was asleep. The Tombstone EPITAPH reported the flood, the story recounting heroic efforts on the part of a Mr. Salcido owner of a lodging house. He was awakened by the roar of the waters and ran to each room, warning occupants to flee. "He had cleared the rooms and was leaving when the flood struck the front door and filled the house with water before he could get to the back exit to open the door and let the water run through. The water was up to his neck in a moment and he struggled until help arrived and saved him. . . . He was taken to Williams' Drug Store where he recovered from his fright. . ."

But nothing that ever happened in Fairbank was more exciting than the attempt to rob the Wells Fargo car at the turn of the century. Sensational at the time, details seemed to have faded away but were unearthed in a 1912 issue of the long defunct REAL MEN OF ARIZONA. "One affray in which Jeff Milton took part proved not to be scatheless, but resulted in victory for him and the breaking up of a most dangerous gang of train robbers that ever infested the Territory.

"It occurred in February of 1900 in Fairbank. Milton was still in the employ of the Express Co. as a messenger (or guard) on the Mexican run from Benson to Guaymas, and on one of his runs he met Bill Stiles a deputy sheriff of Cochise County. Stiles at that time was joined with Bert Alvord also a deputy sheriff. Both were secretly engaged in depredations of their own, themselves keeping discreetly in the background while they planned hold-ups without being discovered. The dividing line between law breakers and defenders was a weak and shaky one in those days and participants in the one activity might the next day join the other side, or take both parts on occasion.

"Stiles told Milton he had arranged a good deal in the desert southwest of Tucson and was desirous of having Milton join him in promoting it. Milton replied that this was impossible, as he was on his way to Guaymas. Stiles then asked "you are sure of that, are you? Well, when you start north again be sure and telegraph me so I can meet you in Benson." Milton promised and Stiles went on his way to plan a hold-up of the Wells Fargo train at Fairbank at a time when Milton whose readiness as a gunfighter was legend would not be present.

"As it happened, however, Milton received a telegram from W. F. Owen, the Express Co. Superintendent, ordering him to return north to take the place of a messenger named Jones who had fallen sick. In his hurry to return he failed to notify Stiles, so when the car marked for holdup stopped in the dusk of a winter's day in Fairbank the man whom Stiles least desired to run up against was guarding the treasure.

"Fairbank was a much bigger place in those days and there was a considerable number of packages to hand out. Milton noticed a considerable number of men in the offing, but presumed them to be cowpunchers. As he stooped to pick up another parcel he heard a voice shout out 'Hands up, there, you blankety blank so and sos!' 'What's the matter?' asked Milton. 'Oh, I guess some of the boys are having a little fun,' answered the agent. 'That's mighty poor fun. Somebody is likely to get hurt around here,' responded Milton.

"He had hardly stopped speaking when the 'Hands up' command was repeated by several voices. And the next moment a number of the men opened fire on him with six-guns and Winchester rifles. The gang was comprised of the Owens brothers, Bravo Horn and a certain notorious bad man, murderer, horsethief and all around desperado named Three Fingered Jack Dunlap. 'Damn it, boys, line up, there,' cried a voice above the fusilade. Milton was shot at the start by a ball that shattered his arm just above the wrist. Another ball knocked off his hat and grazed his skull. Tumbling back into the car he jumped for his gun which was ready and loaded and returned to the door. It was so dark, with people running about, some shooting, that it was impossible to know which were friends and which were enemies. Lead pelted the air in all directions, a perfect storm of bullets rained toward him and riddled the car.

"One ball knocked a lump of flesh out of the same arm already wounded. Then still another entered the arm, ranged upward through the bone and shattered an artery. At this juncture he managed to raise his gun and deliver what turned out to be the most effective blow of the whole battle, shooting Three Finger Jack fatally, though the bandit did not immediately die. Milton, fearing he would die or at least faint away, took the key from the treasure safe and tossed it outside into the darkness.

"When the bandits entered the car they took him for a dead man, searched him and the car for the key. They had not provided themselves with dynamite, and having fully counted on capturing the messenger without a struggle they were forced to abandon the robbery. Only a short time had elapsed since the start of the robbery but they had already remained too long. The excited town was already gathering men to battle the gang. Three Fingered Jack was lifted onto his horse, lashed to the saddle and the gang dashed out of town.

"Retarded in their flight by their wounded companion, they heartlessly abandoned him to die. He was found in the brush about nine miles away next day by one of the posses that was scouring the country. He lived long enough to make a confession. A general rounding up of the gang followed. Bill Stiles turned state's evidence, the others were given long terms in the penitentiary. Since then there have been no further attempts to rob a Well Fargo car.

"Milton was given the best attention locally, then hurried to a hospital in San Francisco where surgeons decided they would have to amputate the arm in order to save his life. When this news was transmitted to Milton he protested, 'Now Doc, what good would I be without my arm? If you cut it off the first thing I'll do when I get out is kill the man that did the job, that goes!' The arm was not amputated, Milton lived and regained partial use of it. He later joined the U.S. Immigration Service as a rider along the border."

The ARIZONA GUIDE, published in 1940 credits Fairbank with a population of 50. As of now, no such number is in evidence, though the store still operates in a small way, as does the postoffice. There are a few trailer houses parked back in the mesquite brush. But Fairbank now is a very different place from the roistering stage and train stop it was when Three Fingered Jack, Bill Stiles and their gang attempted to hold up the treasure car there.

THIS STORE, still operating, served Fairbank in early days. Of adobe construction, it has changed little from times when travel consisted of mule trains hauling ore from mines at Tombstone to mills at Contention City.

GLEESON, ARIZONA

The robin's-egg magic of turquoise lay hidden in the story of Gleeson but old Chief Cochise and the white man he trusted gave the town a gaudier color—blood red.

The Spanish had originally mined turquoise in the Dragoon Mountains as had a primitive race of Indians before them. The Spanish were a hard lot and subjected the aborigines to a state of slavery but were never able to extract from them the secret of where the real treasure of the blue-green gemstone lay. When the white man came and tried to win over the Indians with double-dealing tactics, Apache Chief Cochise, who had intended to be friendly if his tribe was let alone, rose up in all his savage wrath.

Up to 1860 Cochise had not actually molested any Americans but when he was taken into custody and accused of having conducted a raid on a ranch near the spot where the mining town of Gleeson was later built, he escaped his captors and made up for all the trouble he had not caused, spreading murder, rape and destruction among the ranchers.

For a long time he holed up in the Dragoons in an almost impregnable fortress. He held the U. S. Army at bay for ten years, yielding only through mediation with the one white man he trusted. This was Tom Jeffords who operated a stage on the old Butterfield line, long so vulnerable to Apache attack that drivers never traveled the route without an armed guard always on watch.

Jeffords had lost twenty-two of his men to the Apaches but nevertheless rode alone into the hideout of the old chief to see if he could arrange a peace. Cochise was so impressed with the man's bravery that he did pledge a personal pact with him and made him a blood brother. Jeffords was then able to negotiate a meeting between Cochise and General Howard. This resulted in a treaty, one of the terms being that Jeffords be made an Indian agent.

Shortly old Cochise died and was buried in the Dragoons. Only one white man knew just where and that was Tom Jeffords. He never revealed the secret although he lived forty years longer. The area was abundantly endowed with a type of live oak yielding an edible acorn, called "beyota"

OLD GLEESON GENERAL STORE was buy center of trade and word-of-mouth news when ranching and mining were important. The adobe building has coat of stucco for elegance. Louvre with fan for ventilation was added in days of electricity. Arcade with awnings of corrugated sheet metal was also latter day, luxury for loiterers on benches once lining wall. Live oaks gave shade and *beyotas* — edible acorns gathered by Apaches.

WELLS WERE NOT TOO DEPENDABLE in long dry summer of Dragoon Mountains. Town is filled with adobe ruins such as that of old saloon shown here, fallen to reveal view of Gleeson General Store.

OLD FASHIONED ICE BOX leans tipsily outside ruined house, well preserved in dry air. Shrub in background is mesquite, common in southwest desert areas. Belonging to legume family, nourishing seeds were ground, made into small cakes and baked for Indian's staple food. Plant grows into shrubby tree, is armed with vicious thorns, preventing cattle from grazing, is difficult to control.

by the Indians who gathered them in quantity everywhere but in Stronghold Canyon. It remained inviolate and would indicate this is the spiritland of the old chief.

With Indian troubles fading out the white man's thoughts again turned to the legends and tales of turquoise, gold, copper and silver to be found in the Dragoons. Some of all these treasures were located and the town that sprang up at the site of discovery was named Gleeson after one of the miners.

The town grew but never had a real boom. The area was already on a solid basis with cattle raising and moderate mining prosperity was taken in stride. The biggest boost to the economy came with the entry of Tiffany's of New York. This company proposed to mine turquoise on a big scale but the location of really valuable deposits remained elusive and after some desultory efforts, with only a small quantity of fine turquoise to show, Tiffany's left the scene. So did everyone else in time; even the cattle ranchers gave up as water grew more and more scarce. Only a family or two remain in the area.

29

GOLDROAD, ARIZONA

Sensible people, and those in a hurry to get from here to there, take the newer U. S. highway 66 from Kingman to Needles. But Ghost Town hunters branch off to the right five miles from Kingman. After a stretch of interesting, flattish desert the old road climbs breathtakingly toward Sitgreaves Pass, 3,500 feet above sea level.

Almost directly, upon starting down the other side, appear traces of buildings, the outskirts of Goldroad. Trickling downward to an only slightly wider stretch of canyon, the small stream of remnants spreads out a little into the main part of what was once an impressive mining camp.

At the close of a bonanza period of prosperity, with the price of gold making all further operations unprofitable, the buildings were sacrificed to avoid taxes. Since many structures were of adobe and stone because of limited supplies of timber, these unburnable ones leave fairly substantial ruins.

Vegetation surrounding them is of the sparsest, but is most interesting. There are many Ocotillos, Chollas and others, all full of thorns. The cliffs form walls all around and even a casual survey reveals mine shafts, heads, mills and dumps dotting the steepest walls, some clinging precariously after the fashion of those in the San Juan Mountains of Colorado.

EVEN THICKEST STONE WALLS crumble under onslaught of years. Pathetic remains were once home to miner's family, now offer scant shade to Gila monsters, rattlesnakes, rodents. Canyon in background holds main town and mines. Distant mountain range extends to Colorado River.

TWO-YEAR BOOM TOWN

Harshaw, Arizona

The Harshaw mining camp in southern Arizona was built on a solid silver foundation in the center of the Patagonia Mountains. Midway between two main river valleys, it lay athwart the path of history, each movement of people passing that way leaving its mark. Indians living along Sobaioura Creek called the area "Enchanted Land" because of streams flowing generously with clear water which provided an ample growth of good grass. Spaniards came later but stayed only long enough to call those Indians "Patagonias" for their reputed large feet.

The padres who arrived next considered all of Primeria Alta a fertile field for conversion, creating devils for the Indians to labor against for more than three hundred years. Then Spain relinquished the country to the Republic of Mexico which put the padres out and their adobe structures untended, to melt away and leave only peach orchards here and there. Mexican families settling in the narrow canyon where the boom town of Harshaw would spring up, found some of the gnarled trees and named their village Durazno for "place of the peaches." With the Gadsden Purchase which made the Patagonias part of the United States came "yankees" with pick and shovel, including David Tecumseh Harshaw.

One of the stalwarts who left comfortable homes in the east to hunt for gold in California, Harshaw was born in New York in 1828 and just 20 when he traveled overland to work in Nevada County mines, probably at Grass Valley. At the outbreak of the Civil War he joined First California Volunteer Infantry mustered at Oakland and was promptly sent to Tucson.

After the war Harshaw traveled around looking for a good place to raise cattle, finally settling in the San Pedro Valley of southern Arizona with about 1000 head. On these forage lands the young veteran found good deposits of gold and silver, in the Santa Ritas, not far south of Tucson. Nell Murbarger in her definitive *Ghosts of the Adobe Walls,* classic of Arizona's mining days, gives reports from the Tucson *Arizona Citizen* in 1875, that "David T. Harshaw brought in a sack of dust and

nuggets weighing $843, the result of four days' labor for three men . . . the Santa Rita placers are entitled to rank equal with the best placers ever discovered."

Perhaps Harshaw's claim petered out, possibly he was run off by Indians, but one thing for sure, he was running cattle on lands properly allocated for use by Chiricahua Apaches. When they complained to Indian Agent Thomas J. Jeffords the official summarily ordered Harshaw to take his cattle and decamp. Forthwith he drove the animals to a section of the Patagonia Mountains not far south of the town of that name. With plenty of grass and water Harshaw felt he had greatly improved his position, especially when he could get supplies at the Mexican village of Durazno. Again he found metal, his first claims the Hardshell and Harshaw, just south of Durazno which he worked only long enough to prove their potential worth and then sold both in 1879. Having bequeathed his name on the one-time Mexican village he married Maria Jesus Andrada, sister of his partner Jose, and settled down to operate a stage station at Davidson's Springs where he died in September

NEGLECTED GRAVE in one of the two cemeteries at edge of Harshaw, marker not stating and War Dept. unable to determine cause of soldier's death in mining camp. Only one cemetery here is contemporary with Harshaw's brief period of prosperity, 1879-81. Some tombstones are still in evidence, though almost covered by brush, weeds. Cattle around, drop manure on graves of pioneers.

31

of 1884. His obituary said, "David Harshaw was a typical frontiersman, a man with a big heart, the very essence of noble qualities."

And his name was used with electric excitement when that same year the Southern Pacific entered Tucson and a boisterous boom began at Harshaw nee Durazno. In 1880 James Reilly, editor of *Territorial Expositor* of Phoenix, described it as easily the biggest camp he had ever seen outside of Tombstone. That same year managers of the mines arrived with much needed eastern capital to open a large scale development, their chief investment being in the mine located by David Harshaw, consisting of three parallel ledges from 5 feet to 25 feet wide. A gang of men was hired to grade off a section of steep hillside for installation of a new reduction mill scheduled to arrive in due time by railroad to Tucson.

Within six months the 20-stamp Hermosa Mill was crushing 75 tons of ore every day, making it the largest producer in Arizona. Editor Reilly now wrote that any attempt to evaluate potential wealth of the Harshaw properties would be "preposterous." Silver was soon pouring out to the tune of $365,000 every month. 600 people had arrived to share in the boom, most of them adventurers from 35 states and 3 territories according to the Census Schedule of Arizona Territory of 1880. China, India and Mexico were also represented, several dozen from Ireland.

Only 100 men listed themselves as miners. 24 called themselves grocers, the same number liquor sellers. Restaurants employed 35, laundries 11, the others accounted for in such businesses as livery stables, blacksmith shops, wagonmakers, freighters, barber shops. A few candid individuals listed their calling as faro bank dealers and speculators. There was a "bell hanger," whatever occupation that was. Those were male registrants and as for the 64 females, only two kinds of work were given. Most of them were housewives, 4 forthrightly calling themselves prostitutes. Mexican women predominated, most of them mothers with 59 young children. The Harshaw population was youthful, Mike Fagan, large and powerful ex-peace officer, was the oldest man in town at 45.

A newspaper was started, several hotels and as one Tucson reporter wrote it, "every other establishment in town a saloon." Harshaw was undeniably a real city but this status lasted little more than two years, for two reasons. Silver veins grew thin, then pinched out to almost nothing. The largest mine, the Hermosa, which employed 200 men, closed down, retaining only a skeleton force to guard property and make small exploratory borings for the vanished silver vein. The second disaster was a flood caused by cloudbursts in the Patagonias which poured a huge wall of water down the one street in the narrow canyon. A muddy, boulder-carrying deluge tore out all but the more sturdy stone structures, some of them standing today. The ones destroyed were rebuilt with lumber but a bad fire consumed them, the stone buildings again spared. This gave little incentive to rebuilding and Harshaw died as a town.

The *Arizona Weekly Citizen* of July 7, 1888, reported, "A few of the buildings are still standing in a good state of preservation, though unoccupied for several years. . . . About nine families now live in Harshaw." As of today a census would show about the same population, most of the people Spanish-speaking Mexicans (see Boot Hill).

CATHOLIC CHURCH, one of Harshaw's solidly built stone edifices, commented upon by newspapers of Tucson and other cities. Escaping flood and withstanding less dramatic ravages of time, stone walls are being exposed by cracking plaster coating.

JEROME, ARIZONA

The little movie house was well filled that night some twenty years ago. Every now and then a jolting motion shook the building, an effect to be taken as an earthquake anywhere else. The patrons here paid little attention to shuddering floors and when the show was over they headed for the exit doors. The sidewalk which had been only a few inches above the doorsill when they entered was now nearly two feet higher, or more accurately, the theater floor was that much lower. A few of the more elderly had to be helped up to the higher level but no one was unduly excited, the phenomenon of sliding and moving buildings being too ordinary an occurrence in Jerome.

The jail had started to behave the same way a few years before, settling a few feet downward, the little concrete building pulling away from the sidewalk. Steps were made down to the new level while the now sobered drunks inside talked about their free ride. Then with more slips and slides the jail was so far below the street, a new street level had to be established. As the years went on, successively lower street levels had to be made until the calaboose was closed. However, this was not because Jerome was tired of building new streets for it but because there were no more prisoners among the few Jeromans.

What caused all the shimmeying of the earth?

HIGHWAY BELOW is only "through street" in Jerome. High school on point in middle distance, once filled with local youngsters, is still used by 850 students coming by bus from communities in Verde Valley — Clarkdale, Cottonwood, Clemenceau, etc. Top buildings are 1,500 feet above lowest. Smelter in Clarkdale may be seen in distance, Oak Creek Canyon visible on clear day.

JEROME as seen from below shows fantastic panorama of deserted hotels, theaters, schools. Good stand of pine trees once surrounded city, killed by fumes from smelter which has since been torn down, replaced by huge one in valley. Adobe structures once swelled limits of town, ruins of some seen at center and lower left.

The geological reason was Jerome's situation directly upon the large Verde Fault, a major cause of subterranean movement. Then the town was undermined with a complex of more than 85 miles of mine tunnels.

Add to this the fact that the "overburden" of loose rock and soil on top of a solid layer of rock which lay under the town was penetrated by heavy winter rains and leakage from the aging water supply pipes, with all the water collecting in a saturated layer on the rock. And compounding the natural earth shocks were those from frequent explosions in the mines and one mammoth one in the powder house. Small wonder Jerome progressed downward as well as ahead.

John Figi, custodian of the Art Gallery welcoming Jerome's visitors, says these movements are trivial in light of what went on in former ages. "At one time Mingus Mountain, on the side of which Jerome is built, was 12,000 feet higher than it is today. A prehistoric cataclysm flung the top off and pitched it into the Verde Valley, the sandstone and rock hills you see there being the result. The plant down there is making cement for the dam in Glen Canyon and if removal of material is carried on at the present rate for fifty years, they will reach the layer thrown off from here, the top of Jerome's mines, so to speak, and

it will be a tremendously rich layer of copper as exploratory diamond drillings have shown. The large Daisy mine which used to produce so heavily is probably the top of the decapitated vein."

The earliest use for the colorful ores of the Jerome site was by Tuzigoot Indians in 935 A.D. These aborigines found vivid surface outcroppings in blue, green and brown which, when powdered, made fine war paint and in times of peace was useful for pottery coloring. The first Spanish explorers centuries later were friendly with the natives and shown the deposits. It was tough going up the steep sides of Mingus Mountain but the Spaniards were spurred on by thoughts of gold. When they saw the deposits owed their color to baser metals, they turned back in disgust, giving the country "back to the Indians."

A later visitor to the site was Indian scout Al Sieber, who in 1872 found evidence of Indian mining in the primitive rock tools and crude ladders made of juniper pegs. Sieber, however, was no miner and made no effort to capitalize on his find.

In January of 1876 a small party of prospectors from Nevada headed by Capt. John Boyd and John O. Dougherty arrived in nearby Prescott and listened to the tales of copper wealth on Mingus Mountain. They reached the place but seem to have been unimpressed with the area that was to yield half a billion dollars in copper with gold and silver paying the refining cost. Later that same year came more curious and enterprising visitors, ranchers John Ruffner and his friend August McKinnon. Although the two did stake out several claims, they were primarily ranchers and snapped up a buying offer from Territorial Governor Frederick E. Tritle of $2,000 for the claims, getting $500 cash, the rest to come.

Even now there was no development rush, Tritle finding it took more money than he had to open up the claims and get going. But about the time he was ready to throw up the sponge he met an angel in the form of a New York lawyer, Eugene Jerome (who was the grandfather of England's Sir Winston Churchill). Jerome had money and was willing to sink it in a rocky hole on Mingus Mountain but there was a string attached. He was positive a town would develop there and he thought it would be fitting and proper to have it named after him, and so stipulated in the contract. Tritle was willing, or felt he had no choice if the mine was to be developed.

Yet nothing much happened. It seemed necessary to build a smelter to refine the undeniably rich ore and an impossiblity to get such a thing hauled that distance over rough or nonexistent roads. But in 1882 the Santa Fe came to Ashfork and Tritle, with the lawyer's money, built a wagon road from the railhead 60 miles to his property. Parts for the smelter at last arrived and a fabulous mining town was born.

In 1893 the United Verde Copper Co. was incorporated. At this time the town had four hundred people and six saloons. For years an almost continuous wagon train brought food, water, fuel and mine supplies to the settlement that was progressing as it clung to an all but vertical mountainside. In 1900 a contract was let to supply Jerome with water on a regular basis with a 200-unit mule team. The contractor? Pancho Villa.

The population was cosmopolitan to an extreme. Represented by closely knit groups were Italians, Mexicans, Swedes, Yugoslavs, Bohemians and Welshmen. A large English-speaking section was squeezed into a small space on the red splintered rocks of Yeager Canyon, Slavs filling the Hogback and Mexicans overflowing their adobes along Bitter Creek. No

HUGE OPEN-PIT OPERATION of Phelps Dodge Corp., part of old United Verde workings shown behind buildings in telephoto lens. At left center is "Traveling Jail" which has slid downhill from street above and right. Front center is unique church built by Mr. Sabino Gonzoles, Mexican Methodist minister, who felt "urge" to construct building of any material available including railroad ties, powder boxes and old mine timbers. Construction was from 1939 to 1941. Rev. Gonzoles preached last sermon late in 1952, just before mines were closed down.

9
7
5

JEROME
POPULATION
15,000
10,000
5,000
1,000
GHOST CITY

matter what group or location a man lived in, he had a magnificent view of Verde Valley with its red backdrop of Oak Creek Canyon or could look directly down on his neighbor's roof, perhaps scratch matches on his chimney, and on the other side would be the basement of the next house. Only one main street existed, wrapping itself around the crest of the ridge and most cross streets were steep stairways. Some so-called ones were almost impossible to negotiate—and there were no busses or streetcars.

Jerome suffered from labor troubles. The first strike was in 1907, a success for the men which reduced the ten-hour work day to eight and raised wages to $2.75 a day. The next disturbance was not only unsuccessful but took on some comic opera aspects. In 1917, just before the United Verde was bought out by the huge Phelps Dodge Corporation, the I.W.W. started a strike. The men not only ceased to work but staged demonstrations and street battles. The trouble ended when several hundred miners and imported agitators were taken out of the company-owned houses on the hill, loaded on boxcars under the persuasion of guns and other weapons, hauled out into the southeastern Arizona desert and left to sizzle with their sins.

1925 was the top year for Jerome, after which production began to shrivel, closing several of the smaller mines which could not afford operation without rich ore, and then some of the larger ones. In 1953 Phelps Dodge permanently closed the big mine and that was the end of Jerome as a city. Only 100 remained of the 15,000. After this low ebb a few tourist attractions were organized, such as an art gallery, restaurants, etc. The post office is still active, the figure of 300 accounting for all residents now.

Visitors arriving from either end of town, from over Mingus Mountain from Prescott or from Verde Valley, will find the big camp most rewarding. The streets are still such in name only and could lead the unwary motorist into some cul-de-sac of a yard too narrow to turn around in, such as the street leading past the Catholic Church. The automobile should be

JEROME JAIL has slid downhill nearly 300 feet by stages, each new location requiring new street for access. Original level is at upper left, part of street showing. City had ample water supply, enough to keep several swimming pools filled in heyday. Leakage from pipes from artesian springs 14 miles away on Mingus Mountain was partly responsible for unstable ground, a handicap added to natural earth fault and mine explosion.

parked at the bottom of town with wheels against a wall or curb and excursions made on foot, return to the car then being downhill. Otherwise the experience is like descending into Grand Canyon with the return all uphill.

As John Figi said: "Of course if mining should be revived here people would not build on this steep mountainside, but settle on the level ground below. Modern cars would easily reach the mines where the haul up the road used to require at least one team of horses, several with a good load."

In 1884 Senator William A. Clark of Montana showed an interest in the properties since they had begun to pay off. He took a lease on them long enough to assure himself that he had a good thing, then he bought the project, lock-stock-and-barrel. Clark poured a million dollars into the development of the copper mines during the next twelve years.

Now tier upon tier of houses was glued to the 30-degree angle of the hillside, for married men and their families, the immense stone Montana House housing a thousand single men—the largest building in Arizona. Even so, a large number lived in tents and shacky houses of bone-dry lumber. Most of this section went up in smoke in the last series of fire ending in 1899. That same year Jerome was incorporated as the fifth largest city in the state. The mine was to become one of the largest individually owned copper mines in the world.

Near the immense Verde development another vast copper deposit was opened up, the faulted top of what was to be the famed Little Daisy. The ore body was located by George Hull and J. Fisher in 1912 and the richness of the Daisy May was almost unbelievable. Where ore at a value of five percent paid well, here were 300 feet of rock with an assay of fifteen percent at the 1,400-foot level of the mine, then 40 feet of forty percent and at the 1,500 level, five feet of ore with a fantastic copper content of forty-five percent. The Company—The UVX—built a smelter at Clemenceau in the valley and by the end of 1938 production had grossed $125 million.

By 1929 the population of Jerome was 15,000 and included a working force of 2,345 men. More copper was coming out of Arizona than any other state, the Verde operation alone producing as much as $29 million a single year. Gone were the days when building brick was hauled by four and six teams of horses up the single steep road from the kiln in Verde Valley. No longer was it necessary to use the ingenious but inadequate system of converting surplus steam into power to drive the dynamos for electricity. Jerome never had gas. It jumped directly from kerosene to electricity.

Culture was not lacking during the halcyon days.

The miner could attend a lecture by Miss Hollister of Phoenix under the auspices of the W.C.T.U. or a box social put on by the Ladies' Guild of the Episcopal Church. Better attended were the less socially accepted functions.

OLD MOVIE HOUSE slides downhill at rate of inch in two months, may remain stationary for long period, then skid twenty inches in short time.

STATELY COLUMNS STAND at entrance of immense grade school, are slowly crumbling. Structure was closed when large mine operations ceased.

ONE MAN REGIMENT

Pete Kitchen Ranch, Arizona

The Apaches came down "like wolves on the fold" and Arizona ranchers felt the bitter sting of defeat and death. But not Pete Kitchen. He said his hogs looked like walking pincushions with all the arrows sticking out of them and he saw to it they did not stick out of him. "So many men lost their lives in the neighborhood," said Thomas Casanega, who married one of Kitchen's nieces, "if all their bodies were laid side by side like railroad ties they would make a track from Nogales to Potero."

Pete Kitchen was the very essence of stubborn resistance. Although under almost constant attack by Apaches he stood his ground among ranchers who gave up the struggle. The few settlers courageous enough to hold out for a time said of him, "To the Apache he was more terrible than an army with banners."

Frank Rockwood in his book *Arizona Characters* says Pete Kitchen was the connecting link between savagery and civilization. Kitchen left some memoirs showing how clear is this delineation of the man's make-up. He kept much fine stock at his farm near the Mexican border, the fat animals a constant temptation to early cattle rustlers. When

HOME of self-sufficient rancher Pete Kitchen. One of the oldest in Arizona, adobe building was set up in 1850s. It stands several hundred feet from rancher's "fortress" and just left, out of photo, is private cemetery for unknown number of men who dared attack doughty pioneer.

he missed one of his favorite horses and found well-marked tracks pointed toward the border, the outraged rancher got on another good steed and set out after the thief. "I caught up with him some distance south of the line," he wrote, "and put my gun on him, making him return with me. After tying the man to a tree branch overhead with a rope around his neck, I laid down to rest. When I woke up the horse he had been sitting on had wandered some little distance, and much to my surprise, the rope around his neck had strangled him."

Although savage natives killed most of his neighbors, tortured and murdered his favorite herder and slaughtered his stepson, Kitchen fought on. In time the Apaches got the message and left him in comparative peace. He gave all victims of carnage on his ranch decent burial in a private "Boot Hill" near his little adobe ranch home. Not knowing who most were, he did not identify the graves but wife Dona Rose, a deeply devout Catholic, religiously burned candles for them in hope of salvation for their souls.

PETE KITCHEN FORTRESS on rocky knoll with view of fields. Contemporary wrote, "There is a sentinel posted on the roof, there is another out in the cienaga with the stock. The men plowing the bottoms are obliged to carry rifles cocked and swung to the plow handle. Every man and boy, and indeed the women, had to go armed. At the fort there are rifles, revolvers and shotguns along the walls and in every corner. Everything speaks of warfare and bloodshed."
When photo was made in 1964 building housed museum operated by owner Col. Gilbert Proctor who kindly allowed author to camp beside it. Historic structure is now operated by Henry Molina family as one of several Casa Molina restaurants in area. Mundane use seems almost sacrilege but occupation of any sort almost guarantees preservation, abandonment leading to swift decay.

McCABE, ARIZONA

McCabe, the Bradshaw Mountains, had its deep-well mystery but there is no cloud of uncertainty about its final demise. And it did not deserve such a fate. It was a family town, suffering a stroke when the gold faded out, was then inundated by an angry flood.

When gold was found in the creek in the late 1860s, there was a rush to get in on the first easy placerings, after which the town was almost deserted until the mother lode was located. A more permanent town then grew up as hard rock mining progressed with several deep shafts bored and a number of stamp mills erected. A two-story brick building on a gentle rise above the creek bed was the largest and most impressive in town. It housed a large general store and several smaller businesses.

Most of the miners were married and as a family town McCabe did not have the usual shootings and scrapes of early Western camps. One old timer described conditions as "dull". "Oh, there was always the hell-raising town of Providence. It was barely over the hill and within easy walking distance. A man could get anything he might want there and some things he didn't, like a broken nose or a slug of hot lead." But McCabe virtuously preserved its reputation as a "clean town."

A good-sized school house stood just above the store and across the road. On the summit of the hill was the immense building housing all the company offices with refinements not found in most camps, including a granite fireplace, showers and flush toilets. A concrete water tank, perhaps two hundred feet across, was built just below the building yet high enough to supply the town by gravity. The water was not palatable because of heavy mineral content and drinking water was hauled up to the town by mule team, one driver in early days a Mr. Conley, helped by his son Earl.

A Swedish miner, Oscar Johnson, was the principal in McCabe's mystery. A loner, Johnson seemed to be doing very well at his claim. He was a hard worker, rising early as smoke could be seen coming from his shack on the north bank of the creek, and almost furtively, said curious observers, Oscar would emerge and head for his well. He had dug it himself, saying the water hauled into camp was too expensive, but the suspicious watchers remembered he had spent an inordinately long time at the digging, that he had removed far more dirt than the comparatively high water table would require.

The morning visits to the well, when Oscar would draw up a full bucket, seemed innocent

UNIQUE MONUMENT stands securely in cemetery on right side of difficult dirt road — first indication that there are traces of Mc-Cabe. Burial ground is deeply eroded by run-off waters, some graves washed entirely away. Monument is cast in one piece from some zinc-like metal, rings when rapped with knuckles. Placed in 1906, marker has enduring qualities but may overturn when foundation breaks down.

LIKE A MONUMENT to past mining glory, granite ruin of elaborate fireplace stands at summit above McCabe. On site stood large office buildings of mining company. Not far away is evidence of showers, granite floor area having drainage hole. Close by are shattered fragments of porcelain flush toilet, a mining camp rarity. Water was available from huge storage tank, circular basin some two hundred feet across. This was for domestic use and mill operations only, drinking water hauled in from stream.

enough, but there were those frequent night trips too, with a lantern. Unable to stand the suspense, one man stationed himself behind a bushy manzanita and waited. After dark Johnson emerged from the cabin with a ladder and a lantern, taking them to the well then returning for a heavy bag. He lifted the well cover and let down the ladder, descending with lantern and bag. The watcher waited for a long time it seemed until the miner came up, pulled up the ladder and went to the cabin. Rumor was quick to say Oscar Johnson was hoarding his wealth in the well but the incident was more or less passed by as just another peculiar trait of the recluse.

Then one day someone asked: "Say, where is Oscar Johnson? There hasn't been any smoke coming from his chimney for days." On a Sunday morning several men went to the cabin, found no Oscar Johnson but evidence he had not been there for several days. When a week went by and the man did not put in an appearance, a party investigated the well and reported there was a side tunnel about six feet down. With a lantern a man explored the tunnel and found a large room which showed every evidence of recent use but was entirely empty. Had Oscar been murdered and his wealth stolen? There was no sign of violence at the cabin or around his workings. No answer came. The industrious and secretive Scandinavian was never seen again, the mystery never solved.

One day in the late summer of 1937 black clouds gathered over the Bradshaws. It was the season for

OLD SAFE near general store appears to have been blown open. Resting on bed of clean gravel, surrounded by manzanita chaparral, it gives no further clues of violence.

rain, Arizona's mountain areas getting an annual fall of 25 to 30 inches in fall and winter. But this storm was heavier than most, the deluge concentrated in the several canyons that fed the stream pouring down through McCabe. As the waters rose in their narrow channel, some of the bulkheads against the rocky walls began to give way, timbering being carried far down the stream. As dirt and rock caved in, a temporary dam was formed and when the torrent built up enough pressure, it washed out the barrier and a huge wave came down on the town, brushing aside all buildings. No one was hurt, for no one was there and the damage was not known for months. McCabe was a ghost town and had been for years.

When the waters subsided, many buildings on higher ground still stood. The general store with stout brick walls was almost intact, the shed at the rear still housing a fabulous collection of buggies from earlier days. Groceries and valuable merchandise had been hauled away before the flood but shelves of faded, outdated goods still remained. The school house stood on the rise across the street, blackboard walls still bearing chalked problems and grammar lessons.

Since then time, storm, decay and vandalism have taken their inevitable toll. The general store has been leveled, safe falling into the hole that was the cellar. The school was wrecked for lumber which was hauled down to Humboldt. There are even now a few shacks and many ruins showing where mills and a brick kiln once stood. On the side of one hill above the stream bed is a row of large settling tanks. Another larger tank, excavated from native rock and lined with concrete is high on the opposite side of the gulch and above is all that remains of the office buildings, the ruin of a big granite fireplace. This is the lonely lair of a ghost.

MINERAL PARK, ARIZONA

What the Hualpais Indians of this part of Arizona were usually called cannot be printed here. It was only when the early whites felt charitable they referred to the low-grade tribespeople as simply "Wallapais." The Mineral Park *Mohave Miner* constantly complained; "There are more drunken Wallapais women on the street than there are drunken Wallapais men." The best that could be said of them was they were peaceful when sober and never attacked the citizens of the remote mining camp in northwestern Arizona.

Mineral Park's other newspaper, *Alta Arizona,* ran a news item January 28, 1882, concerning a near violent encounter between Wallapais Charley, by way of being a minor chief of his tribe, and Jeff, another Indian. Ordinarily the best of friends, they imbibed too much firewater and when an agrument developed, Charley drew his pistol. Before any blood was shed, Under Sheriff Collins intervened, dragged the pair into his office, gave them a good talking to

HOME-MADE HEATERS were popular in country where stoves were all but impossible to obtain due to expensive transportation. Juniper trees were main fuel, hills near camp cleared of them.

and confiscated Charley's precious gun. The next day Sheriff Robert Steen received this contrite letter:

My Friend Bob Steen

Won't you be so kind as to send me my pistol. I will not carry it into town any more and will behave myself and be a good Indian. Tell me where I can come into town and oblige

Your Friend Wallapais Charley

The first prospectors in western Arizona were soldiers attached to Fort Mohave on the Colorado River or disappointed miners from the California gold fields. Some of them found gold in the blistering foothills, one discovery located where Oatman later mushroomed. The Moss mine developed there and among others those at Gold Road attracted a rush of hopeful, would-be miners. Many found treasure there, others reaching out to make discoveries nearby.

These activities were in the early '60s and a few years later several mines were located at the site of Mineral Park but were not worked extensively as the hostile Hualpais, who were picking out some turquoise, forced the miners to flee. Later some whites took out limited quantities of the semiprecious gemstone.

Ten years later, so many whites had infiltrated the area a truce of sorts was established. Before long, rich silver deposits were uncovered in the Cerbat Range, the mines centered in a beautiful parklike, juniper-covered bench on the western slope, the name Mineral Park as apt as any given to western mining camps. Not only were gold, silver and lead deposits rich and varied in the "Park" but the stream flowing through the town was so permeated with mineral solutions and salts it was unfit to drink. Potable water had to be hauled from a canyon several miles away. By 1874 Harris Solomon was running a regular mule train carrying the supply from Keystone Spring.

Once established, Mineral Park boomed. By 1880

ADOBE RUINS BLEND WITH BACKGROUND, sun-baked bricks matching color of parent earth. This material was much used in areas of scant timber, little lumber available and that high priced. Cerbat Range in which Mineral Park lies is rich in cacti. Shown in foreground is patch of prickly pear, *Opuntia engelmanii*, bearing yellow, water-lily-like flowers, deep red pears which are edible. Behind these are clumps of staghorn chollas (choyas), *Opuntia versicolor*, whose main characteristics are barbed spines with easily detached joints often adhering to stock animals and carried away to start new plants where they drop.

there were four saloons, a restaurant, blacksmith shop, hotel, school and several stores, the earliest influx from less glamorous camps nearby which were soon all but deserted. Anyone wanting to get to the camp from the east was faced with a formidable problem of transportation. He had to travel across the northern part of the United States on the Union Pacific to San Francisco, get down to Los Angeles and overland to

Yuma. Here he would transfer to one of the flat-bottomed steamers which paddled up the Colorado River as far as Hardyville. If lucky, he would not have to wait more than a week for the stagecoach to Mineral Park. And this ride was not exactly luxurious, the roads only dim trails over sand or rock and cactus-studded hills where in summer it was well above 100°.

Supplies had to be sent over this same circuitous route or transported more than four hundred miles over alkali and sand deserts. It is no wonder commodity prices were so high. Bacon cost $1 a pound, sugar 35 cents, flour 50 cents in a day when the miner earned $3 for ten hours' work.

And occasionally prices were used as weapons by saloons. At one time when most of the saloonkeepers tossed a quarter into a lard can for a shot of whiskey, one rebel was charging only half that, Spanish *real* with a value of twelve for a dollar. These "pieces of eight" were commonly called "bits," accounting for the western use of "two bits."

Two of Mineral Park's merchants were always at each other's throats in this same manner. Krider Bros. openly advertised they would not only equal other prices but undersell anything offered by their aggressive competitors, Welton and Grounds, and carried on a running feud with merchant J. W. Haas. Being postmaster and having the post office in his store from '79 to '86, W. M. Krider had a distinct trade advantage.

In casting around for an excuse to quarrel with Krider, Hass accused the postmaster of withholding his mail, this openly in front of the store. Insulted and infuriated, Krider lifted his cane and fetched Haas a smart one on the cranium. Haas went berserk, drew his gun and fired wildly. Krider returned the fire and also missed. In the post office at the time, Sheriff Steen ran out and grabbed both contestants by their collars, marching them to the calaboose where the pair passed the time arranging lawsuits for assault with attempt to commit murder. Both were released on $3,000 bail. The *Mohave Miner* which chronicled these events failed to tell the rest of the story.

By 1884 there were 500 registered voters in Mineral Park with, no doubt, as many women and children. The Chinatown had several opium dens, as well as stores and laundries. At first the opium houses were ignored, then tolerated with distaste and finally a marked increase in young addicts was detected, the greatest evil being they were spending their money with the Chinese instead of the white saloon and bawdy house keepers. The white madames, some carrying considerable weight in town politics, demanded that boys who smoked the poppy stay away from their girls.

In July of 1884, the *Mohave Miner* was needled into carrying scare headlines: "This Menace To Our Youth Must Be Stopped." It is to be assumed the opium dens were closed, for Wilfred Babcock, who worked and lived in Mineral Park during the period after the newspaper blast, could not recall any.

The town continued to grow by leaps and bounds. Lumber was always scarce and high priced, a great drawback to progress. There was a sawmill in the Hualpais Mountains forty miles west of the Park but by the time this essential material reached its destination, the cost was $125 a thousand. In spite of this, building went on apace and Mineral Park could boast of several hotels and office buildings to house "the many professional people who have moved here from Cerbat, Mohave City and Hardyville," as the newspaper had it. It soon took over as county seat from Cerbat. A fine courthouse was erected and, beside it, the jail. Wilfred Babcock remembers the jail doors did not open or close easily for some time.

First newspaper was the *Wallapais Enterprise*, started June 1, 1876 by John Leonard and Chauncey F. Mitchell and dying soon. Two later ones, the *Alta Arizona* and *Mohave Miner*, were contemporaries for a time and bitter rivals for subscriptions. The former was beset by a plague of drunken printers, the two who

OLD CEMETERY retains original juniper trees spared from axes. Some graves date back to '70s. Enclosure in center is unique in style. On grave in foreground grows beavertail cacti, *Opuntia basilaris*.

drank only water from the spring getting the type set and keeping the presses going. After a few spirited years of refuting each other's statements, the *Alta Arizona* left the field to the *Miner*.

Issues of this paper in '84 stated in glowing terms the many plans for expansion. A new hospital was to replace the one that had burned. It was hoped all patients could be kept and treated under one roof where part of them were cared for in the Palace Hotel. The old school building had been purchased by the school board to make an expansion possible, including a 220-square foot extension for the teacher's platform so she could look over the heads of her older and taller pupils.

Because of the price of lumber, many buildings were made of adobe. The locally popular Sheriff Steen's family had one of these for their home. Early one morning during a rare rainy spell, the Chinese cook at the Palace Hotel passed the Steen house on his way to work and saw it had collapsed in the night. Frantic diggers found the small girl of the family still alive, her younger brother almost doubled up under the weight of the adobe bricks but still breathing, the remainder of the Steens dead. Both children survived.

It cannot be said religious influence was very strong in the Park. There never was a regular church, traveling ministers sometimes preaching in a pool hall or hotel. The community did make one gesture heavenward by organizing a non-sectarian Sunday school. The *Mohave Miner* beamed paternally: "It is very important to the children as well as the community whether they shall be trained to be gentle, kind and good or allowed to grow up in evil, vicious habits, a curse to themselves, their parents and their country."

A bank was also missing from the camp. Miners had a haphazard system of leaving part of their money with storekeepers for safekeeping. In 1883 the *Miner* agitated for a bank with a capital of $50,000 to $100,000 but no bank ever appeared. Another plan for the building of a toll road from Mineral Park to Free's Wash, southwest of the present Kingman, also came to naught. It was to be called the Mineral Park and Wallapais Tow Road, the idea proposed by R. H. Upton and S. Owen who got as far as drawing up a partnership February 1, 1875 but built no road. However, several stage lines were eventually established, two of them running between Prescott and Hardyville on the Colorado River, making Mineral Park a station. Hugh White and Co. ran a small express and passenger service from Prescott to Mineral Park, Mohave City, Hackberry and Hardyville. A. L. Simonds advertised his Mineral Park and Kingman Stage would transport passengers between the two towns for $2, a four-hour, fifteen-mile trip.

The town which had been so hampered by transportation problems was thus overjoyed when in 1880 there were rumors that the Atlantic and Pacific Railroad was being put through northern Arizona. The rumors became facts and in '83 the railroad passed a point within fifteen miles of Mineral Park. Plans were carried out to improve the road to this point so as to take advantage of cheap rates for shipping ore and concentrates. Where the new road ended at the tracks, a depot and loading platforms were built, additional buildings put up for stores and a hotel. Several Mineral Park business concerns moved there, others establishing branches in Kingman, the new station stop.

When Kingman began to be noticeable as a town, the *Miner* predicted caustically the place would "soon be taken over by the horned toads." After a few months it took a neutral attitude and soon it was carrying more ads and news from Kingman than

ORE CAR abandoned beside narrow gauge tracks once carried quantities of rich gold- and silver-filled rocks. Prior to building of stamp mills, ore had to be rich to pay for immense cost of shipping overland to Colorado River, thence by barges to Port Isabel at mouth of river on Gulf of California, down Gulf to Port Arena and up coast to San Francisco where it was shipped to Swansea, Wales. When Selby smelter was built in San Francisco, shipping costs were reduced to $125 a ton. On February 12, 1876 a five-stamp quartz mill was put into operation in the Park, could get high price for crushing. After other mills were built, prices were forced down but never to low level, partly because of water scarcity for wet operation to reduce dust hazard.

NAMES OF MINES around Mineral Park include the whimsical Metallic Accident and Woodchopper's Relief as well as Lone Star and Fairfield. Keystone was first important lode, found in 1870 by Charles E. Sherman, producing gold and silver, giving name to Keystone Springs, only source of good water for town.

from home. In 1887 the paper moved to Kingman where it still operates.

Before long there were many vacant buildings in the Park. Several structures were burned and others vandalized, some adobe buildings collapsed for lack of repairs and Mineral Park took on the aspects of a ghost town. Kingman had been agitating for some time to get the county seat position and in November of 1886 a general election to decide the issue gave 271 votes for Kingman, Hackbarry 132, Mineral Park 99 and definitely out of the running. The town would not give up, however, especially since the supervisors had been so slow in calling for a recount of votes. Official results were not presented until December 31, on demand of County Supervisor Samuel Crozier.

What happened next spelled the final doom of Mineral Park's status as county seat. Shortly after midnight a party of Kingman men, their patience exhausted over the obstinate refusal of Mineral Park to comply with orders to give up the records, piled into a wagon and set out on the four-hour trip to the dying town. Arriving in the early morning hours, they proceeded to the courthouse and broke down the doors. They loaded all essential records into the wagon, returned to Kingman and set up the legal procedures necessary to the operation of the county seat.

Population in the camp was now further depleted and only a little mining activity remained. Even this went out in time and Mineral Park was very dead for many years as all buildings fell away, were burned or wrecked for valuable lumber.

At present one mine is again functioning across the creek of the bitter waters, near the old cemetery so picturesquely hidden in the junipers. These old trees and the fence posts near them, full of hollows and holes, make good nesting places for the profusion of Western Bluebirds which have forsaken so many other areas.

47

HOW HE WON THE BATTLE AND LOST THE WAR

Mowry, Arizona

It was certainly a duel in the sun and it might have been one to the death. For there was a challenge in the true spirit and tradition of gallantry. It was accepted and seconds appointed. The duelists met and the former lieutenant fired. But it was not a very good rifle and he was not a very good shot and his antagonist was not a very serious enemy. So instead of killing him he went over and shook his hand.

Dramatic discoveries of silver in the Patagonia Mountains in 1736 brought a crowd of treasure seekers and caused King Philip V of Spain to claim the area as his own. According to persistent rumors the mines at Mowry were originally worked by Jesuit priests. If so their efforts were forgotten but still evident when a pair of Mexicans came along about 1857.

These men from south of the border (16 miles away) were sharp enough to discover that working a silver mine was not as easy as panning for gold, that it would require capital and machinery far beyond their means. They sold out at the first offer, from officers stationed at nearby Fort Crittenden. The Americans found the same problems, that they had no cornucopia that would effortlessly pour forth riches in gleaming silver. And when they saw they could not work together they gladly accepted the bid from Lt. Sylvester Mowry, also at the fort.

DANCE HALL, one of best preserved structures in extensive town growing up around Sylvester Mowry's extremely rich silver-lead mines, only metropolitan center in area. It had hotels, saloons, gambling places, stores, almost all built of adobe. When this photo was made in 1963 buildings were good enough to merit listing as "complete town for sale" in Tubac real estate office. By 1967 porch had collapsed, more plaster fallen, but still structurally solid. Tree is one most characteristic of area—interior live oak (as distinguished from California coastal tree). Live oak has evergreen, holly-like leaves, small acorns.

Mowry resigned from the army and devoted his energies to the mine. One of his problems was the roads were little more than trails and there would be no railroad for many years. With a crew of Mexican peons he started deepening the shafts and tunnels and before long his men were ascending ladders with astoundingly rich loads of silver-lead ore. This looked like success and he renamed the Patagonia mine for himself. As the Mowry it would produce over $1 million in one three-year period.

Galena was the ore, at first roughly refined in Mexican blast furnaces at Lochiel on the border, the lead and silver bars weighing about 70 pounds, shipped to Europe and sold in England for $200 per ton. But shortly pure silver was being cast locally into bars worth from $200 to $300 and used as a medium of exchange in an area still lacking in currency.

With the fantastic success of his mines making headlines in Eastern and European press, Mowry received many offers to speak in public at good fees. He turned the management of the mine over to several good men and went on what amounted to a chautauqua circuit. In one speech he declared that all streams in Arizona teemed with fish. However the eastern audience evaluated the overstatement, one Edward Cross of Tubac, Arizona, correspondent of the St. Louis *Republican*, bristled indignantly. In printed comment he ridiculed Mowry's brash utterance, saying he had found a few fish as long as his fingernail, that these must be the "Mowry trout."

Stung by the article, Mowry surprised Cross by demanding satisfaction in a formal duel. Reluctant but game, Cross met his challenger near Tubac (an old town near the Mission Tumacacori). The affair was widely publicized and attended by a gallery largely from Tucson, gamblers from mining camps having a field day placing bets.

Chosen as weapons were Burnside rifles and neither mine owner nor newsman knew much about using them. The first three shots went wild

COMPANY OFFICE interior, deteriorating but for Civil War vintage, still in good condition. Picture taken in 1963 shows usual adobe and plaster construction, streaks on wall seen thru door at left made by water leaking from roof.

MAIN GUARD TOWER overlooking Yuma Territorial Penitentiary. Gatling gun here frustrated most escapes. Water was pumped to tank under platform. During Civil War Sylvester Mowry was confined in this notorious prison, charged with treason, Union government maintaining mine owner provided lead bullets to Confederates. (For story and other photos of prison see **Tales the Western Tombstones Tell.**)

all his energies to them he might have made it through the war but there was talk about his sympathies being with the Confederate forces. A Rhode Islander by birth with no record of antipathy toward the Union cause, his continued public utterances were somehow construed as treachery to the North.

On June 8, 1862, Sylvester Mowry was arrested for treason. Gen. Carlton ordered the accused made prisoner on charges that Mowry had rendered aid and comfort to the enemy by producing for Confederate armies bullets manufactured of lead from his mines. The Union government seized them and confiscated all silver and lead produced.

The prisoner was immediately taken to Yuma and thrown into its notorious, dreaded territorial prison, it being reported he was "closely confined" which indicated incarceration in the "Hell Hole" or dungeon. There he languished until November when he was suddenly released and informed there was not a shred of evidence against him. In spite of complete exoneration Mowry found himself destitute, with no hope of any property being restored to him.

He brought suit against Gen. Carlton and the government for $1 million but all efforts to collect were frustrated especially after the mines were sold at public auction for $4,000. Some historians claim he was paid damages but others dispute this. Most agree Mowry went to London, England, where he died in poverty in 1871.

and then Mowry's gun failed to discharge. The seconds agreed he was entitled to another try but as he raised the weapon he saw Cross with arms folded, bravely ready for the bullet. Firing the rifle into the air, Mowry walked over to Cross and extended his hand. Both declared themselves satisfied, and later both made public retractions of their bitter statements.

Mowry's mines were producing $1,000 a day when the Civil War broke out. Had he devoted

CENTRALLY LOCATED building assumed to be mine company office, photo taken in 1963. Roads wind thru town as main street, visitor continuing along good surface about 1 mile, taking left fork up hill, exploring manzanita brush at left, will bring him to cemetery. Just back of point from which photo was taken is fork leading sharply left and steeply up nearer hill. About ¾ mile up slope are located big Mowry mines and small village dating from World War I days, now as deserted as main town.

OATMAN, ARIZONA

Oatman was named for a family which had camped near Gila Bend in 1851. It consisted of the mother and father, two daughters and a son. The Oatmans were attacked by a marauding band of Apaches, the parents killed, the boy, Lorenzo, beaten to unconsciousness and the girls kidnapped. When a detail of soldiers was sent out to effect their rescue, the sisters, Olive and Mary Ann were hidden by their captors at a small spring a half mile north of town and then spirited away. Mary Ann died later, but Olive was released in 1856 and joined her brother at Fort Yuma. She married John Fairchild in New York State in 1865 and died in Texas in 1903.

In its earlier days Oatman boasted a narrow gauge railway. It ran from the mines to Fort Mojave on the Colorado, to which point supplies were ferried from Needles, California.

During this period of ascendancy, Oatman took $3,000,000 in gold from its sterile, craggy site and boasted two banks, ten stores and a Chamber of Commerce.

"MOST FAMOUS SALOON IN ARIZONA" is proud boast of few remaining residents. Structure was known as "Mission Inn," upper floor once rested on ground, was raised and new section built beneath. Some differences of opinion exist as to purpose of many cubicles, each with one of numbers 1 to 18, upstairs. Some say they were "offices," others "gambling joints" or "apartments." Quartzite obelisk "Elephant's Tooth" looms in background.

QUARTZSITE, ARIZONA

Hi Jolly and eighty camels crossing the desert sands of Arizona furnish the color behind the settlement of Quartzsite at Tyson's Well. The camel caravans did not stay in the country but Hi Jolly did, to act as scout for the army and he lies buried in an unmarked grave in the local cemetery.

The town came into being because gold was found between that spot, Ehrenberg and La Paz. While never a mining camp it was an important stage stop, at first with no name but because of a well there and a man named Tyson the first settler, it became known as Tyson's Well. When the Indians began a series of attacks on the few residents, an adobe fort was installed with a few soldiers and the place became Fort Tyson although it was never a formal army fort.

In time the settlement needed a post office but authorities rejected the name Fort Tyson as having no standing. The white nature of the prevailing country rock suggested "Quartzite" which name was accepted, but somewhere along the line an "s" was inserted and the infant town became officially Quartzsite. This was the area adopted by Hi Jolly who had been Hadji Ali in Syria.

About 1855 the United States Government decided to use camels to open up the road from Fort Defiance to the Colorado River, the country almost all desert. Civilian Gynn Harris Heap was sent to the Middle East to procure camel herds and bring them home. He centered his search in Smyrna, Turkey, and frequented a grog shop called Mimico Teadora near the famous Caravan Bridge where Arabs and Greeks gathered in friendly talk.

Here in late 1856 Heap met his man, one Hadji Ali who had spent most of his life with camels, half of it driving or buying them for others. The first packet of camels had been readied for the voyage and Hadji Ali was ready to leave with them on his great adventure. Instead he was sent into the interior of Asia Minor to secure a second herd and then accompanied it to the United States, arriving at Indianola, Texas, February 10, 1857.

Hi Jolly as he now was called never spoke much of his past but friends and army men knew his father was an Arabian who had participated in a raid on a Greek island and taken a native girl as a trophy of war. She became Hadji Ali's mother and for a time he went by the Greek name Philip Tetro, later changing it when he embraced the Mohammedan faith.

The two shipments of camels comprised groups of thirty-three and forty-seven, several females bringing forth young aboard ship. The herd was divided into several units and under Arab drivers taken over snowy mountains, through pine woods and over deserts, covering about twenty-five miles a day. The camels did not protest at the heavy packs but the drivers did. One by one they quit but Hi Jolly stayed on to break in new drivers from army personnel.

The camel project seemed to be going well but the Civil War broke out to end it, road building and all. The camels were offered as "surplus" but there were almost no takers. The animals required special handling, were crankier than mules and panicked other stock. Turned loose to fend for themselves they got along with varying degrees of success. Myths and legends about the strange beasts grew rapidly, one concerning "a great, rusty-red animal" seen mysteriously with a dead rider strapped to its back. As the beast roamed the wastelands pieces of the body were torn off against brush and cacti until only the legs and then only the feet remained. At last someone shot the wanderer which by then carried only the rawhide bindings. Another engaging legend was offered by Indians. One camel was foolish enough to defy the spirits of thunder and lightning, was turned into stone and the origin of Camelback Mountain near Phoenix explained.

With the abandonment of the camels, Hi Jolly was out of a job, but not for long as he was too good a man as scout and guide in Northern Arizona with which he was now familiar. He keeps appearing in stories about the subjugation of the Indians by the army and the rounding up of cattle and horse thieves.

About 1871 a band of Apaches stole over a hundred head of horses, mules and cattle from the

Bowers Ranch in Skull Valley, killing the herder in the process. Hi Jolly was working at Fort McDowell and was sent out as tracker for a cavalry company. He came across the trail but could not persuade the commanding officer it was the right one. Disgustedly he returned to the Fort and when the soldiers returned the officer was arrested and courtmartialed.

On April 28, 1880, Hi Jolly was married to Gertrude Serna of Tucson, in that city. The marriage started out well but the Greek-Arab was a born nomad, the trait kept alive by years of scouting and prospecting. In 1894 he reported in Yuma that he had located a rich deposit of tin in the Plomosa district. He had been living in the Tyson's Wells area, he said, and made the discovery in seeking medical aid for a sick prospector who had been working with him. His final wanderings were confined to the Tyson's Well or Quartzsite area where he died, December 16, 1902.

MONUMENT TO HI JOLLY, dedicated January 5, 1936. Built by Arizona Highway Department, copper camel at apex was made in Highway shops at Phoenix. Memorial stands in Quartzsite Cemetery where, in unmarked grave, lies famed camel driver, scout and prospector. Base rocks are black lava of the area, next above snowy quartzite, then band of petrified wood. Rounded log section near right corner is spectacular specimen, ruby red in color, proves vandals sometimes have self-control. In copper container at base are Hi Jolly's government contracts, ashes of Topsy, one of his camels which died at Griffith Park Zoo in Los Angeles, and his total wealth at death — sixty cents.

SALOME, ARIZONA

The Salome Frog, second in fame only to Mark Twain's Celebrated Frog of Calaveras County, was the creation of Dick Wick Hall. He made the frog known locally through the pages of his little weekly newspaper, the SALOME SUN, then in the late '20s broke him into the big time in the SATURDAY EVENING POST. The character was his talisman, symbol of his free spirit and sense of humor as big as the desert itself.

"The Salome Frog is seven years Old," he explained in one of his sketches which was accompanied by a cartoon showing the frog with a canteen on its back, "and even though he can't swim it isn't his Fault. He never had a chance, but he lives in Hope. Three years ago Fourth of July Palo Verde Pete shot off a box of Dynamite and the Frog thinking it was Thunder, chased the Cloud of Smoke two miles down the road, hoping it might rain. He is older and wiser now, and is getting like the rest of the Natives, he just sits and Thinks."

The frog of Salome wasn't born in that town, Hall went on to explain. He found its egg in Owens Valley in California and thought at first it was a wild duck egg, but on the way home it hatched and proved to be a frog. The creature was nurtured on loving care and bottled Shasta and Pluto water which explains why it grew up to be so healthy and active.

If not the founder of Salome, Dick Wick Hall was at least its moving force with his newspaper and service station where he sold "Laffing Gas." As De Forest Hall he was born in Creston, Iowa, 1877. After college he served in a war and collected rattlesnakes in Florida. At a Nebraska State Fair he was so entranced by a display of the Hopi Indians of Arizona, he set his sights on the northern part of the state, arriving there at twenty-one with $14.35 in his pocket. Very soon he was among the Hopis as a census taker and the Indians liked him so well he was taken into the tribe. Wearing Hopi garb, he studied their habits, customs and ceremonies including the sacred Snake Dance. Close observation of their drawings, petroglyphs and symbolic designs may have influenced his later use of sketches in his mimeographed paper the SALOME SUN.

After the Hopi interlude, Hall settled down for a time on a small ranch in Pleasant Valley, the area long the scene of a range feud between cattle and sheep ranchers, theoretically finished with a full-scale battle in 1887. Smaller outbursts continued periodically but Hall, growing vegetables for the community, was never involved. "I was never shot at," he said. "I guess good gardeners were too scarce."

Then came a stint on a construction job, followed by something more fitting to his talents. He was made editor of the WICKENBURG NEWS-HERALD, a paper of shaky stature which did not strengthen

BLUE ROCK INN, operated in days of Dick Wick Hall by Mrs. E. S. Jones and her three daughters. As girls married, husbands provided extra help when business boomed as highway was built by town. Hall wrote free "ad" in his paper: "All inside rooms have Running Water ready to run on Very Short Notice and by coming at the right Season of the Year you can have whichever You Prefer—Hot or Cold (always hottest in summer). Only the Ground and Atmosphere are provided with outdoor Rooms, as no covering is Needed in the summer Season which is often quite Long."

DICK WICK HALL'S MODEST HOME also served as shop where he mimeographed famous little paper, the **Salome Sun.** In 1926 Hall went to Los Angeles "unwillingly" to have dental work done and while there doctors discovered a far advanced case of Bright's Disease from which he died. His body lies under monument in front yard, shaft built of pieces of valuable ore which mining friends contributed. Two small boys guided photographer to spot, took exception to his pronunciation of town's name—Salomay—informed him correct way to say it was—Salom.

financially during his tenure. No doubt he contributed color with such doggerel as:

"The past ten months serve to remind us
  Editors don't stand a chance.
The more work the more we find behind us
  Bigger patches in our pants."

During his stay in Wickenburg he used the alliterative "Dick Wick" as his name and was Dick Wick Hall the rest of his days. Also during this period he was bitten by the prospecting bug and the condition became chronic. He wrote home so glowingly of his new love, Arizona, his brother Ernest (later to be Arizona's Secretary of State) joined him and the two started combing the surrounding hills with pick and pan. An acquaintance, one Shorty Alger, lit his fuse in a gopher hole in the area just west of Wickenburg and exposed a pocket of gold assaying $100 to the pound. The news set off a minor gold rush but Dick, being astute and on the spot, filed on 100,000 acres of desert land with his brother as partner.

Shorty's fifteen-foot hole soon yielded $30,000 worth of gold, then pinched out. With almost everyone going home, Dick stayed on and began the drilling of a well, determined to develop a town in

the area. Natural promotion qualities asserted themselves and when the well produced, he formed the Grace Valley Irrigation district.

Having struck some color close by he started a mine called the Glory Hole and as a few buildings sprang up, a town of sorts was born. The railroad was being run through from Wickenburg and he induced a merchant friend, E. S. Jones, former owner of stores in Wickenburg and old Congress, to set up a new one on his property to serve the railroad men and anyone happening along. The location was half a mile below the well and mine, more convenient to the railroad, so the buildings of the first settlement were moved down and new ones added. The tiny hamlet was named Salome for Grace Salome Pratt, wife of one of Dick's mining partners, Carl Pratt.

One addition to the slowly growing Salome was a boarding house and hotel run by Mrs. Jones and her three daughters—Evvy, Lucy and Dorothy. Another was a post office with Hall as temporary postmaster, and a saloon. Salome did not support the latter and it was reopened as a school. The first teacher was one of the Jones girls whose married sister in Wickenburg had several children of school age. When the roster got low the teacher would call her sister to send down the number needed to fill the necessary quota of eight.

Part of this time Dick Wick Hall was busy traveling through Louisiana, Texas, Utah, California and Florida promoting other interests which included mines, oil wells and real estate. When the highway was built close to Salome, paralleling the railroad, he saw possibilities in a gasoline station and garage, and began staying home to develop them. The road was rough and many tired travelers elected to spend the night at the Blue Rock Inn — the boarding house and hotel. Salome had been built north of the tracks and as the highway was run south of them, the store was left "stranded" as it were. Mr. Jones' enterprising sons-in-law, of which there were several by now, tried to prevail on the old gentleman to move the store to the highway. The patriarch was adamant. "Nothing doing. Let them come over here. They know where we are."

It was to publicize the gas station that Hall started his famous one-sheet mimeographed "newspaper" where the Salome Frog found a home. It was only one of many quizzical characters to appear on the pages. As prominent was Salome herself. She was early separated from the lady of the same name, being a ribald caricature of the Biblical dancer. Hall's masthead was varied, most often reading: "The Salome Sun, where she danced," followed by the disclaimer: "It wasn't my fault. I *told* her the Sand would be too hot without her shoes." Many free "ads" were shaped up to the benefit and sometimes embarrassment of the parties involved. One issue said you could always have hot or cold running water at the Inn, provided you came at the right season. Of the fertile soil around Salome, Hall wrote: "The Melons don't do too well here. The vines grow so fast they wear out the melons dragging them over the ground." He also said: "Salome's population has increased 100% a year — 19 people in 19 years", and one of his many comments about the aridity of the region was: "We plant onions between the potatoes, they make the eyes of the potatoes water enough to irrigate the garden." He made crude little maps for his customers at the Laffing Gas Station with a small line under them — "This map doesn't show all the bumps and curves, but don't worry, you will find them all right."

Salome today is still about the same size but many of the buildings are unoccupied. The vitality of the town faded with Hall's death in 1926. But both the town and Dick Wick Hall's spirit come to life each fall, September 10, with an old-fashioned pit barbecue, square and folk dances for the farmers and cattlemen for fifty miles around. They come with their families and relive the times of Dick Wick Hall. The paved roads are about the only difference from the days when he was writing:

"This very old Typewriter I learned to Type on has lost lots of its teeth. It was so Old and so many of its Letters were Gone that I got used to hitting the Capitals where the little ones were gone that I can't get Out of the Habit."

STORE ON HALL PROPERTY was set up by his friend E. S. Jones, former merchant of Wickenburg and old Congress, in 1906. Post office was added shortly, Hall serving as temporary postmaster. Little false-fronts stand silent and empty, slowly falling victims to weather.

STANTON, ARIZONA

"From Monastery To Murder" could have been the title of a biography of Charles P. Stanton if he could have found anybody to write it. By one means or another, always devious, he got what he wanted which was to be "king of the camp" and was the most hated and feared man in the Antelope Valley.

Stanton began his adult life in an atmosphere of rectitude as novice in a monastery but was soon expelled on charges of immorality. Drifting west he passed in and out of many mining camps, always learning some new way of making a "fast buck", preferably by latching on to some innocent's hard-earned cash. Then he struck the Antelope Valley and saw opportunity with a big "O".

The Rich Hill district with the Congress, Weaver, Antelope and Octave mines in Antelope Valley, was one of the several productive placer areas discovered by the Pauline Weaver party in the early 1860's. When the stage line through the Valley established a regular stop there, the place took the name of Antelope Station. The usual saloons, boarding houses and stores grew up along the placer beds, centering around the general store of the popular partners, Wilson and Timmerman.

In Antelope Station Stanton settled in a small cabin near the partners' store. His first intention may have been to pan some of the easy gold in the creek but if so the noble desire was short lived. More to his liking was the Wilson and Timmerman business.

He started a well-planned, three-way plot, pitting the partners against another Antelope resident, William Partridge. Hate was worked up between Partridge and Wilson, then Stanton slipped the word that Wilson was out gunning for the other. Partridge flared up, took the initiative and shot the merchant in the street in true Western style. Partridge was convicted of a murder and sent to the penitentiary largely because of adverse testimony by his supposed friend, Charles P. Stanton.

Smugly, he now began to lay plans to shorten the future of partner Timmerman. Sure enough the man was found dead one day, a coroner's jury unable to say whether the death was suicide from grief over his partner's passing or simply an accident.

Up to now Stanton had not been suspected but when he took over the store and claimed the partners had left it to him, people began to wonder. After a continuing series of mysterious acts of violence, all happening to those who stood in Stanton's way, suspicion became certainty. But his power and influence was so great no one dared to lift a voice—no one except Barney Martin who was heard on several occasions to say: "Something should be done about Charles Stanton."

Then one midnight a stranger knocked at Martin's door and gave warning. "A lot of strange things have been happening in this town, what with people getting killed and all. Get your family out of here before they are all murdered."

OLD CONGRESS HOTEL is still in use as private residence. Giant saguaro cacti were planted as small seedlings when town and hotel were flourishing. Holes in upper areas made by woodpeckers as nests are often occupied later by elfin owls. Cactus plant forms hard, air- and water-tight linings around pockets, once used by Indians for water bags. When photographer set up tripod in yard it was filled with milk goats, all scampering out except one curious maverick.

Martin was no personal coward but he knew he couldn't keep guard over his family the clock around. So he sent a man on horseback to tell his friend Captain Calderwood that his family would be arriving at Calderwood Station in a day or two, then he piled his family into a wagon and left town.

Linked with Stanton's nefarious interests were the Valenzuela brothers who were to come up short in the holdup at the Vulture mine. These two desperadoes in company with several others followed the Martin wagon and forced it off the road after it was well away from the camp. The entire family was then murdered, dry brush piled on the wagon and the whole set on fire. When the Martins failed to appear at Calderwood, the captain sent out a search party which traced the wagon tracks to the scene of carnage.

Yet nothing was done to check Stanton's supremacy for fear of reprisal. Instead of suffering for his misdeeds he now took over the whole town, even changing its name to his own. Feeling secure as "king of the camp", Stanton began pressing his attentions on a beautiful Mexican girl, Froilana, daughter of Pedro Lucero who was leader of a gang of toughs in neighboring Weaver. The girl had different ideas and no intention of submitting to him. Stanton, not used to resistence in any form, forced the issue. The next day in his store, he turned to face what he thought was a customer and quickly saw it was the girl's brother Jose. Before Stanton could draw his gun, Jose put two .44 slugs into the chest of the man who had wronged his sister.

Fleeing from the scene, young Lucero met a friend coming down the trail who inquired the reason for all the hurry. "I have just killed Stanton," he replied, "and I am hurry up to get across the border." The friend caught his arm. "Wait. Don't go. We will get up a reward for you."

58

"A spiral of gray smoke . . . but there was no fire!"

TOMBSTONE, ARIZONA

Edward L. Schieffelin of Tombstone, Arizona, and Bob Womack of Cripple Creek, Colorado, had several things in common. They were prospectors at heart and each had a stubborn faith in the ultimate riches of his chosen locale. Each did, in time, see his dream fulfilled in a fabulous strike but there the parallel ended. Bob never did do much with his strike because he drank too much and could not interest big money for proper developments of his find. Ed, on the other hand, made the proper contacts right away, kept control of the several companies he formed, and was a prime figure in the development and history of his city.

As prospectors found out, locating a rich vein is one thing, mining it is another. In the case of placer gold, a lot of the stuff may be found loose in the creek bed and may be had for the panning, but hard rock mining is something else, particularly in the case of silver. When Ed made his find he had done his searching all over Oregon, California and Nevada, at last bearing down on a restricted area in southern Arizona, the fringe of hills bordering the San Pedro River. For a long time the search was as fruitless as the others but now he didn't move on. Settling down to a dogged, systematic scrutiny, he went over the ground almost inch by inch. It wasn't easy. Plenty of

WEARY OLD SADDLES in harness house of O. K. Corral bear mute testimony to hard usage in days when chief means of transportation was riding horse. These were used by Wyatt Earp, McLowery brothers, Clantons and others of the day.

O. K. CORRAL supported large blacksmith shop, used several anvils. This one saw service over long period in '70s and '80s. Most of auxiliary tools are intact and in their original places.

rattlesnakes and gila monsters lurked under every other bush but the most dangerous hazards were bands of marauding Apache Indians. This tribe had more tenaciously and vindictively resisted the white man than any other. And, in fact, the stronghold of the head man of all the Apaches, Cochise, was in the Dragoon mountains, only a few miles from the San Pedro.

Ed tried to work the country under the protection of a group of soldier scouts stationed at Fort Huachuca, but felt too restricted, and informed the men he was going to set out on his own. Asked what he was really looking for, he told them that he expected to find something very useful in the valley. Loud laughter greeted this evasive answer and one of the soldiers said, "Sure you will and it'll be your tombstone."

In approved fashion, Ed persisted in looking for "float" and then searching for the lode or vein from which it came. And finally, there it was, a rich vein of silver, close to the hideout of the Apaches in the Dragoons. The grim joke about

his tombstone had rankled, likely because it could so easily have materialized, and he felt a deep satisfaction in naming his claim "The Tombstone." With help in the form of his brother, Al, and one Richard Gird, a clever mining man, he located several other silver deposits, among them the Lucky Cuss and the Tough Nut. This last had an erratic breaking of the lode in every direction, due to faulting.

A real problem developed in trying to enclose the best of these in the amount of ground allotted to a claim, 600 by 1500 feet, a "tough nut" to crack. Actually, the first find, the Tombstone, proved to be not so rich as he had hoped, and was soon sold for just enough to get a little capital. Then they sold another one, the Contention for $10,000. This last sale was soon regretted, the Contention

OLD CHAINS ARE DRAPED across hitching rail of O.K. Corral Stable. Original building was in bad state of repair few years after famous shooting scrape in yard, was repaired and restored with authentic atmosphere. Visitors can now browse around stable and yard almost hearing again fusillade of shots.

BOXES IN TINY BIRD CAGE THEATER were taken at $25 a night and often for a whole week during popular presentations. Theater made no pretensions at elegance, shows were frankly burlesque of most rowdy type. Girls doubled as performers, waitresses and anything else requested of them. Opened December 26, 1881, it was never empty, was a place where lonely, thirsty miners or tired businessmen could always be comforted. As girls served drinks to patrons during prelude to performance, they sang the bawdy songs of the day, giving the place its name. Stoutly built of adobe it is well preserved and the visitor today can wander around the tiny floor and stage where performers of another day cavorted.

YARD OF O. K. CORRAL. Adobe wall and big swinging gate are much as they were in days of famous fight here, October 27, 1881. Fight climaxed long standing feud between Ike Clanton's cowboys and three Earp brothers. Clanton's gang had been vowing to "get" the Earps and had so annoyed the Marshal and his brothers that he decided to put an end to it once and for all. As the brothers and Doc Holliday headed for O. K. Corral they saw Sheriff Behan trying to keep the peace by asking the Clantons and McLowerys to disarm. When the Marshal and his party got near enough, he added his order, "Boys, throw up your hands, I want you to give up your shooters." At this Frank McLowery drew his weapon but was a split second too slow, was shot just above the waist by Wyatt Earp. This set off a barrage of gunfire. When the smoke cleared away three men were dead and two wounded. Only Doc Holliday escaped unscathed. The *Epitaph*, Tombstone newspaper of the day, reported that, "The shooting created great excitement, and the street was immediately filled with people. Ike Clanton (who had run from the fracas) was captured and taken to jail. The feeling of the better class of citizens is that the Marshal and his posse acted solely in the right in attempting to disarm the cowboys and that it was a case of kill or be killed."

yielding $5,000,000 in the first five years. This gave them a better idea of the value of what they held, and they refused an offer of $150,000 for the others, deciding they had enough money to go ahead. Big money interests now invested in the operation, as long as they could not buy it outright. This is the point where the careers of Ed Schieffelin and Bob Womack diverge.

By this time, all sorts of stores, offices and saloons had grown up near the diggings, and the motley collection had taken on the status of a city. Because of the slope of the land, streets were laid out at an angle from cardinal compass directions, numbered streets are intersected by Toughnut, Allen, Fremont and Safford. Allen became filled up first and remained the main street. The O. K. Corral, the Bird Cage Theater, Cosmopolitan Hotel, Campbell and Hatch's Pool Hall and many more places of dubious respectability mingled with stores along Allen Street.

The original prospectors, miners, assay men and other hard working gentry now gave way to a new crop of characters. This new crop was made up of men like Wyatt Earp, Doc Holliday, Bat Masterson, Luke Short and Turkey Creek Johnson. Johnson had come from Deadwood with a ready made reputation as a gunslinger, and his confidence in his own aim was such that he invited his opponents to meet him in front of the cemetery. Since he, himself, served as volunteer sexton, he figured to save himself some foot work.

The year 1880 alone saw 110 liquor licenses issued for honky tonks along Allen Street, until every other structure was a saloon. There were fourteen faro joints which never closed.

The biggest tide of population came sometime in the decade between 1880 and 1890, rising to about 15,000. Even with such a large proportion of the lawless, enough remained to support four churches, several dancing schools, along with a Masonic Hall, and quarters for the Knights of Pythias. Catering to culture was the Tombstone Club, this was a sort of library where many periodicals and books were rented, and where meetings were held to discuss plays, politics and the more genteel aspects of life in Tombstone. Somehow, these latter seem never to have been very prominent in the history of the place.

It seemed that there was an inexhaustible supply of silver in the mines, and the shafts went deeper and deeper. Then came catastrophe.

Abundant courses of water were encountered at these lower depths, and the mines filled. Huge pumps had to be installed. One, The Grand Central, stood thirty feet above its foundations and cost $300,000. It worked fine but the water went down slowly, in spite of an enormous outpouring at the mouth of the mine. Only when other mine owners began to celebrate did the horrible truth dawn. The Grand Central was draining all the mines in the district! Not only that, the others refused to share in the expense.

Pumping however, continued until 1885, when the old enemy, fire, struck and razed the pump house. A year later fire hit the Contention operations destroying the pumping works and forcing closure. Then, at long last—cooperation. A consolidated pumping system was set up and in 1901 sunk a main shaft to the depth of 1,080 feet, bringing out 8 million gallons of water a day. Tombstone got on its feet again and resumed the pleasures of the Bird Cage Theater, bawdy houses and saloons.

As the single male population had been increasing so had that of the prostitutes. A fair number of these were employed at the Bird Cage, where the girls acted as performers and danced with the customers "so as to promote friendly relations." Another group worked and lived in a house managed by a madame. Others, more independent or not up to the required standards, kept their own cribs, and sat at the doors to attract busi-

HEARSE MADE FREQUENT TRIPS to Boot Hill, sometimes several in one day as when Billy Clanton and McLowerys were buried there. Vehicle rented for those whose friends could afford it, where undertaker was employed and c a s k e t provided. More victims of bullets or mine accidents were merely laid in pine box and carried over. Even box was of skimpiest construction as lumber was a scarce and expensive commodity. Nearest timber was many miles away in high mountains. Any shipment of lumber had to be guarded as it came into town to prevent highjacking.

**TOMBSTONE WAS ORIGIN-
ALLY IN PIMA COUNTY,**
with seat at Tucson 73 miles
across Whelstones. As town expanded in population, new
county of Cochise was formed,
and courthouse of adobe built on
Fremont St. Increasing prestige
demanded finer edifice, and this
structure was put up at corner
of Third and Toughnut Streets.
It no longer serves, county seat
having been transferred to Bis-
bee.

ness. Still others walked the streets and went after customers avoiding a split of their earnings with a procurer.

Seldom did anyone hear of a surname for the girls. Nicknames prevailed, such as: Rowdy Kate, Dutch Annie, Blonde Marie, Irish May and Crazy Horse Lil. The land on which Dutch Annie built her brothels was owned by Wyatt Earp and leased to her.

The smaller respectable section, residences of families, etc., tried to edge as far as possible in the other corner of town, still not very far away, as too much expansion would go over the edge of the mesa.

This last flurry of boom and optimism was all too short, and signs of decay began to creep in when the inordinate cost of operating the pump-

ing system began to overtake income. The town was already on its last legs, when in 1914 the big Phelps Dodge Corporation bought equipment of the Tombstone Consolidated Mining Company at a receiver's sale for $50,000, sounding the death-knell of active mining for Tombstone.

The "town too tough to die" still lives, in a sense. It offers much to the visitor, a good many of the buildings so steeped in the rowdy history of the famous place still stand.

Ed Schieffelin lies now on the hill above town, near his first discovery. Over his grave is a stone marked "This is my Tombstone." His funeral was the largest ever held in town. The next largest was that of Dutch Annie, "Queen of the Red Light District," attracting a procession of 1,000 buggies, and most of the business men and city officials.

Arizona

NO LAW BUT LOVE

Tubac, Arizona

The story of Tubac is interwoven with those of southern Arizona's three most important missions, San Xavier del Bac, Tumacacori and Guevavi (often spelled Guebabi). San Xavier, poetically referred to as the White Dove of the Desert, has been in almost constant use and is possibly the most beautiful and finest example of mission architecture in the United States. Tumacacori, victim of Apaches and vandals, is a pathetic shell, yet retains a certain nobility. Its ruins are arrested from further decay by its present status as a national monument. Guevavi, older and never as large nor as solidly built as the others, has all but disappeared, its adobe walls melted to mere mounds of mud. Of the seven missions established by Father Kino during his service within the present

boundaries of Arizona, only these three were known to have been in operation at the time of his death in 1711.

Missions and ranches of the Tubac area were constantly exposed to murderous Apache raids during their early years and were all but inoperative by 1851. In that year, Pima and Papago tribes joined forces in an earth sweep just north of the Mexican border. Priests who had failed to escape were killed and Spanish silver-mining equipment, in operation since 1736, was destroyed. The next year a presidio, or garrison was established at Tubac, with soldiers offering a measure of protection to what few farmers remained. By 1753, the priests had returned to their devastated churches.

The earliest history of Tubac as a settlement isn't clear, but its name originated from a Pima

SOME GRAVES in old Tubac cemetery are marked but whole sections lack any identification.

word meaning "a burned out place." Located beside the Santa Cruz River, it is bordered on the west by the Diablito Mountains and on the other horizon by the Santa Ritas. The river, now a trickle at best, was a dependable stream in the days of Tubac's prosperity, even justifying the building of grist mills along its banks. By 1776 the town was the center of an extensive farming, cattle raising and mining community. In that year, Anza chose the fertile spot as a gathering place while he planned his push on to San Francisco. Already distinguished as being the oldest town established by white men in Arizona, Tubac became the first Mormon settlement in the state just 100 years later.

Shortly after the arrival of the "Saints," there appeared a man who later would be called the "Father of Arizona." This was Charles D. Poston, who with his friend Herman Ehrenberg prospected the neighboring mountains in 1854. Poston found sufficient indications of mineral wealth to warrant his being chosen to lead an expedition sent out two years later by the Sonora Exploring and Mining Company, which developed into the Heintzelman mine.

During this period, Poston was put in charge of the town's 800 souls, four-fifths of them Mexicans. Invested by his company with the title of Alcalde, the new mayor instigated a unique monetary system in use at Tubac in 1858. Since almost the entire populace was illiterate, paper money called *boletas*, bearing pictures instead of numbered denominations was used. A pig signified 12½ cents, a calf 25c, a rooster 50c, a horse $1.00 and a bull $5.00.

Poston wrote of the community at this time, "We had no law but love and no occupation but labor; no government, no taxes, no public debt, no poli-

RESTORATION at Tubac has been generally well done, building of this wall not finished where lamp post is inserted. Many other adobe buildings need repairing or complete rebuilding. Insertion of wheel in adobe wall is anachronism not appealing to purists.

FRAGMENT of original Mexican Presidio near modern museum. Soldiers stationed here protected residents from vicious Apaches for comparatively short period.

tics. It was a community in a perfect state of nature." So natural were some of the relations between young couples at Tubac—who merely set up housekeeping without benefit of clergy—that Poston inquired the reason. "It's a long journey to the nearest priest," they said, "and the father charges a fee of $25, which we cannot afford."

Poston then took it upon himself to perform marriages, claiming he was legally authorized to do so because of his government position. Instead of charging a stiff fee, Poston performed the rites free, even presenting the happy couples with a gift. In addition to marrying "new" couples, he married many who had already had offspring and wished to make their children legitimate. So popular did this service become that strange faces from surrounding areas began to show up at his office. "I had been marrying people and baptizing children for two years and had a good many god-children named Carlos or Carlotta, according to gender, and had begun to feel quite patriarchal," he commented, when the blow fell.

Bishop Lamy sent down to Tubac a priest named Macbeuf, the Vicar Apostolic of New Mexico. According to the Bishop, Father Macbeuf was to "look after the spiritual condition of the people of Tubac." Extremely conscientious, the priest followed the precepts of church law to the letter. The few sheets in town were commandeered to make walls for a confessional; he made parishioners wait until noon for the breakfast blessing, and he or-

dered that his followers have nothing to do with the Alcalde who had been so grossly encroaching upon the rights of the church. But worse yet, he informed his distraught congregation that marriages and baptisms that had been performed by Poston were illegal, that many were living in adultery. Then, going to Poston, he informed him that he had ordered the sinful cohabitors to suspend connubial relations forthwith.

In his journal, Poston says of the situation: "I knew there would be a riot on the Santa Cruz if this ban could not be lifted. Women sulked; men cursed, maintaining they were entitled to the rights of matrimony. My strong defense was that I had not charged any of them anything and had given them a treat, a marriage certificate with a seal on it made out of a Mexican dollar and had forged on an anvil." Still, though the Pope of Rome was beyond the jurisdiction of even the Alcalde of Tubac, he could not see the way open to a restoration of happiness.

"It would never do to let the population of the Territory be stopped in this way," he continued, "so I arranged with Father Macbeuf to give sanctity of the church to the marriages and legitimatize the little Carlos and Carlottas with holy water at a cost to the company of $700." This rectified the matrimonial situation along the Santa Cruz River and all were again satisfied." (Reprinted by courtesy of *Desert Magazine*.)

OLD RAILROAD CAR abandoned among much other rail equipment, mining machinery. Artifacts at Twin Buttes cannot be approached too closely, all sections behind fences. Photo made by special permission. Cactus plant is Opuntia species, this one with slabs of brilliant cerise-purple.

GHOST BEHIND BARBED WIRE

Twin Buttes, Arizona

Copper mining began in what was locally called the Borracho Mines some time in the early 1870s. Located in the mountains 26 miles southwest of Tucson, Arizona, miners named the town that developed Twin Buttes for a pair of nearby peaks. Mining there was sporadic for the first three decades, as little money was available to small-time Mexican operators and digging was done mostly by pick and shovel methods. When the copper veins thickened, activity increased until the deposit pinched out. Then everybody indulged in a siesta.

Near the turn of the century "The Three Nations" began wide-scale operations in the mines. American John G. Baxter, Irish Michael Irish and Scotch John Ellis, seeing what they called "an inexhaustible

supply" of copper ore, began by prospecting both old and new workings. Results were so encouraging and news releases so enthusiastic that a group of Milwaukee financiers bought out the whole thing, incorporating the Twin Buttes Mining and Smelting Co. with assets of $1,000,000 under the laws of Arizona Territory. Before incorporation was fully accomplished, the new company's prospectors made a happy discovery. The Morgan Mine had an ore body 95 feet deep, 25 feet wide and 300 feet long, with ore assaying 10%.

That same year, the company made plans to build a 500-ton smelter and construct a railroad from Tucson to the now roaring copper camp. The railroad would supplant transport by wagon and team and the new smelter would handle the huge amounts of ore pouring from the Morgan Mine and that royal trio, the Copper King, Copper Queen and Copper Prince.

By this time, Twin Buttes had acquired a newspaper, but it wasn't printed in town and it wasn't intended for local consumption. The *Twin Buttes Times*, edited and printed in Milwaukee, was aimed at stockholders. Bubbling with enthusiasm and carrying the Twin Buttes dateline for authenticity, it delivered the glad news that not only would the new railroad carry ores and supplies for Twin Buttes itself, but already applications were being received from other mining districts with requests for spurs. Among these, the *Times* said, were the Helvetia Mines in the Santa Ritas and the Lincoln Mining Company, which consisted of 31 claims in the Sierrita Mountains. The paper continuously stressed forthcoming benefits of the railroad because under territorial law, the Twin Buttes Mining and Smelting Company had to establish a second corporation, The Twin Buttes Railroad, in order to build the railroad. So stockholders, traditionally

OCOTILLO, technically Fourqueieria splendens is widespread throughout warmer sections of southern deserts. This one near Patagonia is in full display of scarlet bloom. Plant is not related to cactus tribe, has own method of coping with scant or non-existent moisture. In rain, regardless of season, shrub puts forth leaves, flowers. Here foliage has dropped to be replaced by bloom.

dazzled by an aura of rich paying mines, had to be infected by railroad fever, too.

Contrary to dire predictions, the projected railroad was actually built. The new Twin Buttes Railroad, connecting with the Southern Pacific in Tucson, ran in a southerly direction through Santa Clara Valley to Sahuarita. Then, swinging westerly in easy grades and curves, it ascended to Twin Buttes. Shortly after leaving Tucson, travelers on the railroad were treated to a close-up view of Mission San Xavier, that dazzling "White Dove of the Desert." The railroad advertised that it was prepared to accept general freight such as hardware, machinery, milk, cream and meat, the latter three items, it was stressed, at "shipper's risk." For the first few years, the railroad was a huge success. Twin Buttes Mines shipped large quantities of ore of types not handled at the local smelters, freight and passenger business was good, and some of the spur extensions were actually constructed.

Then, around 1907, the line unaccountably laid off employees and some freight shipments were "lost." Dissatisfied customers complained of poor service and high rates. In a few months both mine and railroad companies were overdrawn at the bank. About this time, a Twin Buttes Mining and Smelter stock offer was made of 250,000 shares at 60 cents, the offer almost immediately moderated to 40 cents. There were few takers. Bad times had hit Twin Buttes.

By 1910, the original company was pretty much disbanded. John Ellis, one of the "Three Nation" men who had gone along with the Twin Butte setup, married in Tempe, then returned to Scotland, where he died in 1909. Michael Irish married in Tucson, then took his new bride and copper wealth to the old country. But the other member, John C. Baxter, stepped in when the company closed down operation of the Twin Buttes properties and together with Ed Bush, reopened the Morgan. The start of World War I gave their new company a big boost and the railroad once again carried a car of ore every week. This boom was temporary, however. After the war, things again declined at the Buttes.

As deposits grew thinner, general economic conditions grew steadily worse and soon Twin Buttes became a ghost town. The railroad also faded into a shadowy spectre. Of the town, little is left, and this unreachable behind barbed wire. (Reprinted by courtesy of *Desert Magazine*.)

VULTURE CITY, ARIZONA

In the center of a sun-baked plaza in Vulture City stands an imposing group of ancient stone buildings and in the floor of the central one is a cavernous stone-lined pit covered by a heavy iron door. At the height of activity at the Vulture mine in the 1880s the buildings also housed the general and assay offices and the stone chamber was used to store gold bullion for safekeeping until it could be shipped to Phoenix.

There was the day three horsemen with two pack horses rode up to the front of the bullion room. Two were the brothers Valenzuela, Inocente and Francisco. When they leveled guns and roughly demanded the iron door be raised, a guard and the superintendent protested. They were both shot and killed on the instant. While one of the bandits held a gun on the rest of the office force, the other two went into the bullion room, lifted the conveniently unlocked door, removed $75,000 worth of gold bars and loaded the boxes on the pack horses. Gunfire now broke out on both sides. A bullet hit one of the bandits who dropped to the dust while the other two fled with the gold.

A posse was hastily organized but by the time the pursuers caught up with their quarry the loot had been buried. The leader of the posse shot one of the desperadoes but was held back from killing the other who fled into the mesquite. For two months the fugitive was hounded but eventually he thought it was safe to return to the spot where the bullion was hidden. As he started to lift out the heavy bars, he was shot and fell across them.

For a few years after this the bullion was shipped out by Wells Fargo carriers. The stages were repeatedly held up, drivers killed and the gold carried off. This happened so often Wells Fargo officials declined to haul the cargo and the mining company resorted to packing it on horses over rough and devious routes across the desert. After these safe carries, the gold was sent over the road again and on the very first trip the stage was held up, both driver and guard killed.

This was the way things went at the Vulture from beginning to end. Violence of every sort haunted the mine, its many operators and the men who worked in the tunnels. Danger from raiding Apaches was everpresent, guards with ready rifles being stationed on the knolls surrounding the workings. Even so more than four hundred whites were killed by Indians in one fifteen-year period. Near the point where the road turned toward town, the Wickenburg-Ehrenberg stage was once ambushed, six passengers killed, two escaping. One of these was a woman who later died of her wounds. Robbery, murder and rape were so frequent in the camp itself that at least nineteen men were hanged from the gnarled ironwood tree in the plaza.

It all started with Heinrich Heintzel who had known there was a nice vein of coal on his father's land in Austria and had always wanted to mine and sell it, the family finances seeming ever at the vanishing point. His father stubbornly refused and after his death young Heinrich found out why. He dug some coal and sold it only to learn government agents would imprison him for not turning it over to them. He fled to America, changed

PART OF VULTURE CITY. On descending hill where are located deep shafted mine, shops and mills, much of town comes into view. Group of stone buildings at left faces other direction on central plaza. At extreme left is store, next taller structure contained general offices, smaller one next is bullion room with vault in floor, last is elaborate assay office with almost all equipment still intact. During one period of ore shortage several buildings were torn down, walls put through mill and much gold recovered. Present mine owner estimates "there are 25 to 35 thousand dollars worth of gold in the walls of these buildings remaining." Just beyond is frame building housing mess hall. Others are bunk and tool houses. At extreme right small stone building with vanishing shingles may have served as jail. At its left corner is hanging tree.

his name to Henry Wickenburg, headed for the West and started prospecting in Arizona.

He arrived in Yuma in 1862, having made arrangements to join the party of Major Van Bibber at La Paz to prospect in Peeples Valley. Low water in the Colorado delayed the boat so long young Henry found the major had departed without him. He started out after the party.

Here was a man fresh from a foreign land attempting to penetrate two hundred miles of strange desert land alone. It was an incredible effort but young Wickenburg accomplished it, finding Van Bibber and the others camped in Peeples Valley. They prospected along the Hassayampa River with little or no success and in 1864 several members gave up, the party reduced to six. While they stayed in the river camp to decide what to do next, the young and persistent Austrian headed his burro toward a peak, near which he had heard was a vein of gold.

He stopped a short distance from the peak and set up a semi-permanent camp with a small tent. After several days of prospecting he wanted to sweep out the floor, and since there were many vultures circling around, he shot one to get a wing for a good broom. The wounded bird was thrashing in the dust and as he killed it he saw under the fluttering wings bright glints of gold, Wildly excited, he gathered up several pieces of the rich ore, returned to his companions and filed a claim with them. All

went to work on the site but the drudgery and lack of water discouraged the five partners and after ten weeks they decamped.

Wickenburg named his mine and the lonely peak Vulture and set to work by himself. All winter he used pick and shovel to remove surface ore, stuffing it into rawhides and packing it on the backs of two burros to the Hassayampa, twenty miles away.

Mining the ore was not too difficult for at first he did not have to go below ground. The lode was almost pure quartz, actually projected from the ground to a height of eighty feet, the ridges providing roosting places for the vultures, and extended horizontally three hundred feet, sixty to eighty in width. This exposure of such rich, gold-bearing ore was unique and would affect the history of Arizona for years.

Being unable to hand crush his ore and pan it in the river with any efficiency, Wickenburg employed Charles Genung to help him build an arrastra, the crudest type of grinder. After Henry had sluiced some of the product in the river water, he was convinced he really had wealth if he could only mine and recover at the same time. So he engaged several willing men to do the digging, hauling the ore down to him at the stream where he built several more crushers. This was Wickenburg's first mistake and set the pattern for a whole series of heartbreaks.

SUPPER REMNANTS LEFT FOR 21 YEARS. When gold mining was curtailed by government some "bootlegging" was being done here under guise of milling ore hauled in from old copper mine nearby. Informed of illegal gold operations here, U. S. inspectors stopped the men but allowed them to get supper. After hurried meal culprits slipped away to neighboring Bagdad copper mine where they were employed, went to work on morning shift.

Since he had never had an assay run, Henry did not know just how rich his mine was. As the prospectors and miners dug into the lode they soon ran into ore worth $100,000 to the ton or better than 25% gold. It was too much to keep men honest and they diverted the richest ore, sending the rest down to the boss.

In spite of this there was enough good ore arriving at the Hassayampa to warrant the building of real stamp mills by various firms. One was erected and operated by the Goldwater brothers who owned the large store in La Paz and later in Ehrenberg. Before long there were four hundred and fifty wagons hauling ore and eighty-five mills to grind it, a far cry from Henry's sledge hammer days a short time before.

Lack of water at the mine was a continuing problem. It had to be hauled from the river and cost ten cents a gallon for both men and mules. The animals hauling the water got very thirsty in the dust and heat and drank most of it. And they also ate much hay which could not be grown in this sterile rocky area. Eventually the water problem was solved by pumping it from the Hassayampa and feed was produced in the fertile Salt River Valley, a small village growing up there. The first building was Hancock's Store and the name of the town became Phoenix.

Wickenburg had sold out his interest in 1865, the price supposed to have been $85,000, $20,000 as a down payment. Almost immediately the buyer, B. Phelps of New York, began to haggle with the Austrian saying his title was not clear, partly because of the long lost partners. Believing he could win the case against the big corporation, Henry hired lawyers and sued, spending almost all his $20,000, but the courts held for the company. Broken in spirit, Wickenburg retired to an adobe house by the river.

During the litigation the company had taken out $1,850,000 in gold, built a huge mill at the mine and was erecting many stone buildings as offices, bunk houses, stores and homes for married workers. Adobe structures also sprang up by the dozens until Vulture City was a city in fact.

After a few years of prosperity B. Phelps sold out, having run up against a fault which cut off the main Talmadge vein. The new owners were furious but helpless, having bought the property on the strength of known richness. After many exploratory thrusts they located the continuing vein but then new faults were encountered and the mine

"MILLION DOLLAR STOPE" was so large miners were forced to leave heavy pillars of rich gold-bearing rock as ceiling supports. When later owners began mining out pillars, thousands of tons of rock collapsed into pit, forming huge "glory hole." While some surface ore has been removed since, artificial crater is essentially due to fall of roof.

changed hands again. Subsequent history of the workings followed this pattern until one lucky owner noticed the vein was widening and becoming even richer. The stope got so wide rock pillars were left to support the ceiling composed of many tons of earth and rock. This section was called aptly "The Million Dollar Stope". Then a new owner, a Canadian named McClyde, found himself running short of ready ore to keep the mills going and started mining out the pillars. Before salvage was completed the entire roof fell in, creating a gigantic "glory hole". Many pillars of high assay ore were lost, as was any possibility of locating the direction of the lode.

In 1931 "Rawhide Douglas" put down a shaft near the present well in an effort to relocate the

main body of ore but without success. The present mine owner, Dr. George H. Mangun says: "No one has ever located it. None of our present fancy electro-magnetic and electronics devices has been able to give us any clue. This makes the seventh time the lode has been lost due to faulting in prehistoric times."

During the life of the Vulture mine it has yielded $17 million in gold. Any estimate as to how much this would be increased by persistent "high-grading" could only be a guess, but some old timers say the true total would be near $100 million.

And the discoverer of all this wealth, Henry Wickenburg, lived out his embittered life in the adobe shack down by the river. His health gradually failed and meager savings disappeared. Early in July of 1905 the Austrian, born Heinrich Heintzel, walked out of his home, stopped under a large mesquite tree and blew his brains out. The weapon, an old style revolver, was very likely the same one with which he killed the vulture that showed the way to it all.

19 MEN MET DEATH HERE. During Vulture's early turbulence most murderers and horse thieves came to gruesome end dangling from stout branch of hanging tree. Fights among citizens or workmen resulting in death were condoned but not shooting of residents by strangers. 19th victim of noose was man whose attentions to comely woman were resented by husband who marched culprit to tree at gunpoint. Limb is conveniently low but as one old timer remarked: "We got their feet off the ground." Tree is large specimen of Olneya Tsota, locally called ironwood, general designation for several tough-wooded desert trees.

WEAVER, ARIZONA

Pauline Weaver was Tennessee born in 1800, the father a white man, mother the daughter of an Indian chief. Pauline was destined to be honored by having the name Weaver used for a mining camp, not because Pauline was some girl wonder of Arizona but because *he* was a military scout and public benefactor. The Indian mother named her baby Paulino which became Pauline in usage. Although a strange sounding name for a rugged character, it was not an uncommon one among half-breeds. Weaver however was to distinguish himself from the ordinary.

The boy started his wandering career as soon as he cut loose from his mother's buckskin "apron strings", ranging from home to Puget Sound and into Arizona. On the great ruin of Casa Grande one can see written on the walls: "Pauline Weaver was here — 1832" but he cannot be blamed for desecration. Pauline could not read or write.

In 1847 General Stephen W. Kearny hired him as military guide to lead the Mormon Battalion from New Mexico to California, rewarding him with a land grant in the area of present Banning. But the man was not a farmer and headed back to Arizona. In common with other "mountain men" he carried several weapons — his long-barreled, muzzle-loading flintlock gun, later a percussion cap type, then there was his bowie-type knife for skinning, butchering and eating.

While many of these men traveled in bands for safety. Weaver, like Bill Williams, preferred going it alone. One memorable exception was his gathering a party including Major A. H. Peeples, Jack Swilling, several other whites and some Mexicans. They were at La Paz after the discovery of gold there but came late and were not satisfied with what they found, pushing on through the arid desert region toward the Bradshaw Mountains. They reached a good stream of water, shot several antelope and made camp. The stream was named Weaver Creek in honor of the guide and the location Antelope Valley. This spot later became Stanton.

Next morning the horses were missing and the Mexican aides were sent after them. Covering the high hill nearby and beyond it, they not only found the animals but an abundance of *chispas*, nuggets the size of pebbles. Gathering a handful, they returned with the horses and told their story. Without waiting for breakfast, Major Peeples rushed over the mountain shoulder and picked up $7,000 in gold before returning to camp.

History says the men soon cleaned up the surface deposits but neglects to state if they ever had

FOUNDATIONS FOR MILL BUILDINGS in Weaver contain much native rock, not much scarce cement. Little adobe structure, center background, is typical of area where lumber was unobtainable. Formerly roofed with brush and mud, new mining activity at turn of century saw sheet metal roof as replacement, and even this has suffered from ravages of time. Building served as store, is lone survivor of business section of once flourishing camp, now only waste of rubble and brush. Tiny cemetery has no headboards standing now but in 1918 thirty-five were counted, all bearing legends: "Died with his boots on."

STONE POWDER HOUSE barely retains heavy iron door. Site is immediately below Weaver, likely chosen as safe distance. Large saguaro cactus may easily be several hundred years old and weigh several tons, is supported vertically by heavy woody-fibered structure, rest is pulp composed mostly of water. Rock intrusion in background is home for countless rattlesnakes, area known as "Rattlesnake Haven."

breakfast. As soon as the news got out a horde of whites and Mexicans burst on the scene in a full-scale gold rush. The mountain became known as Rich Hill, the mushrooming collection of adobes as Weaver Camp, later Weaverville, then Weaver. As men swarmed in, each claim was limited to 200 square feet and claim jumping was common.

When the camp's short life came to an end, the placers alone had given up a total of $1 million and lodes were found both at Weaver and the neighboring camp of Octave. The latter was appropriately named as eight partners found deposits.

Not having a miner's temperament, Weaver departed quickly. In 1867 he was again hired as a guide and attached to Camp Lincoln, later Camp Verde. Refusing a bunk in the barracks he occupied a tent outside the reservation. On the morning of June 21, a soldier was sent to see why the guide had not reported as scheduled and found Weaver dead in the tent. Everything was neatly in order

and the body wrapped in a blanket. Weaver had apparently been sharing the tent with an Apache and a year or so before had received an arrow in the shoulder. The shaft was removed but the head remained and this was thought to have caused his death.

He was buried with military honors by the companies of the 14th Regiment stationed at Camp Lincoln in the cemetery there. In 1892, after the Indian scares had subsided, remains of all military personnel including those of Weaver, were removed to San Francisco yet Weaver was not to rest there but to be a wanderer in death as he had been in life. In 1928 a movement was started in Prescott to bring the remains to the spot where in 1863 he had made as permanent a camp as he ever did. The spot is on the grounds of the Sharlot Hall Museum in Prescott, and is marked by a large stone bearing a bronze plate inscribed: "PAULINE WEAVER — truly a great man."

COMBINATION STONE and dugout buildings served as business section in better days of large gold mining camp of Octave, close neighbor of Weaver. In 1863 rich gold placer beds were discovered in Weaver Creek by party of eight men to commemorate their number.

MILL AT OCTAVE was built in expectation of many years of production by quartz veins, which were exhausted by end of century. Even so, Octave mine, consisting of two shafts 1,300 feet deep, turned out more than $8 million.

MEMORIES GHASTLY & GHOSTLY

WHITE HILLS, ARIZONA

In a truly desert setting, five miles from the highway, lie the scattered remnants of one of the wildest camps in Arizona.

This was White Hills, so named for the backdrop of blazingly white, rocky ridges. The buildings are few and lean toward each other, as if seeking support in their senility.

There is little rubbish in White Hills. The dooryards seem to have been swept recently; the glaring sand is smooth and neat. Many Joshua trees and bisnagas, the barrel cacti, have grown up to form landscaping.

CEMETERY IS OVER-GROWN by "Bisnagas," barrel cacti. These are of type reputed to have saved many desert travelers from death by thirst. If the top is chopped off, the interior pulp mashed into a hollow, copious juice collects and is perfectly potable, if somewhat insipid.

"FRONT YARD" OF miner's cottage in White Hills is paved with dazzling white gravel, landscaped with typical desert plants, cacti and gnarled Joshua trees.

The place was not so tidy in the 1890's. There were 1,900 rough-and-ready miners then, not to mention their unsavory hangers-on. Water was brought in from distant mountain springs, but who drank it? Not many, judging from the piles of whiskey bottles on the fringes.

Rats were a serious problem in the town, living sumptuously on the garbage left everywhere. Cats were imported, to become a problem in turn when they multiplied apace, as cats will do. These then became targets for gun practice, their neglected bodies adding to the general stench.

The town suffered a number of cloudbursts, furnishing an embarrassingly large amount of water all at once, to the point of washing outhouses into the open desert.

Wandering around the immediate vicinity reveals innumerable mine headings, shafts and tunnels centered by the mill ruins.

NEW MEXICO and TEXAS
GHOST TOWNS

ALMA, NEW MEXICO

Into Alma's brief period of life was crowded more turbulence, murder and bloodshed than fell to the lot of any other comparable town in New Mexico. Apaches almost continually harassed the village; any brief respite from Indian raids was filled with internal strife between ranchers and holdups by bandits.

The original plans for Alma were more than peaceful; in fact, the town was laid out along communal lines. No mining was involved at first; this meant no influx of single men to allow for saloons and brothels. Only families would settle here in the fertile and well-watered "Frisco Valley" and farm the land. Cabins would be built close together for better protection from Indians; the farms would surround the homes; everything seemed ideal.

Maurice Coates, one of the dreamers, was born in Canada in 1856. He was a drifter and in his wanderings became a friend of James Keller who also was heading westward. They stopped in Prescott, Arizona, for a while where they decided that farming was their forte, then retraced their steps to the San Francisco Valley, New Mexico, where they found land that was suitable at the edge of the Mogollon Range, named for Don Juan Ignacio Flores Mogollon, Governor of the Province of New Mexico, 1712 to '15. Together with two other interested men, Capt. J. G. Birney and

Robert Stubblefield, they laid out plans for the town and called the place Mogollon. The same year, 1878, control of Mogollon was bought out by Capt. Birney. Since he had never liked the name Mogollon, he rechristened the infant settlement "Alma" for his mother.

And now the bloody period began. W. II. McCullough, a native New Mexican, was the first man to sell the founders on the idea of settling in the state, and had been one of the original farmers of the valley. Almost immediately after the change in ownership, he, with Birney and Prescott, were slain by a party of sheepherders which included whites and two Pueblo Indians. The sheepherders had learned that the Alma men were going to the Adams diggings in Arizona to see what was going on there, and an ambush was laid for them on the assumption that they would be carrying quite a lot of money. They figured, rightly, that Navajos who had recently been on the warpath would be blamed. The true story came out in '86, when the remains were found and one of the Pueblos, conscience stricken, confessed to the deed. He was convicted of murder by the tribal council and put to death by his own people. Before he died, he implicated the other members of the party and they were pursued by the sheriff but never caught.

Although trouble with Pueblos and Navajos con-

81

tinued, the real terror was furnished by Apaches. One evening five of them made a raid on James Keller's ranch and killed several of his cattle. Infuriated, he swore to kill every one of the Indian party, and started after them, alone. When he caught up with them unobserved, he thought better of it and returned to Alma for help. Reinforced by several men, he took the trail again, and since the Indians had not suspected they were being pursued, they were soon overtaken by the avenging settlers. The tally at the end of the battle, three warriors dead and one wounded. The latter died while fleeing the scene, his body found the next day. The raid had been a costly one for the Apaches, but the significant factor in the whole episode was that one of the slain Indians proved to be Toribo, son-in-law of notorious Victorio. His slaying would not go unavenged.

As soon as the news reached Victorio, the Chief began to lay plans to wipe out the entire settlement of Alma. He went to the camp of a sub-chief called Steve to enlist help. When Steve refused, realizing that slaughter of the whites would soon bring the wrath of a battalion of soldiers on his head, the furious Victorio retreated far enough to assemble his

warriors and then attacked his erstwhile friend. The battle of Apache against Apache ended in humiliating defeat for Victorio, and in addition the loss of several of his best braves. Smarting, he killed and scalped the first two white men he ran across. Their names are not known, but two of the same party escaped— George Mehams and Eli Mader. These men made their way to the nearby mining camp of Cooney and spread the news. The founder of this community, Sergeant James Cooney, with a couple of miners named Chick and Brightman and other man unnamed, took off after the Indians. In the meantime, Victorio had found more willing allies than Steve's warriors, the more terrible Geronimo and Nana. Their augmented force was too much for Cooney's party, Brightman and the unidentified miner being killed and scalped. Cooney and Chick fled to Alma, arriving there in the dead of night.

Alma now made preparations for an almost certain attack, and agreed to make a fort of the Roberts home, that being the most likely to resist a siege. Cooney, having alerted the settlers in Alma, was anxious to return to his own town and with one volunteer, left for the camp named for him.

BLACKSMITH SHOP under large trees at outskirts of Alma where travelers stopped to have wagon wheels fixed, horses and mules shod. Dry climate most of year often made iron tires come off wheels. Tire was laid on ground, elevated about eight inches by rocks, fire built under and around. When metal was well expanded, tire was slipped over wheel and hammered on. Blacksmith shop was owned by partners, Dan Russell and William Antrim. Antrim had courted and married Katherine McCarthy, mother of Billy the Kid, in Sante Fe, March 1, 1873. Billy was then 14 years old and extremely fond of mother, resented intrusion of Antrim. Two got along in armed truce. The Kid hung around the blacksmith shop and affection of a sort grew between them so when Garret killed the Kid everyone thought Antrim would go gunning for the killer. He eventually went to Adelaide, California, died and was buried there. Shop was converted to garage in earliest days of autos, "antique" pump added to front of old smithy.

They got safely away about eight o'clock. At ten, Apaches appeared on the hillside east of Alma and opened fire on the Roberts cabin. One wagonload of four whites, the Meador family, had just arrived at the refuge and had not yet entered. They were unable to get out of the wagon because of the firing by the Indians. Suddenly to everyone's astonishment Mrs. Meador grabbed a rifle and began returning the fire. In the resulting momentary confusion, a woman opened the cabin door, and all slipped in, though not before Mr. Meador lost a lock of his hair to a bullet whizzing by. Another missle went through the bonnet of the lady opening the door. The river was on the opposite side and the women managed to get some water collected in kettles and pans before they were spotted and fired upon.

The siege was now on in earnest and firing was general. The first Indian casualty resulted when a brave couldn't resist the temptation of a beautiful horse tethered in the open. When he exposed himself to reach for the bridle, a well-aimed shot from the gun of Jim Keller felled him. One of the men in the cabin, a Mr. Wilcox, made the mistake of standing up to make sure the Indian was really dead and was himself slain by a bullet through the heart.

It seemed necessary to summon aid some way, so Keller and Pete Carpenter managed to slip out as soon as it got dark and made it to Silver City, unharmed. From there a rider was sent to Fort Bayard where a rescue squad was organized and joined by a reinforced group of civilians from Silver City. The men rode the seventy-two miles when they were forced to rest their horses. They then made the distance to Bush Valley where they expected to change horses, but were dismayed to find that Indians had run off all available mounts, some thirty horses. They were now out of provisions as well and managed to collect three days supply while their horses rested. At last they reached the outlying ranches near Alma on May 14th, 1880. The next day they forced the besieging Indians to retreat to the mountains, and the first siege of Alma was over. Altogether thirty-one whites had been killed in the area during the uprising. These figures included Sergeant Cooney and his volunteer, who had been waylaid on the return to Cooney and killed. Their mutilated bodies were found by the rescue party. Cooney was buried in a solid stone "tomb" close to his mine and town.

As soon as Alma had a chance to relax a little it went ahead. July of '82 showed a population of more than three hundred. A school was built, taking care of sixty-eight children. James Meador built the Hotel de Brunswick. An organization called the Minute Men was set up and the men trained regularly so as to be ready for the next Indian attack. Church services were held in the schoolhouse by a circuit rider, and later by ministers from neighboring Cooney and Mogollon. One of the residents wrote a letter to the editor of the *Albuquerque Journal* in 1883, stating "our town is made up of thirty-five houses well constructed of adobe and lumber. We have two business houses doing general merchandising business and in connection with the same a good saloon and card rooms. . . . Two saloons, one owned by D. A. Bechtol who smilingly caters to his many friend's desires in the shape of liquid refreshments; the other mentioned above." Two blacksmith shops and a large general merchandise store in a newly constructed adobe building completed the inventory.

The same year saw another Indian attack. This one was on a ranch near town and Judge McComas and his wife, who had stopped there overnight on a trip from Silver City, were killed and their six-year-old son carried off. The boy was never seen alive again although many stories persisted about him. One was that the boy's head was bashed in when it seemed certain that the party would be attacked by whites, another that the chief of the Indian tribe in later years had red hair and blue eyes and was presumed to be Charley McComas.

In another siege most of the settlers remained awake all night waiting for an imminent attack—all but a Mr. Herr who slept with a large revolver under his pillow. Circumstances, however, weren't conducive to anything but the most restless slumber, and his turnings worked the pistol out from under the pillow. When he arose in the morning, he knocked it down. It fired and sent a bullet through his head.

At various times troops were stationed in Alma to guard against Apaches. During the worst of Geronimo's raiding, two troops of the 8th cavalry made their headquarters at the big W. S. Ranch, remaining for some sixteen months.

Before and after, never during, these occupations the town became the hangout of the notorious "Wild Bunch" made up of Butch Cassidy, Tom Ketchum, Toppy Johnson and the others. William Antrim, father-in-law of Billy, the Kid, was a resident of Alma and the Kid stayed there with him for a time. Another familiar figure in Alma was that of "Mountain Man" Ben Lilly. He was supposed to have killed 110 mountain lions during his time there, earning for himself $55,000 in bounty money.

All these legendary figures, ferocious Apaches, farmers, saloonkeepers, their shelters and places of business are gone with the wind now. Only one adobe building and the tiny cemetery filled with victims of Indians and murder remain.

New Mexico

TURQUOISE TOWN

Cerrillos, New Mexico

No one can say just when Cerrillos (properly Los Cerrillos, "the little hills") had its beginning. Certainly the diggings there are very ancient, gold and turquoise mined in the low mountains around the town since at least 500 A.D. when Basket Maker Indians were in their prime. A few miles from Mt. Chalchihuitl is a huge pit in the solid rock and across Galisteo Creek and up a winding arroyo is the famed Mina del Tiro, "Mine of the Shaft." All evidence is that prehistoric Indians were the miners. History comes into somewhat sharper focus with the likelihood that those gold and silver ores assayed by Spanish prospector Espejo in 1582 came from the Little Hills.

Indian revolutionist Po-pe led his tribesmen against the hated Spanish in 1680, driving those not murdered out of the country. Setting up new quarters at El Paso del Norte Spanish fugitives forgot all about mining or at least made no further attempts to regain the turquoise and gold at Los Cerrillos, all locations being lost.

Three hundred years after Espejo, in 1879, prospecting Americans rediscovered precious metals and blue turquoise at Los Cerrillos and the ancient diggings. A rush followed with more than three hundred men swarming over the little hills. Not long after this the Santa Fe Railroad came through, setting off an even larger boom, satellite towns like Bonanza and Carbonateville mushrooming briefly. It was during this heated period that eastern capital came in to reopen the old turquoise mines, the two largest being the Tiffany and Castilian. An 1899 report listed New Mexico's production of turquoise as worth $1,600,000, most of it coming from Cerrillos, Yankees having dropped the "Los."

With production of metals and blue gemstones lessening, the town began to fail after the turn of the century. There was some activity as long as neighboring Madrid flourished. When tipples there ceased to load coal cars and the railroad curtailed operations, something in Cerrillos died too. It has withered since although a tavern still serves an occasional thirsty rancher or tourist, a general store and restaurant open part time.

OLDEST BUILDING remaining in Cerrillos, it is presumed. Pine logs from mountains were squared with broad axe, laid up with minimum notching, wide chinks filled with mud. Portion at far left received coat of elegant plaster in later years.

CHRONIC DIFFICULTY holding back full development of milling rich ore from mines in high country near Cimarron was lack of consistent water power. Invention of new "impulse type" of water wheel by Lester Allen Pelton in Camptonville, Calif., 1878 was hailed as answer to problem, since wheel required only small volume of water for operation. Although much of metals mining boom in northern New Mexico was already finished by then, some Pelton wheels were imported, proved to be only another disappointment. Though jet of water could be small it had to be directed at cups with great velocity not obtainable at all times.

CIMARRON, NEW MEXICO

"A house is not a home", said a certain madam of distinction, but it is possible to have a home with a house in it. Cimarron land owner Lucien B. Maxwell had one. The mammoth house, as large as a city block, was essentially a hotel containing quarters for Maxwell when he was not riding over his vast domain, as well as gambling rooms, saloon, dance hall, billiard parlor. Then there was the special area reserved for women of special virtue — and they were permanent fixtures. Once a girl was installed in these lavishly furnished rooms she was allowed to leave only if she were not coming back.

The Maxwell estate was three times as large as the State of Rhode Island, comprising 1,714,765 acres. Besides Cimarron, the area included the sites of Springer, Raton and Elizabethtown in New Mexico, spreading well over into Colorado to take in Segundo and other towns. French trapper Don Carlos Beaubien and his Spanish or Mexican partner Guadalupe Miranda, applied for a grant in 1841 and used the land as their own although legal title was held up for 41 years. An ex-trapper, hailing from Kaskaskia, Illinois, Maxwell came exploring, joined General Fremont's expedition and married Luz Beaubien, Don Carlos' daughter. In 1849 the couple settled on the Beaubien-Miranda Grant, and upon the father-in-law's death in 1864, bought out the other heirs, becoming the owners of the largest land grant in New Mexico.

Maxwell's family included four daughters and a son Peter, whom the father despised because the boy would not share his interests and "wasted his time with worthless friends." Maxwell did favor one daughter, Virginia, but when she met Captain A. S. B. Keyes, associated in Indian Agency operations, father objected violently to the romance, but finally did give grudging but unforgiving consent to the marriage. The wedding on the top floor of the estate granary was a brilliant social event — but Lucien Maxwell did not attend.

When he first took over the grant, Maxwell lost no time in getting a herd of cattle established and with complete control of it, industriously increased the herds by setting up individual ranchers with their own cattle, tenants to make payments on a share basis. It was typical of the times that no contracts were ever drawn up, all agreements being verbal.

At about 6000 feet in elevation most of the grassy meadows around Cimarron were assured of ample rainfall for good pasturage and Maxwell's herds flourished. He quickly had a surplus to market, the main outlet a scattered group of accessible army posts. He sold only the extra cattle to their commissaries, keeping his best animals and upgrading the remaining stock. And he maintained a diversity in the stock, saddle and work horses grazing in the pastures, more hilly sections supporting flocks of sheep. There was even a large goat ranch, its manager to be well known in later years as Buffalo Bill Cody.

But Maxwell was not content with agrarian

projects. Noting the many prospectors, trappers and travelers along the Santa Fe Trail who were camping just anywhere, he decided to build a huge stopping place for them. It was not a humanitarian gesture to shelter them from rain and snow. This was business. He would provide amusements for these lonely men, liquor to warm their bellies, faro, roulette, monte and female companionship — to divert the flow of gold to Santa Fe.

The Maxwell House was built in 1864 and was soon the center of social life in northern New Mexico, as well as the principal "wayside inn." The old registers contained some prominent names but if a guest chose not to sign for reasons of his own, he was not refused. Davy Crockett — the desperado, not the legendary character of an earlier era — Kit Carson, Clay Allison and Buffalo Bill, who occasionally came in from the lonely post on the goat ranch to live it up a little, were a few of the famous guests. Cody's visits were not all dalliance as it was in Cimarron he organized the first of his Wild West Shows.

There were some shooting scrapes in the Maxwell House, particularly in the bar and gambling sections, but participants were quickly ejected or carried out, Maxwell not tolerating such nonsense as it was bad for business, he said. But bullets flew freely elsewhere in Cimarron. One man who seemed to attract them was burly Mason Chase, red-headed son of a rancher. On one occasion there was a "shivaree" going on at the Cosgrove house. It had started as a celebration for a newly married couple but had gotten out of hand from too much red eye.

Young Charles Cosgrove stepped outside to run off the demonstrators when Mason Chase came along wanting to know what the party was all about. The infuriated Cosgrove, assuming Chase was the instigator, raised his gun and fired point blank at Chase's heart. But the red-head stayed upright. Recently made deputy sheriff, he made notes on his job in a thick notebook carried in his breast pocket and it received the bullet. Later he complained he could not read some of the writing in it.

Not so lucky was bandit Davy Crockett who had the town of Cimarron and countryside under his control. In September of 1876 he met up with Deputy Sheriff Joe Holbrook. It was a case of which man was quicker on the draw and Crockett was buried on Cimarron's boot hill. Friends placed a headboard at his grave but vandals later carried it off as a souvenir.

Clay Allison was another badman who kept the town in a turmoil. Historian Charles Siringo

OLD CIMARRON JAIL has heavy plank door with tiny barred window. From this opening peered long succession of outlaws, murderers, horse thieves, many emerging only for noose around necks.

"credits" him with eighteen victims, the most modest estimates being ten. J. Frank Dobie, beloved western writer who passed away in 1964, said of Allison: "He was quixotically independent in interpreting what constituted his rights. The more whiskey he drank, the more rights he possessed and sometimes when he came to town he bought a great deal of whiskey. He was generous with it, however, even insisting on his horse enjoying a fair portion."

Allison was twenty years old at the start of the Civil War and he joined the Confederate side. Captured by Union soldiers, he was convicted of spying and sentenced to be shot. He was held in a makeshift prison and although six feet two and weighing one hundred and eighty pounds, he had deceptively small hands and was able to slip out of his handcuffs and escape.

Allison liked off-the-trail types of duels when

involved in quarrels. He once got his adversary to stand at one end of a freshly dug grave facing the pit, Allison at the other, winner to cover up the loser. Another was brought on by Allison's killing Pancho Grieg in a flareup over a billiard game in Cimarron's St. James Hotel. He remarked it sure was a hot day and taking off his hat, used it for a fan and with a tricky movement drew his gun under cover of the hat, shooting Pancho dead.

Sheriff Mace Bowman told Allison his actions in the affair were not entirely ethical and suggested the gunman give himself up. Allison had a proposition ready. He and the sheriff would lay their guns on the bar of Lambert's Hotel (officially the St. James). They would stand back to back and at a given signal, walk twenty-five paces. Then at another signal they would rush for their guns. The sheriff allowed this was a reasonable arrangement, possibly because he knew Allison had accidentally shot himself in the foot not long before and might be handicapped. He figured wrong. Allison won the dash and leveled his gun at the sheriff. Bowman then stood straight, exposed his chest and said: "All right, shoot me, you ....!" But Allison admired such courage and answered: "Mace, you're too brave a man to die," placing his gun back in its holster. The two then shook hands and justice, frontier fashion, was done. Allison's death came some years later in ironical fashion. The gunman was full of whiskey and driving a team of four mules

CENTURY OLD GRANARY and grist mill was built to hold and grind grain produced on Maxwell Grant. It seems as solid today as when built in 1864, all floors solid and safe. This view shows north or rear, facing on nearby Cimarron River. Front side once had ramp affording access to second floor. Wedding of Virginia Maxwell and Capt. A. S. B. Keyes was held here.

when the wagon hit a sharp bump. Allison was bounced out and the wheels of the heavy rig rolled over his head, crushing it "like an eggshell," said the freighter traveling with him.

The Las Vegas GAZETTE took a laconic view of the goings on at Cimarron, reporting once: "Everything is quiet at Cimarron. Nobody has been killed there in three days." The town boasted of fifteen saloons where gunmen could get their courage up, four hotels, a post office and a miniature printing plant where a weekly paper, the Cimarron NEWS AND PRESS, was published. The spindly hand-press was said to have been first used by Padre Antonio Jose Martinez to print his little Taos paper, EL CREPUSCULE. One day the NEWS AND PRESS incautiously hit the street with an editorial blistering some of the gunmen terrorizing the town. That night the ouraged outlaws broke into the newspaper office housed in the Indian Agency headquarters and smashed the press, dumping the wreckage and type cases in the Cimarron River.

The mother of Mason Chase was one of the forthright women in Cimarron. On an autumn day when the leaves were yellowing, the apples in her little orchard ripening, she shook the branches and let the fruit fall into her apron. A wildcat on an upper branch suddenly dropped on the woman, clawing and biting her. After getting her hands on the animal's throat, she squeezed the windpipe until the struggling cat went limp. Then Mrs. Chase calmly gathered the scattered apples into her apron and went home.

And it was Mrs. Chase's daughter-in-law, wife of Mason, who was struck by lightning and lived, although doomed to carry a lifetime reminder of the incident. Hope Gilbert, now of Pasadena, California, who lived in Cimarron as a child, heard the story from Tom McBride, born on the Chase ranch. Before she was married, Nellie Curtis Chase traveled with her family to a dance about five miles from home. She rode on the front seat of an open spring wagon beside the driver and her sister. The sky was ominous when they started and during the rain a flash of lightning made a direct hit on the wagon. The mule pulling it was knocked to the ground and the dog running alongside killed. The driver was stunned and Nellie appeared dead, clothes burned from her body, gold necklace melted and imbedded in the skin. Unconscious for several days, the girl survived but all the rest of her life the mark of the lightning-fused necklace remained around her neck.

Lucien Maxwell stayed with stock raising and

MECHANISM ONCE OPERATING grinding stones, still intact on floor above, was powered by generous water flow diverted from Cimarron River. When Lucien Maxwell was made head of U.S. Government Indian Agency, he dispensed flour and provisions to Utes and Apaches from store in granary. Well educated, six feet tall with fair complexion and blue eyes, friendly "White Father" was highly regarded by Indians who felt protective toward Maxwell ranch, on at least one occasion preventing raid by hostile tribe.

inn keeping, and succeeded mightily. He employed five hundred men on the ranches, several thousand acres of rich land producing hay and other crops. His contracts with the government expanded and money poured into his coffers, which was in truth a cowhide trunk in his bedroom, the rancher having little faith in banks.

In the middle '60s gold was discovered on various streams within the Maxwell Grant boundaries. At first these were kept secret, the discoverers fearing ejection and reprisals from the big boss. But when the news did leak out, he took no action and the three men involved in the earliest workings formed a company — head officers: W. H. Moore,

William Koenig and John Buck. Without opposition the outfit successfully mined its claims.

Then even larger deposits were found by two other partners — Brownson and Kelly — in nearby Moreno Valley, but the tiny stream there failed to supply enough water for washing operations. The finders staked their claims, however, and dreamed of obtaining water by diverting some of the flow of Red River in Taos County. Such a scheme would require a big fund but the men set about organizing a stock company to finance the ditch.

First they approached Maxwell with an offer of stock in the company and the man who had done so well at ranching and cattle raising made his first big mistake. He invested heavily in the venture and as the company began to run out of money long before the ditch was finished, he was approached again for further funds. The project took $300,000 for completion and it is probable Lucien Maxwell supplied most of it.

The NEW MEXICO MINER reported: "It was a colossal undertaking . . . a marvelous piece of engineering. The ditch forms three-fourths of a circle in its length of skirting along the edge of the mountains, bridging ravines and gullies." But the article left out some painful details such as the fact that so many leaks developed along the long canal that little water arrived at the lower end. Although extensive repairs were made with expensive maintenance kept up, it was never a success, but considerable gold was extracted with its aid. Some time later the MINER was forced to modify its opinion, stating: "The Lynch Ditch which carries water from Red River to the Moreno placer mines at Elizabethtown is to be sold next month at a sheriff's sale to satisfy a judgment and cost aggregating $7,000."

From one disastrous debacle, Maxwell turned to another. He started the First National Bank of Santa Fe, charter granted in December, 1870. It took him only a year to discover banking was somewhat more complex than stuffing money into a cowhide trunk and he sold out at a heavy loss. Now he was approached by a group seeking to finance the building of the Texas Pacific Railroad and the man born to raise hay and cattle invested $250,000. When it failed, Maxwell retired to his ranch to lick his wounds. In 1870 he sold his grant, lock-stock-and barrel to a group of financiers for around $750,000 and moved to Fort Sumner, which had been demili-

tarized and offered for sale by the government. Maxwell bought the part having buildings and other improvements, remodeling the officers' quarters into a luxurious home with twenty rooms. Here he lived in semi-retirement until he died in 1875, leaving his property to his son Peter.

Peter Maxwell was described as a "well meaning, inoffensive man, but very timid" by John W. Poe, deputy of Lincoln County sheriff Pat Garrett. On the hot night of July 14, 1881, Peter had given sanctuary to the notorious gunman Billy the Kid, who was on the run after being convicted of murder and sentenced to hang in April at Lincoln. He escaped from jail there, killing two guards as he fled. Garrett and his deputies tracked him to Fort Sumner and the Kid was slain by Garrett in young Maxwell's bedroom. He was buried in the old military cemetery where Lucien B. Maxwell already lay, and where Peter was buried at his death.

Cimarron had its turn, from 1872 to 1882, at being county seat of Colfax, a county credited with having more of them than any other in the country. Elizabethtown was one, others Springer, Raton and even little Colfax almost made it. By 1880, Cimarron was getting somewhat ghostly, becoming a true wraith after removal of the county seat. Twenty-five years later the St. Louis, Rocky Mountain and Pacific Railroad built a spur line to Cimarron and Ute Park, causing the old town to come to life, particularly the section across the Cimarron River on the north side where real estate operators bought a townsite and erected hotels, stores, selling lots and houses to people who arrived with the rails.

Today there are still two Cimarrons, "old" and "new", divided by the river. All the historic buildings remaining are on the south side, including the jail and the famous 100-year-old granary built to hold the wheat produced on the Maxwell Grant. The notorious St. James Hotel, where owner Herbert Lambert, "had a man for breakfast twenty-six times", still stands in somewhat altered form as does the Don Diego Tavern. Across the street are the all but obliterated ruins of the Maxwell House.

Not far away is the Philmont Ranch, originally Kit Carson's Rayado Rancho established in 1849, later owned by Waite Philips. In 1941 the ranch was turned over to the National Boy Scouts. Now thousands of boys hold their annual Jamborees there, few realizing the aura of history surrounding old Cimarron.

DAWSON, NEW MEXICO

In a day when almost everybody burned wood in their stoves, J. B. Dawson was called a crackpot since he scraped chunks of coal from the surface of his farm land. Then out of curiosity, some of his neighbors asked for samples to burn and were pleased enough at the results to avoid the chore of bucking wood and buy the black fuel from Dawson.

J. B. Dawson, with his homestead, was one of the ranchers with a few hundred acres each who were giving trouble to the Maxwell Land Grant Company which had bought an immense tract from Lucien B. Maxwell. Having neglected to look into the matter of all the ranchers living on the land, they had no way of knowing who was a legal owner and who was merely squatting.

When the company saw the ground was heavily laced with coal, it hankered to develop the vein but the attempted eviction of Dawson brought him up fighting, claiming he had bought his land from Maxwell although admitting the transaction had been purely verbal, sealed with a handshake. Maxwell, he said, always did business that way, and the company officials found he was right.

Dawson was disposed to settle the matter with six-guns but consented to abide by a court decision. He hired attorney Andrieus A. Jones who was well aware of Maxwell's real estate deals. The case was tried in the fall of 1893 and decided in favor of

Dawson. The New Mexico Supreme Court held that the company could not prove that Dawson did not own the land, or mineral rights thereof, an important point since the coal deposits were the crux of the whole argument. Maxwell, of course, could not testify as he had died eighteen years earlier.

The trial brought out some facts that further added to the company's discomfort. Dawson stated he had paid Maxwell $3,700 for what he thought was 1,000 acres. The lawyer proved the date and amount were correct but the parcel of land embraced 20,000 acres.

Dawson set about marketing his coal in a big way, with his neighbors the Springers, selling the coal-bearing area to the newly organized Dawson Fuel Company for $400,000 and $5,000 for a township site. He held out 1200 acres on which to build a home, wishing to retain "a little open space around the house." By advice of counsel Dawson had all transactions in black and white with all signatures duly witnessed. But his wife would not sign until she obtained full rights to sell all milk, for a period of ten years, the anticipated town of Dawson would need. J. B. conceded.

Much of the development was under the control of C. B. Eddy, president of the El Paso and Northeastern Railroad, the man who had changed his mind about running his rails to the mining camp

SOLID STONE BARN for sheltering horses and equipment of Phelps Dodge Corp. was retained by company among others for huge cattle ranch when property was sold. This was in 1950 and sounded death knell for Dawson.

of White Oaks, feeling officials of that settlement were holding him up on land for right-of-way and depot. (See Ghost Town Album — Ed.) The railroad had gone to Carrizozo instead to tap coal beds there. These deposits proved shallow and now Eddy was anxious to recoup his losses in the expected deeper veins at Dawson.

On June 17, 1901, the Las Vegas OPTIC reported: "President C. B. Eddy of the El Paso and Northeastern, accompanied by a party of other railroad men, visited Colfax County last week to inspect the Dawson coal lands recently purchased by the El Paso and Northeastern road. Mr. Eddy, in an interview with a reporter with the Las Vegas OPTIC, stated that the money is on hand for the construction of a railroad to the coal fields, and the likelihood is that the railroad will miss Las Vegas a distance of fully twenty miles. A township has been purchased and laid out at the Dawson ranch by the new owners of the Dawson coal fields, as Mr. Eddy is a town builder and boomer who always gets there in his projects. It may be predicted that the new town in Colfax County, through his efforts backed by the railroad he represents, will become one of the most important towns in New Mexico." The company showed a capital of $1,900,000 divided into 10,000 shares with headquarters at Alamogordo where the railroad company already maintained offices.

The same year saw incorporation of the Dawson Railroad Company, also with headquarters at Alamogordo, with plans to build a railroad 130 miles long from Liberty to Dawson, taking advantage of some stretches of lines already constructed or building. Its heads were most of the people who had bought the Dawson coal lands.

Things began happening fast on that ground. By August 1, 1901 a crew of fifty miners was on hand to work the first vein outcropping. A sawmill was busy turning out lumber for houses and by the end of that first year Dawson was well on the way to becoming a city and center of the largest coal mining operation in New Mexico. A post office was established with George T. Pearl the first postmaster. There was a wine and liquor store owned by Henry Pfaff, a large store called the Southwestern Mercantile Co. The town doctor was H. K. Pangborn. By 1902 Dawson's population was 600, with 40 children in the new school. The place had a fine, stimulating climate, there was plenty of work for everyone and Dawson seemed blessed above many other towns. Yet it was doomed to suffer a series of tragedies that shadowed its history to the end.

The first of these struck on September 14, 1903. A fire and explosion in Mine No. 1 took a comparatively light toll, three trapped miners being killed, the bodies shipped away to the nearest known relatives. The worst blow did not come for ten years when Dawson had its cemetery.

1905 brought a newspaper, the Dawson NEWS, with enormous expansion of population and mine operations. There were now about 2,000 people living in the town and many new homes constructed. The Dawson Hotel got a 70-foot addition. Capacity of the coal washer was increased to 250 tons an hour, total number of coke ovens to 124. The mine company owned huge kilns, built mainly to produce bricks for coke ovens and chimneys. Coke, the solid portion remaining after coal is subjected to intense heat in a closed retort, was a major export to smelters and foundries all over the southwest. It burned with a pure flame without gas or smoke, being nearly pure carbon.

About this time the giant, omnipresent Phelps Dodge Corporation began to show a strong interest in what was going on at Dawson. It sent one of its best men, Dr. James Douglas, to the camp with the result the company bought the operation and organized the Stag Canyon Fuel Company, capitalized at $5 million. Under the new management the town expanded even more to a population of 3,500 and the "palatial" Dawson Theater was completed at a cost of $40,000.

Dawson's bawdy houses were forced to build additions to accommodate the large influx of single miners. Trouble ensued, as evidenced in an item in the Raton RANGE, August 15, 1907: "Lizzie Zeller, an inmate of one of the houses in the red light district of Dawson, was shot by Tom Jenkins over the accidental shooting of John Jenkins, his brother. John and Lizzie were in friendly dispute over a gun when the weapon went off and shot John. When Tom heard his brother was wounded he went to the house, called for the woman, called her vile names and shot her. He was placed under arrest. . . The Zeller woman will be taken to her home in Las Vegas for burial."

The camp was largely populated by foreign born workers — Greeks, Slavs, Italian, French, Welsh, Scotch, Mexicans, Germans, Japanese and Chinese. Most of the single men, and those who had to make a stake before sending for their wives, lived in a separate section called Boarding House Row. Greeks and Italians were numerous enough to have their own divisions, presided over by a boarding boss of their own nationality, since many had not yet learned to speak English.

The kilns supplying bricks for construction of coke ovens and chimneys also turned out material for rebuilding and modernizing the old frame school houses, one of the largest being Dawson High School with forty teachers. The Dawson Hospital, with a staff of five doctors, maintained a complete laboratory, with surgery and X-ray equipment. Buildings on the grounds housed nurses and other employees, kitchen, laundry and dispensary with registered pharmacist.

On April 6, 1913, the Raton REPORTER said: "The Phelps Dodge Company that owns the Stag Canyon Mines at Dawson has planned the reclamation of an immense area of land in the vicinity of Dawson by means of a reservoir and a system of ditches and canals, which when completed will be one of the largest irrigation projects in the country. The contract amounts to $350,000."

It was during this period of abundance and prosperity that Dawson suffered its worst catastrophe. On October 20, 1913, a tremendous explosion in Mine No. 2 clogged the entrances and entombed 300 men, killing 263. The blast came at 3 p.m. There were no warnings, no escaping gas or rumblings, only a sudden roar.

Relief and disaster crews were rushed from neighboring towns — Raton, Trinidad, Blossburg, Brilliant, Gardner, Van Houten and Morley. Even a relief car was sent from Denver. By 11 a.m. next day 22 men were accounted for, with 16 alive, and it was hoped this ratio of men saved would prevail, but as the days dragged on the recovered dead outnumbered the living. Rescue crews worked around the clock, rows of bodies brought to the surface grew longer, distraught wives and family members clogged and impeded operations around the mouth of the mine. Two of the rescuers were themselves killed by falling boulders in the shaft. Immense mass funerals were conducted for the victims and row upon row of graves dug, making it necessary to extend the cemetery far up the hill. Wholesale burials were not completed for weeks.

Even after such a calamity life and coal mining went on in the camp and in time, some of the festivities. The camp had always been a good show town and traveling theatrical companies found good audiences even shortly after the disaster.

The NEW MEXICO MAGAZINE, San Diego Exposition Souvenir Edition in 1915, carried a story on Dawson. It included such comments as: "Many a little flower garden surounds the cottage. Sometimes the earth where the cottage stands is hard and stony, and then it is a common thing for the resi-

dent of that house to wall his yard with stones, and then haul in rich earth for his garden. Men do not do these things when their tenure is uncertain. They keep their lawns cropped and the window boxes with their bits of bloom neatly painted. They do good work in the mines and are happy . . . the houses themselves are worthy of comment. There are no shacks. There is no poorer section, although there is a separate quarter for the non-English speaking. . . . .

"The Church, like the schools is financed by the company. There is only one, the Church of All Creeds, but services of several denominations are held in it. Rev. Harvey M. Shields, an Episcopal minister is in charge of regular services, but a Catholic priest holds services in the camp once a month. A Catholic church is being built." The Catholic church was completed in 1917 and dedicated to St. John the Baptist, with the Rev. Joseph A. Couturier, O.M.I. as first pastor.

Safety measures were heavily increased after the disastrous explosion and subsequent accidents were comparatively minor, fatalities few. But in February, 1923, another ruinous explosion took 125 lives. Again the cemetery had to be extended to allow more space for more rows of graves, the mass burial scenes of 1913 repeated.

No further tragedy took place until the one of February 25, 1950. On that date the people of Dawson were told the Phelps Dodge Corporation would close down all operations of the Stag Canyon Mining Co. The announcement meant the death of the one industry town. The reason for the closure was simple — the increasing availability of a new fuel for smelters and foundries, natural gas. Specifically the enormous Phelps Dodge copper smelter at El Paso, Texas, which had been consuming most of Dawson's coke output, now found it more expensive to produce than the handily obtainable natural gas.

When the final blow fell at the actual closure on April 30th, many residents had already left and vacant houses showed curtainless windows. The only surviving operation, and that a temporary one, was the Frontier Power Plant which served Dawson and surrounding area with electricity. It operated until a stock pile of surface coal was exhausted.

On June 6th, the National Iron and Metal Company of Phoenix, Arizona, bought the deserted town of Dawson, wrecking and removing all machinery and buildings. A few houses were spared, these and the land having been retained by Phelps Dodge for a large cattle operation.

ELIZABETHTOWN, NEW MEXICO

This is the country of "The Big Ditch"—and traces of it still show after almost a century. A rare visitor may stand in the deserted ruins of Elizabethtown, where it nestles in the high bowl between the peaks of McGinty and Baldy Mountains, and visualize activity when they brought water to Humbug Gulch.

The gravels of that mountain gash were rich in gold but water was either too scarce to work them or flash flooding in the spring damaged equipment. "We've got to have an even and regular water supply or quit," the miners said. So they did it the hard way, digging the eleven miles of "The Big Ditch" by pick and shovel and a few sacks of blasting powder from the source of Red River. It cost $280,000 but saved the camp.

On July 9, 1869 when the first water hit Humbug Gulch there was a wild celebration but it was short-lived. The flow slowed to a dribble with dozens of leaks showing up along the route. Patching remedied the loss temporarily but crews had to be established at intervals along the waterway with cabins for living quarters to make constant repairs to insure the steady flow of 600 inches. And even then it became necessary to divert more water from Moreno Creek and Ponil River.

Elizabethtown is situated five miles north of Eagle's Nest Lake and some forty miles northwest of Cimarron. The boom began in the middle 1860s when Ute and Apache Indians were relatively peaceful, wandering over the slopes of Baldy and McGinty Mountains. One of them showed up in Fort Union with a specimen of float so rich it set off a rush of the first magnitude, swelling the town on the slopes of Baldy to 5,000 people.

The first men to track down the location where the sample had been picked up were William Kroenig and William Moore, whose small copper mine was named the Mystic Lode. While that first sample of rock was rich copper ore, and the first diggings had been for copper, this find of gold changed the whole scheme of things. The original metal was forgotten and from then on, E'town was all gold.

By the spring of '67, locations had been made at Michigan Gulch, Humbug Gulch and Grouse Gulch,

LOG BUILDING was erected at time of E'town's greatest expansion, when group of five men with sluice 90 feet long were taking out $100 a day in gold for each man, worth $20 an ounce just as it came from dripping gravels. Quartz lode assayed $2,000 per ton and no one bothered with anything skimpier. Almost all frame buildings in town have crumbled away.

the latter containing the phenomenal Spanish Bar. All measurements were made from a large willow tree on the banks of the central stream. The town was named for the eldest daughter of William Moore, Elizabeth, who later became a schoolteacher in the town, shortened to E'town. The camp grew so rapidly it was soon the seat of Colfax County, an honor lost later to Cimarron.

During the best years there were three stagecoach lines, to Springer, Trinidad and Questa. There were saloons and three dancehalls, two hotels, five general stores and later several boardinghouses. One hotel operator was a Henry Lambert who had once cooked for General Grant and Abraham Lincoln. In the fall of '71 he went to greener pastures in Cimarron where he opened the celebrated St. James.

In 1868 the editor of the *Sante Fe Gazette* wrote: "The first house (in E'town) was built by John Moore who furnished the miners with provisions on credit, thereby enabling them to open up the country. Elizabethtown now has 100 buildings." A later article stated: "The new city of Elizabethtown continues on its course. The weather is cold; the cool winds from the snowcapped peaks cause us to huddle around the blazing pitch-pine fires of our fellow townsmen, Messrs. Sears, Pollock, Draper, C. E. Pease and Harburger. Occasionally, we find our way to the Mayflower Saloon. where we warm the inner as well as the outer man. So pass the long winter evenings. Prices are very reasonable for a mining town. New arrivals are an almost everyday occurrence. Denver and vicinity are well represented among the new arrivals. I perceived Doc Howe of prospecting celebrity whose manly form and gentlemanly address is truly an honor to the place he has left. There is very little mining property for sale. Claim owners generally think we have a good enough thing to warrant them to suffer a New Mexico winter in order to be on the ground when the water comes . . . . A stage line has been established between Elizabethtown and Maxwell's by V. S. Dhelby and Co. who intend to commence running a tri-weekly line in a few days." Toward spring came optimism and some advice: "Elizabethtown contains fifty or sixty houses, some of them like the Arkansas Traveler's house, roofless, for the weather is too severe to complete them . . . . There is considerable bustle and business in the air to be seen and especially should you go into Abor's Saloon you will be convinced that it is a stirring place. There are several stores, two restaurants and many saloons, as also a drug store, a billiard table, a barber shop and gambling houses where a miner can deposit all his hard-earned earnings of weeks in a few hours. That house across the street in which you see two smiling faces you will do well to give it a wide berth, as you will be richer in pocket, better in health and wiser in mind."

Those early days of the boom town were filled with such robbery, murder and pillage as have rarely been equalled. One badman was Long Taylor. He stood six foot seven inches, was easily identified but not often caught. In '73, in company with one Coal-Oil Johnny, he held up the Cimarron stage in the narrow passage known as the Palisades, escaping with some $700. George Greely ran one of the most profitable saloons but was constantly in trouble because of a hot temper, taking no "guff" from anyone. On Independence Day, 1886, he called a customer on the carpet for a fancied insult to one of his several "lady friends." Infuriated, the man rushed out, returning in a few minutes with his Winchester. Firing point blank at Greely, he turned to make his escape but was stopped by a flying tackle at the door, later serving time for murder at the penitentiary in Santa Fe.

Perhaps the most gruesome episode was staged at the height of the town's heyday when rooms were scarce and no questions asked about them. A stranger would come into camp, rent a room in the boardinghouse operated by Charles Kennedy on the side of a steep hill, and disappear. Since no one knew such newcomers, they would ordinarily not be missed. But one was and his friends went to Kennedy's place. They were met halfway by the proprietor's distraught wife, a native New Mexican, who had decided to confess everything.

The Vigilantes were sent for and they slipped in the back of the house. There was Kennedy bending over a fire, burning dismembered sections of the visitor's body, his valuables set to one side. The town had a stout timbered jail but when the murderer was taken to the courthouse for trial, the outraged citizens seized him, tied a rope around his neck and threw him to the ground. Then one man got astride a horse and dragged the unfortunate miscreant up and down the dirt streets until long after he was dead.

McKenna, in his *Black Range Tales* recalls: "Myself and three other men who were footloose and without families pitched together and hired a bull team. Loading up what we needed in the way of food and blankets, we pulled out for Elizabethtown, a gold diggings in the main Rockies, a hundred miles west from Trinidad. It took us about fifteen days to get there, the bullwhacker being in no hurry, for the bulls were poor and the grass was good . . . . It was there I panned my first gold . . . learned what was meant by diggings and stored up bits of mining lore from veteran prospectors. I was told that Elizabethtown was tame when compared to the days of the big rush, when shootings were as common as meetings in the street and saloons. I sat for the first time before a golden campfire and listened to blood-curdling tales of raid-ing Indians, of heartless cutthroats, of daring outlaws, of dashing cowboys, of painted women, of dead shots and regular old sourdoughs and desert rats, some good, some bad . . . ."

And there was the building of the dredge *Eleanor*. In 1901, E'town was still a busy place, its seven saloons always crowded and hotels full. Eastern capital was still interested in organizing companies and gold was still so plentiful it was being weighed out in troy-weight in exchange for such necessities of life as—whiskey. But here and there were reports that a certain placer was petering out, that expensive stamp mills were working on a part-time basis. Some people were even expressing the opinion that E'town might one day be a ghost town. Loud and derisive boos might greet this kind of remark but cold figures gave it credence—that gold production in the camp was not what it had been.

The famous Spanish Bar still harbored as much and more gold in its depths than ever had been re-moved but getting at the deeper gravels was something else. The answer came in the Oro Dredging Co. and the person of H. J. Reiling of Chicago. He had solved similar problems in the mining camps of Montana and felt the only possible obstacle here would be getting two boilers into the camp. These would weigh a total of ten tons and the existing road from the rail head at Springer was a narrow, winding track that ran almost its entire length up the precipitous Cimarron Canyon. Machinery of lesser weight had been hauled up the road and the inadequate bridges and narrow switchbacks could be remedied.

When the first of the boilers was started on its way, hauled by fourteen head of horses, it soon ran into difficulties, a small bridge at the beginning of the route collapsing like cardboard. With this warning, spans over deeper canyons were strengthened and the first boiler was deposited on the bar in two weeks, the second in one. A side benefit of the job was the widened and improved road for daily trips of the stage. During the period the dredge was being hauled two stages had been shuffled, one running above, one below, since there was no passing.

The camp turned out in a body to dedicate the new dredge in August of 1901. Incongruous were the "outfits" worn by members of the party from the effete East who had shuddered their way up the raw canyon. After all, their money had built the dredge, now so proudly floating on its own pond at the lower end of Spanish Bar, and they felt they should be on hand to see it put into operation.

A bottle of champagne was broken on its bow by Mrs. W. A. Moughy of Wooster, Ohio. Since other bottles had already been opened and emptied in more conventional fashion, champagne for the Easterners and whiskey for the men responsible for the hauling and assembling of the *Eleanor*, the celebration that followed the christening was the wildest in the history of the town.

The first few years of work for the big dredge went according to plan. Values of the gravel in Spanish Bar were about $2 per cubic yard and the machine was capable of biting off 50,000 cubic yards a month. Part of this material was from the bottom of the pond and the rest from the banks. Operations were on a round-the-clock basis to make up for com-plete closure during winter.

The high and mighty days gradually came to an end with the failure of easily obtained gold in the gravels. Hard rock mining became more and more expensive in proportion to profits, replacement machinery and labor costing more while the price of gold remained static. The fate of the big dredge paralleled the demise of E'town. The *Eleanor* slowed down and for a few years operated on only one shift, then there were complete shutdowns for a month at a time. The company was extending its operations to the town of Breckenridge, Colorado, and needing more money, mortgaged the *Eleanor*. It was gobbling up the gravels but there was not enough river gold to meet expenses. At last the mortgage was foreclosed and the dredge sold at a sheriff's sale to two optimis-tic gentlemen named J. Van Houten and Charles Springer. For eight years they paid a watchman to live on the gold boat, hoping that one day the metal would advance in price.

As the machinery rusted and the dredge began to settle into the gravel, she was at last abandoned, as was the town itself. Several years later the pilot house was all that was showing above the sand of Spanish Bar. Now even that has disappeared.

FOLSOM, NEW MEXICO

It cost Madison Emery a cow to keep peace with the Indians camped just outside the village. He was trying to explain that neither he nor his stepson had anything to do with the dead buck when there was a sudden rattle-bang of explosions and the peace pipe went out. The "shots" were found to be only rifle cartridges in the stove but the situation was touchy, and well — what was a cow if the Indians would go away?

The town of Folsom, named for President Cleveland's wife Frances Folsom, began as a tiny hamlet close to the present town. Called Madison for the first settler, Madison Emery, the site has disappeared so completely none of Folsom's residents ever heard of it.

When Emery arrived on the scene in 1862 he found the grass in the valley so tall it would hide a man on a horse, the hills covered with a fine stand of pinon pines, streams filled with fish and game abundant. He built a cabin and as more families made homes, stores and other businesses sprang up, he erected a rough hotel.

The frontier town was constantly harassed by Indians and was especially apprehensive when they made semi-permanent camps near the village. On one of those occasions Bud Sumpter, Emery's stepson, found an Indian lying behind the store. He thought the brave was asleep until he turned him over, but he was dead apparently from too much firewater.

Emery feared violence from the Indians who might doubt the manner of the buck's death, invited the chief and council to his home for a parley. Progress was being made when there was a furious fusillade of what seemed to be gunshots and all those present dived for doors and windows. When it was discovered the "shots" were cartridges some prankster had dropped in the kitchen stove, the redmen were persuaded to return and relight the peace pipe. Harmony seemed assured when Emery presented the chief with his fattest cow.

Madison was the nearest settlement to the "Robbers' Roost" just north of Kenton in neighboring Oklahoma. Periodically the notorious Coe and his gang would make a hurried visit to Madison when they scented a raid on the hideout. They would pull up in front of the inn run by Mrs. Emery, order the horses "serviced" at gun point, then repair to the nearest saloon. After tanking up, the outlaws would demand a meal from Mrs. Emery, sleep off food and drink in her beds and sweep away at dawn like so many scavenger crows. Then everybody in Madison breathed easier.

Coe's outlawry got important enough to set the U.S. Cavalry after him. A company from Fort Lyons, Colorado, moved into Kenton, flushed the gang and Coe slipped over to his safe refuge at the Emerys. This time it was not so safe. A detachment from Fort Union, New Mexico, was bivouacked behind a hill. Mrs. Emery fed and wined the bandit and as soon as he was asleep, sent her son Bud on his pony to alert the soldiers. He returned with a guard which arrested Coe. As the badman was led from the house he remarked: "That pony has had a hard ride". To avoid reprisals on the Emerys, Coe was taken to Pueblo, Colorado, to await trial. It never came, his widespread fame proving his undoing. A Vigilante Committee broke into the calaboose at night, snatched the bandit and strung him up, leg irons and all. The mystery of his disappearance from jail remained for years until someone found his skeleton, hardware still attached.

But what lawlessness could not do to Madison, the coming of the Colorado and Southern Railroad did. Because the line bypassed the town just enough to cause it to seek a new site, the original town languished and utterly vanished. At the new location shelters and business establishments were all tents, giving the clutter the name of "Ragtown", but it got a new one — Folsom — when it developed quickly. The rails came in 1887-1888 and by 1895 Folsom had two mercantile stores, three saloons and several other businesses including two houses which were not homes. One reason for the rapid growth was, being on the railroad it had the largest stockyards north of Fort Worth.

But the change in the town was not to the credit of law and order. The first citizen of Folsom was W. A. Thompson, proprietor of the Gem Saloon and deputy sheriff. He came from Missouri under a cloud, charged with the murder of a man and in Folsom racked up a record as lurid as that of any other New Mexico badman, in a state that produced Bill the Kid, Clay Allison and others of that ilk.

One time he shot point blank at an erstwhile friend, killing him and gave as the reason: "The dirty so-and-so had the nerve to get drunk in another saloon." Again, infuriated at a taunt from a local lad in his saloon, he pursued the boy outdoors, firing as he ran. One of the bullets went through the stove of a neighbor but all missed the boy, who escaped. Raging inwardly, Thompson turned his gun on anyone within range including Bill Thatcher, a fellow officer but bitter enemy, and Jeff Kiel who had emerged from King's Store. Thatcher was wounded seriously and Kiel fatally. Thatcher managed to shoot Thompson's gun from his hands, the crazed assailant running into his saloon and barricading the doors.

A crowd bent on lynching quickly gathered outside but short of burning the building and endangering the entire block, they could not get Thompson out. When waiting cooled the mob's temper, Thompson staggered forth dead drunk and collapsed. Authorities took him to the Clayton jail, then to Springer.

Released on bond, he returned to Folsom, sold his saloon and cleared up all personal matters. At the murder trial in Clayton he was acquitted, a verdict that would have been impossible nearer home. He then moved to Trinidad and married the girl for whom he had committed his first murder. The couple later went to Oklahoma where Thompson killed another person and was again acquitted.

In 1908 the town had that new-fangled contraption, the telephone, switchboard being in the home of Sarah J. Rooke on the edge of town. One night in August Sarah answered her buzzer to hear a voice shout that a huge wave from a flash flood was racing down the river and would strike the town in minutes, warning to get people out of town without trying to rescue any possessions. Sarah was too busy to go, but rang one bell after another, as many as she could before the water hit. Her own house was swept from its foundations, girl and switchboard with it. Her body was found eight miles below the town. Most buildings had been carried away and seventeen persons drowned, yet many were saved because of Sarah's heroism. Grateful citizens of Folsom and other nearby towns contributed funds for a granite memorial at her grave.

But Folsom's most prominent citizen was the "Folsom Man", existing only by deduction. Archeologists had long been interested in an arroyo close to the town where they had found superficial evidences of artifacts dating from the Pleistocene or Ice Age, some 20,000 years ago. In 1927 more careful digging revealed a cache of bones belonging to ice age animals, most of them slain by man-made weapons such as exquisitely fashioned lances or spear points, some found among the bones. In several instances a point was imbedded in a bone. Made of flint, they showed careful workmanship, finely fluted along the edges.

Although no human remains were found, the discovery dated the existence of man in North America much earlier than previously estimated, 1000 B.C. It has since been substantiated that these first settlers of Folsom were descendants of wanderers who crossed from Asia over a land bridge, moving on to New Mexico. Although most of the northern lands were still covered by deep ice deposits, there was a corridor of bare ground parallel to the east side of the Rocky Mountains along which men and animals could migrate. Later similar discoveries near the Sandia Mountains, also in New Mexico, suggested an even earlier date for the presence of these immigrants.

BUSY ESTABLISHMENT during heyday of Folsom. Building sheltered Doherty Investment Co., general store, market and early post office. Present one is housed in its own small building, faces imminent closure.

MOST BUILDINGS in Folsom are constructed of stone, have well withstood ravages of time. Water tower, windmill were supported on top of log tripod at left. Folsom is geologically fascinating as Capulin National Monument. Area contains nine small near-perfect craters in addition to Mount Capulin, 8368 feet. Main cinder cone, of recent formation, is one mile in diameter at base, 1450 feet at summit, is considered most nearly symmetrical volcano in this country.

GHOSTS ON THE CREST

Golden, New Mexico

The confirmed "shunpiker" could hardly pick a more rewarding route between Albuquerque and Santa Fe than paved New Mexico State 10. Beginning a few miles east of Albuquerque the road spans a short stretch that leads to highly scenic Sandia Crest, 10,678 feet high, and a chain of some of the most picturesque ghost towns in the state. Here were scenes of successive boom and bust in the frantic search for gold, silver, lead, turquoise and more plebian coal.

The first community reached after turning north from U.S. 66 is San Antonitos, an old village populated mostly by Mexican woodcutters and cattle ranchers. Then comes the ancient site of Paako and gold mining camp of San Pedro where only the old coke ovens remain and these hard to find. After that Golden, the only one now visible of what was a cluster of placer camps.

Adjoining Golden at the north was the earlier town of Tuerto ("one-eyed man," in Spanish) where a boom took place in 1839, ten years before the big one in the California Sierra. But there was an older camp just east, around the shoulder of the cluster of peaks called Ortiz Mountains, 8,928 feet. The city editor of the Albuquerque *Tribune* and writer for *New Mexico Magazine*, Ralph Looney, did much research on the old camps in this area. He reports the fact that Dolores, also called Placitas Viejas ("old placers"), was the scene of the first gold rush in what is now the United States. By way of distinguishing it from the more recent camp nearby, it was at first called Placitas Nuevas and was large enough to support twenty-two stores. Both have utterly vanished and Golden is fast decaying.

When placer gold was exhausted in Lazarus Gulch and Tuerto Creek, miners gradually shifted south, deserting Tuerto and forming Golden, where an old church stood, constructed in the early 1830s. In recent years the structure was restored yet it retains the soft adobe lines of the original (see *Tales the Western Tombstones Tell*). The lady tending the little store in 1966 was quite resentful when visitors called the place a "ghost town" but was quite willing to accept their money. As in all near-abandoned towns considerable vandalism has been perpetrated on buildings and cemetery, but this writer believes those who visit any old town because of its historical interest are not the ones who tear up floors to look for treasure or who smash tombstones. Deliberate destruction is more likely to be the work of casual joy-riders out for a thrill or two, their signatures a scattering of empty liquor bottles and beer cans.

VERY OLD STRUCTURES such as this attest age of Golden. Construction here is primitive, using local materials.

HILLSBORO, NEW MEXICO

Dan Dugan was all for throwing it away and forgetting about it so they could get on with future searching. Dave Stitzel said "No" for a time and then seeing it was no use bucking such Irish stubborness, slipped a couple of pieces in his pocket. The partners agreed on most matters but this April day in 1877 they had run across some float on the east side of Black Range and couldn't see eye to eye on its value.

The two moved on. Discouraged over the poor results of this prospecting jaunt, they were traveling in rough circles intending to return to Santa Rita in the Pinos Altos Range. After more half-hearted poking and picking in the Mimbres Mountains, part of the Black Range, they crossed the valley of the Mimbres River where there was a large stamp mill and the usual assay office. Here they were to rest a few days.

Stitzel slipped away, taking his rocks to the assayer. His partner would only have laughed at him. He was prepared for a delay for even though prospectors were first in line at the office, several days were necessary to run an assay. The pieces of ore must first be crushed into pea-gravel size and ground to powder. A measured amount was then roasted, a "button" of metal melted out and weighed, the comparison to the ore sample given in terms of value per ton. Dugan was impatient to be on his way after hearing what his partner had done. When he got the value news he was impatient to go back. The finished assay ran $160.

The men immediately returned to the float site and established a claim. This first one was called the Opportunity, a second one christened Ready Pay. Both were successful, the first five tons of ore bringing the partners $400. Soon others were flocking in and a name for the new camp was needed. Each man wanted to name the place after his home town. When no agreement was reached, a hatful of names was shuffled and Hillsborough drawn. In usage it was shortened to Hillsboro.

Only seven miles from Kingston, another mining camp, the narrow mountain road through Percha Canyon connecting the two was full of hazards. The road itself was dangerously steep and rough, washouts were common and rocks often rolled down on the coaches, but the most feared danger was that of bandits. There were plenty of

MAIN STREET OF HILLSBORO is unchanged from days when Billy the Kid visited saloons and on one occasion ducked into back room when posse was on his trail.

places along the road where stagecoaches had to slow down to get through and robbers chose these spots for surprise holdups.

Large amounts of gold were often shipped to the railroad at Lake Valley, via Hillsboro, and the return trip was likely to bring the payroll for both mountain camps. Every so often road agents would relieve the drivers of their bullion or money and many were the methods devised for circumventing them. One Bill Holt, a driver for the Orchards Line would make a slit in the collar of one of the horses, remove some stuffing and insert the money in the cavity. Bulky bullion was more difficult to conceal but was sometimes saved by having guards raise their weapons at each narrow pass, ready to fire on any holdup men that might be waiting. The killing of two of them discouraged such surprise parties for a while.

Hillsboro is very quiet now. Enough people remain in the town and surrounding countryside to form small congregations in the two churches, Catholic and Protestant, but very little business goes on and most of the buildings are vacant.

SUBSTANTIAL AND COMMODIOUS JAIL, w a s second to be built in Hillsboro. Original was windowless adobe cell, part of tiny courthouse on main street. This one, built about the same time, 1893, as second courthouse adjoining was erected to take care of flood of drunks, thieves and highwaymen. Latter were constantly holding up the stagecoaches carrying money and gold bullion between Kingston, Hillsboro and Lake Valley, mining towns linked together by common needs. Hoosegow was three weeks' home of Oliver Lee, James Gilliland and William McNutt, in one of most famous murder trials in New Mexico. Prisoners were fed during tenure by Sadie Orchards, retired from stage driving and operating hotel in Hillsboro. Jail is roofless, allowing sun and rain to nourish grass in cells.

MAIN ENTRANCE TO COURTHOUSE, Murder trial for killing of Judge Fountain and his nine-year-old son was held here, although crime supposedly was committed near Las Cruces. Public feeling against the men held for murders was so intense that lynching was feared, and prisoners were moved to Hillsboro under cover of darkness. No trace of missing judge or boy was ever found; for lack of any corpus delicti or evidence of foul play three weeks trial ended in not guilty verdict. Town had been so loaded with curious spectators all hotels were filled and cowboys camped beside their chuck-wagons.

KELLY, NEW MEXICO

The road from Magdalena to Kelly winds steeply up a short canyon and then suddenly becomes a street, narrow and rough, bordered sparsely on both sides by the pitiful remnants of what was once a thriving town of 3,000. Most of these claimed their town was the most orderly in New Mexico. "Gunfighting is out, here. Fights are to be settled with fists, bricks or rocks."

Kelly's beginnings concerned a Civil War soldier marching with the Union Army, he stooped to pick up a rock that interested him. He couldn't conveniently keep it with him, so sent it to a friend, J. S. Hutchason. This friend was so excited about the sample that he immediately went prospecting in the Magdalenas, hoping to find the outcropping from which the float had come. This he never did, not even finding another piece to match the original. But he did stake out a couple of claims, naming them the Graphic and the Juanita.

Hutchason was an industrious man. In addition to blasting out his own ore (oxidized lead-zinc) he built a crude smelter of adobe. He had to ship the resulting lead pigs all the way to Kansas City by oxcart over the Santa Fe trail, but still made enough money to keep going. He sometimes took a little time off and on one occasion was pecking around at the rocks some little distance from the Juanita mine. While studying these interesting specimens he was joined by a friend who had a sawmill nearby, Andy Kelly. Kelly was intrigued but didn't show his interest. When Hutchason returned to work, Kelly staked out a claim to the spot and called it after himself. He worked it for a time, but one year failed to do the legal amount and Hutchason who had kept his eye on the project, stepped in and took over, keeping up the assessment work himself. The ore produced by this mine was carbonates with galena, averaging 50 to 60 per cent of lead, 10 ounces of silver and some copper.

In 1870 miners laid out a townsite, long and narrow in the canyon and named it Kelly for the mine now producing well. In the next period of development, a Col. E. W. Eaton decided to put some money into the mines of Kelly, and leased the Juanita. Almost immediately the more extensive workings ran into a rich vein of silver so good that when the news leaked out, a boom was on its way. Now things happened fast. Hutchason took advantage of the fever and sold his Graphic claim to a firm called Hanson and Dawsey for $30,000, and the Kelly to Gustav Billings

LITTLE MISSION CHURCH of Saint John the Baptist still stands on steep street of Kelly. Once private residence, it was remodeled for church purposes. Mission never had a priest of its own, was attended from Magdalena. Although Kelly is now completely deserted, each feast day of Saint John the Baptist, June 24th, sees little chapel filled with about seventy-five people from all over countryside, gathered to attend Mass.

EXTENSIVE RUINS OF BOARDING HOUSE disintegrates beside quiet street once teeming with activity. Adobe, sun-dried brick, was standard building material in southwest where timber is scarce, stiff clay a l w a y s available. Sometimes adobe was mixed with chopped straw for added strength. Also optional was finishing coat of stucco which could be of mud or plaster. Either way, thick walls p r o v i d e d protection against heat, cold. Indians could not set fire to structures to force evacuation as often happened in case of frame buildings.

for $45,000. To roast his own ore, Billings built a smelter at the edge of nearby Socorro in 1881 and operated it for twelve years. During this period the village in the Magdalena mountain canyon produced most of the lead mined in New Mexico.

Until about 1885 Indian troubles beset the camp. Every so often they would come swooping down the canyon, to be repulsed only at heavy cost. Or they would sneak to the edges of the camp at night, stealing horses and cattle. When at last the railroad reached Magdalena, several cars were kept handy to carry the women and children to safety in Socorro in case of an outbreak.

But Kelly flourished. There was now a Meth-odist church as well as the original Catholic one, seven saloons, several rooming houses and three stores. The three dance palaces supported a goodly number of "frail sisters," some kept in a regular "house," the more independent ones having individual cribs farther down the canyon. Both hotels kept three shifts going on the same beds, the saloons and dance halls on a "we never close" basis.

Jonas Nelson got a short term lease on the Hardscrabble mine and worked it for all it was worth in the time allotted. When he received a check from the smelter, it was so large he was inspired to throw a party the likes of which Kelly had never seen. He built a platform in front of

the mine workings, ordered a special train from Los Angeles. It was a "surprise package" con-taining such goodies as champagne and beautiful girls. The party cost Nelson every cent he had and he had to go back to the pick and shovel, but he always maintained "It was worth it."

In the '90s, sharp-eyed Cony Brown wondered about the greenish rocks so common everywhere in Kelly and sent some samples for analysis. When the report came back, he took a lease on the old dumps and all available workings not in active operation before he made details of the paper known. He had found the "worthless" green rock to be Smithsonite, zinc carbonate, a rare and valu-able ore. This discovery set off another boom.

In 1904 the Sherwin-Williams Paint Company bought the old Graphic for $150,000 and the Tri-Bullion Smelting and Development Company bought the Kelly from Billings for $200,000, build-ing a smelter on the spot. Zinc recoveries made Kelly the leading producer of that metal, output between 1904 and 1928, $21,667,950.

1931 saw the end of the Smithsonite deposits and a few more years ended the workings of the lead-zinc sulphides. While some of the population held on, refusing to believe the town had died, most moved to other camps, or to Magdalena be-low on the plain. At last even the old die-hards gave up, and today Kelly does not have a living soul to shelter.

KINGSTON, NEW MEXICO

A single piece of float exhibited in Denver in 1882, created such a boom in the place where it was found that a whole town was born on the site in a few weeks. The camp was first called Percha City, after Percha Creek, where Jack Sheddon had first found the chunk of rich silver ore. It was surveyed for a town in October of 1882 and by the end of that year 1800 men and some women had moved in. The men consisted of miners and merchants with a sprinkling of gamblers and pimps. The women were mostly the latter's stock in trade, a few others, miners' wives. As the camp settled down to a more steady existence more families became established.

In Kingston's first hectic years, the buildings were of the flimsiest nature, large tents or some combination of fabric and whipsaw lumber. One of the first hotels had walls of canvas and a roof of boards, the cracks in the latter battened to keep most of New Mexico's infrequent rains out. Three tiers of bunks lined the walls. Prices varied, ranging from cheaper shelves above to the more convenient and costly ones below. All patrons were reduced to the same level, however, when frequent shooting scrapes outside sent bullets flying through the fabric walls and everyone dived to the floor and comparative safety. Food served in the kitchen and dining room "annex" came from an outdoor kitchen. Meats on the menu were purchased from the butcher shop near by advertising beef, bear, venison, pork, wild turkey and goat.

At first the camp had no jail, prisoners being tied to a post, gagged if too noisy and at the convenience of whoever was serving as "sheriff," hustled off to the jail in seven-mile-distant Hillsboro. There were no churches for a long time. When the idea of building one occurred a man passed the hat in the saloons and brothels and soon had it filled with nuggets, rings and currency to the tune of $1,500, enough to build a stone structure. One church to 22 saloons was not considered too bad a proportion.

Before the Civil War, the old New Mexican town of Mesilla on the Rio Grande had a little weekly newspaper. The *Mesilla Times* was printed on an old Washington hand press which had been hauled in over hundreds of miles of desert. When that town was captured by Confederates

the press was a victim of the general carnage and wound up in the bed of the Rio Grande. There it lay for several years until an itinerant printer who wanted to start a paper in the now flourishing Kingston thought of it. He got help enough to extract the relic from the sands of the river bottom and hauled it to town. Miraculously, it functioned after some repairs and served to get out a crude newspaper and odd job printing for several years. One of the hand bills produced read:

Ho! For the Gold and Silver Mines of New Mexico
Fortune hunters, capitalists and poor men,
Sickly folks, all whose hearts are bowed down;
And ye who would live long and be healthy,
and happy; come to our sunny clime and see
For Yourselves.

About this time Kingston began having Indian troubles. One day the town found itself entirely surrounded by a ring of the dreaded Apaches on horseback, led by notorious Victorio. Unfortunately for the Indians, they had picked a day some miners were ready to go on a hunting expedition to augment the meat supply. Remingtons were handy and loaded, the aborigines were routed in a blaze of rifle fire in a matter of minutes. The defeat caused a long respite in further attacks, but the miners knew that another attempt to sack the camp would sooner or later be made and kept a constant watch. When Victorio and his men did come whooping in and were again repulsed with heavy losses he called the whole thing off, permanently. To show how big they could be, the miners named their newly completed three-story hotel after the vanquished chieftain calling it "The Victorio."

At its height Kingston was well supplied with hotels, with a smaller one and another built later. In addition there were several dance halls, many stores, the Percha Bank, a G.A.R. Post and Masonic, Knights of Pythias and Odd Fellows halls. By this time there were enough families to require a schoolhouse. All these buildings lined up on both sides of the single street above Middle Percha Creek made a fine effect, Kingston was on its way.

"Pretty Sam" had finished a Casino and Dance Hall during this period of prosperity and the whole town was eagerly awaiting the grand opening, since all drinks were to be on the house. The elegant falsefronted building was on the side of the street next to the creek, and as the ground sloped sharply away, only the front was on the level, while the rear of the bistro rested on stilts above the stream. Since this rear section was not finished in time for the festivities, "Pretty Sam" had a man put a few nails in the door leading to a bridge planned for future construction.

Came the big night and the celebration was at its height. Sam had shrewdly set the date on Christmas Eve. An orchestra had been imported from El Paso, the girls from all but one of the various hook joints were dancing and available. The only reason one brothel was not represented was that Big Annie and her Girls from the Orpheum planned to make a big entrance when the party was at its height, and this they did. There was one miner who was not at the party. Drunk, he had forgotten about the opening and had other plans in mind. Banging on the door of the darkened Orpheum he got madder and madder. It suddenly dawned on him where everybody was and he turned and ran all the way to where the glittering casino was swelling to the joints. Bursting in the front door, his guns blazing, he made even more of an entrance than had the Madame and her girls. Big Annie, however, broke for the back door, followed by the rest of the frolickers. The few small nails might had prevented the headlong plunge of Big Annie, buxom though she was, but the pressure from behind was terrific. The Madame was precipitated headlong into Percha Creek, with a few other celebrants to keep her company.

OLD PERCHA BANK stands just below foundations of Show House where Lillian Russell and her troupe once performed. Bank was center of all business in Kingston, transactions were involving sales of mines and claims. Bank furniture, teller's windows are still intact in structure, but all floor space is taken up with storage of mine equipment. Little ore cart has position just inside front door. Bell was used many years to sound fire alarms and announce arrival of mail. Small trees in front of bank are young specimens of ubiquitous "Tree of Heaven." (Ailanthus altissima). This fast growing, self sufficient tree was originally introduced by Chinese miners homesick for some reminder of their homeland. Seeds blow in wind and suckers spread underground, resulting in widespread propagation. Plants are rapid growers, reaching height of twenty feet in three or four years.

KOEHLER, NEW MEXICO

The swastika, ancient symbol of good luck, seemed to cast its benediction on all of Koehler and its huge coal mines. The emblem was a part of life in the camp, seen on every building and all business correspondence, natural enough as the mining company was named Swastika Fuel Co. All this was pre-Hitler and while all signs and symbols were removed in war time, ghost town seekers may still be slightly puzzled at outlines and evidences of the swastika on some of Koehler's weathered boards.

In the spring of 1909 when the town's spectacular growth was attracting national attention, the Des Moines (Iowa) REGISTER sent reporter Tracy Garrett west to write a feature on it. The article was reprinted in the Santa Fe NEW MEXICAN, June 13, 1909, and later included in the works of historian F. Stanley, pseudonym of Francis L. Stanley Crocchiola. Native of New York, teacher of English, history and other subjects at St. John's College on the Hudson, Crocchiola came to New Mexico for his health, amassing a great store of the state's history and writing many books about it. He cites the REGISTER's story as containing the most vivid picture possible of life in Koehler, particularly on pay day.

"The miners are paid once a month, and though no credit is given, no one need go hungry or thirsty between paydays. This is avoided by a system of scrip money. After a miner has worked three days he can go to the mine office and draw a portion of his "time" in scrip. The scrip is elaborately lithographed paper in denominations of from ten cents to five dollars in scrip and good only for merchandise at the company store or saloon.

"From Raton comes the paymaster on the afternoon of payday. With him is a chest containing about $24,000 and three or four armed guards with six-shooters and Winchesters. The chest is carried into the company store and there closely guarded until 7:30, when the line that has been forming since early evening is permitted to enter.

"At the pay window, or directly in front of it sits Bill Bolden, marshall of the camp, deputy sheriff, gun man, a sure shot, a man who is always cool in danger, mild of voice, quick of action. At Bill's side hangs a six-shooter, but he seldom has to reach for it. Every man in camp knows that he can reach for it with lightning quickness, and no one dares to provoke him into action. A word from Bill Bolden will stop the line of march or a fight. He is all powerful at Koehler.

"For pay day and night and the day following several extra deputies are sworn in. Their badges of office are well filled cartridge belts, six-shooters and rifles. These men are much in evidence around the stores when the $24,000 is being handed out to the laborers. . . The cashier counts out the money, currency, except for the last four to seven dollars, this being paid in silver so the man may have some change handy when he leaves the window. . . .

"On the outskirts of the crowd. pushing and

STOCK PILE of coal at Koehler seems tremendous now in face of little demand, would be mere drop in bucket in days when all locomotives on lines of Atcheson, Topeka and Santa Fe were burning coal. Now little used spur line visible in middle ground runs to mine short distance above.

ONCE HUGE MINE OPERATION just above Koehler is still in limited production. Skeleton crew removes some coal, guards valuable machinery. Sometimes former miners bring children here for visit, try to explain working of tipples, cars, washers, usually meet with lack of interest.

ATS

jostling to keep as near the line as possible, are women of all nations waiting for the breadwinner money, that they may secure their share for the purchase of supplies or perhaps a ribbon or a piece of dress goods. Some, especially the Mexican and Italian women, are gaily dressed, green, red and yellow being the favorite colors, and she who can contrive to have all these colors on wears the happiest smile. One girl of fourteen, who was pointed out as a bride of one week, appeared on payday night in a green satin skirt reaching to but a few inches below her knees, red shoes and stockings, yellow waist, and a hat that combined all colors. As she was waiting for her newly wed husband to draw his wages a withered old lady forced her way through the crowd whispered to Bolden, and the payline was halted. The woman presented a time check for $7.50 and hurried over to the butcher

shop. Again the line moved on. Soon after another woman slipped up to the marshall and the performance was repeated. Every few minutes this occurred, with never a word of complaint from the waiting miners. For these women were the wives of miners who were ill or had been injured. . . .

"The throng of recently paid representatives of a dozen nations left the women and picked their way up the track to where the saloon door stood invitingly open. The saloon is tremendous barn-like structure running more than one hundred feet down a side. Crowded three and four deep about the bar were negroes, Chinamen, Slavs, Greeks and Mexicans, in fact all nations except Japs. The other side of the room is lined with card tables and these two are crowded with players of everything from stud poker to cooncan. Before them sat their mugs and glasses and among them hurried sturdy waiters, selected for their jobs as much for their ability to bounce disturbers as for filling empty glasses. A babel of languages rose from the tables and bar, and could be heard across the prairie and towards the ranches long after the lights of the town were left behind and only the glare from the coke ovens marked for the eye the place where payday night was at its height.

"Sunday the day following pay night was quiet at the town. Riding through the gate that surrounds the camp, there were, however, many silent evidences of the revels of the night before. Empty and broken bottles, articles of clothing and pieces of harness. In the middle of the road, his coat folded carefully over his arm, his hat missing, lay a man, or the wreck of one. The sun shone brightly on his face, but though the hours passed, he did not move. Riders and drivers turned their horses aside, but none touched him. He was not dead, the marshall or one of his deputies would pick him up. 'Every-

thing passed off nice', remarked the chief officer of the camp, as he kicked his boots on the store steps. "There wasn't a killing, or even a big fight, we have an all-fired peaceful outfit here in the lay-out.' " The writer expressed himself as confident however that any lack of fights and killings could be credited to Bill Bolden and his pair of six-shooters rather than to any inherent restraint on the part of the miners.

Koehler had no more fire protection than any of the mining camps and time after time large sections of the town were destroyed, one of the last disasters, in 1923, leveling the large two-story school building that served for twenty years. By the start of the new year the community hall or other structures were sufficiently remodeled to serve as pro-tem school houses.

Yet the town might have saved itself the trouble. The mines closed down in 1924 and that meant desertion of the camp. Koehler became a ghost town

KOEHLER had cosmopolitan population of about 1,200. Houses were heated with free coal, lit by kerosene in early days. When electricity became available company insisted on electric lights, forbade old lamps clung to by many foreign born workers and families. Times also changed shopping habits, residents forsaking local stores to travel to large centers at Raton and Trinidad, Colorado, when rapid transportation became available.

COLFAX PREDATED most of coal towns in Colfax County, was only a stop on the old road to Cimarron, a flourishing supply center while Dawson, a short distance up the canyon, boomed with its coal production. When railroad was built directly to coal mines at Dawson, Colfax declined. Town is now deserted except for family living in old Frederici store, built and operated by father of Fred Frederici, District Judge of Raton, now deceased. Senior Frederici migrated to America from Italy in 1903, remembered when coke ovens glowed at nearby Starkville, Colorado, now "suburb" of Trinidad.

and remained empty for twelve years. Then with some returning demand for coal the owners decided to reactivate conservatively. Mr. J. Van Houten, head of the company made a public statement to stockholders. "As this property has been idle since 1924 many repairs to tracks, buildings and pipelines will be necessary. Considerable new equipment will have to be purchased. For this purpose the sum of $200,000 has been appropriated by the board. By adding production of this mine to that of existing operations, the company's producing capacity will be maintained for many years to come." Mr. Koehler's report went on to stress new expenses added to the company's outlay, such as increased taxes, unemployment contributions, social security costs. "The recent increase in oil prices will help some," he said with a qualifying note, "to what extent remains to be seen."

That was in 1938 and actual reopening of the mine was still postponed. The Atcheson, Topeka and Santa Fe, previously the largest single purchaser of coal for its locomotives, was rapidly converting to oil. More, government control of coal processing was not favorable to mine owners.

Finally, for a few years, the company produced coal again but on a very limited scale. Production in 1954 was only 57,000 tons, almost all used for fuel in neighboring towns. "The railroads are now almost completely dieselized as far as locomotive power is concerned," wailed the president. "We have been unsuccessful in securing any government contracts of consequence. We have tried to interest the authorities in shipments of coal to Japan and other foreign destinations but to no avail."

The neighboring coal camp of Van Houten, one of the largest in the northern New Mexico complex, closed down February 2, 1954. At first related camps felt the closure would improve their own situations but creeping paralysis set in. Brilliant, where investment was over $1 million at one time, was soon affected as was its close neighbor Gardner. It was only a matter of time until Koehler, already ailing, would receive the kiss of death. The same fate was in store for Catskill, Yankee, Blossburg, Carisburg and Morley, just across the line in Colorado.

The common denominator in the death of New Mexico's coal camps was the failing usefulness of solid fuels, variations being only in detail. Where coke was the major product as in Dawson, its use in foundries was replaced by natural gas. Where raw coal was the big export, as in Koehler and other camps, it was diesel oil that rang the death knell.

LAKE VALLEY, NEW MEXICO

On the map of New Mexico, Lake Valley lies at the bottom or south end of an inverted L. Kingston is at the other, western end and Hillsboro at the junction. These three towns in the wild and wooly days of the 1880s and '90s composed the stage route of the Orchard Line.

Sadie Orchard knew it well. She ranks among the most colorful characters of New Mexico's early days. She came to the Territory in 1886 and seeing the advantages of having the only stage line in the region, she and her husband assembled two Concord Coaches and an express wagon as a nucleus. She drove one of the coaches, making the full run from Kingston to Hillsboro to Lake Valley. It

was her proud boast that her coach had never been held up while she held the reins. This could not be said of the stage line as a whole for bandits and Indians waylaid the stage and freight wagons with discouraging regularity. Sadie is said to have shaken her head about the worst stretch on the route, narrow Percha Canyon. "It sure was troublesome for us stage drivers. Indians lurked along the way and the road was surely trying."

Lake Valley hadn't always been the important terminus of a stage line. In the '70s it was only a tiny settlement and few people knew of it. More did very quickly after the August day in 1878 when cowboy George W. Lufkin rode along the

IN OLD LAKE VALLEY CEMETERY some graves like this one of Sarah Collins are fenced. Those graves without protection from digging coyotes became project of Christian Endeavor. Society raised money to place heavy stone slab cover over graves. C. E. also built fence around entire graveyard, keeping out cattle, other large animals. George Lufkin, first discoverer of silver in camp lies here, died penniless, was buried by county.

MAJOR MORGAN MORGANS, veteran of the Union Army ran rooming house in little false front and "annex." By '96 Lake Valley had lost much of population but remainder felt need of religious influence. Town never had church but ladies organized Christian Endeaver Society, bought rooming house, covered walls with oilcloth, hung up seven kerosene lamps, placed chairs in rows. Annex was furnished for convenience of any preacher who might stay overnight. Ordinarily a leader was chosen from members to conduct each Sunday's services. These were non-sectarian; members included Presbyterians, Methodists, Baptists, Quakers, Mormons and Catholics. Dues were ten cents a month, modest sum realized was augmented by bazaars, basket socials. Society was even able to contribute to famine relief for stricken China, flood victims in Monticello, Sierra County, offered food and lodging to any needy persons traveling through Lake Valley by wagon and team.

edge of Black Range, rifle cradled in one arm and loaded for Apaches, his prospector's pick in the other. At lunch time he stopped under a pinon tree. Among the stones scattered about was a piece of float so interesting he put it in his pocket. Later he had it assayed and was told the value of the sample came out several thousand ounces to the ton. Excited, Lufkin got his friend Chris Watson to join him in partnership and the two relocated the source of the sample. They found the spot but no more float. However they did locate several promising claims, one of them near the town of Lake Valley.

Money dwindled and no good vein was forthcoming. The partners sold out to the Sierra Grande Mining Company, made up of a group of Philadelphia capitalists, receiving $100,000 for the claim. This was a good price considering the prospects. The location actually consisted of several shafts and tunnels; one of the latter had hardly penetrated the side of the hill. A lease was taken on this one by a blacksmith named John Leavitt. Two days after the original finders had sold their

claim Leavitt broke through into the most fabulous lode of silver the world has ever known.

It consisted of a hollow in the hillside, a "room" nicknamed the "Bridal Chamber." The cavern had walls of solid horn silver. The total silver removed was 2,500,000 ounces bringing $1.11 an ounce at that time. Before it was all scraped out a spur from the railroad had been extended right into the Bridal Chamber and the rich stuff was shoveled directly into the cars.

Naturally this kind of thing could not be kept a secret, and a rush of prospectors, miners and hangers-on poured into a forty-mile strip along the edge of the Black Range, presided over by Kingston, Hillsboro and Lake Valley.

The Black Range Mining District was officially organized in 1881. Most of the population came that same year, when the Apache troubles were at their peak; no miners cabin or settlers hut was safe from raids by Victorio, or his henchmen, Loco and Nana. In spite of their continuing raids, total production in the period up to 1894 was close to $25,000,000.

One of the smaller towns in the area was Chloride. During the period of intense badgering by Indians, a sentry was kept on constant duty there. Old timers gloried in telling about the time the watch fell to one Schmidt, a German fresh from the old country. He had never handled a rifle but was carefully instructed in its use and reminded that a single shot from the weapon would warn the town that an Apache raid was imminent. About the middle of the night the ominous shot was heard, throwing the camp into the usual panic; women and children were hustled off to the blockhouse built for this purpose. Nothing happened. Pretty soon Schmidt came walking sheepishly into town explaining, "I shot her all right, but I don't mean to do it."

In 1883 Kingston was a hotbed of rustler activity. Organized gangs of cattle thieves became so brazen that they even flaunted their identity to the ranchers they had robbed, as no recourse was possible, short of murder. Ranchers finally appealed to Territorial Governor L. A. Shelton to send a full company of militia, armed to the teeth. The governor ordered Major A. J. Fountain to proceed from Mesilla to the Black Range area. Fountain headed for Kingston with almost his entire battalion, leaving only a skeleton force to guard

the jail at Mesilla. Arriving at Kingston, Fountain found that the ringleaders of the rustlers had fled to Lake Valley. Taking a detail of five men he proceeded toward that town arriving there at five in the morning. He arrested one of the most wanted men without any trouble. This was "Butch" whose real name was William Leland. The other of the desired duo, John Watts, made a run for it, and when cornered lifted his rifle. When he saw that he was outnumbered he put up his hands.

"The two prisoners," Fountain wrote in his report, "were mounted on one horse, unbound. At about 4:30 a.m. after the moon had gone down and before daylight the command arrived at the *cienaga* known as Daly's . . . There I halted the command and ordered the men to dismount and prepare coffee . . . I had the prisoners dismount and asked Watts how he was getting along, he replied 'I want a drink bad'. I told him the men would have coffee in a few minutes. He answered that he didn't want coffee, but whiskey and asked me to allow him to go to a nearby tavern to get some. I told him I could not give him permission and rode off and dismounted."

There was a good deal of confusion while the men were unsaddling the horses and unpacking the mules and in the midst of it someone noticed that the prisoners were hightailing it up the road. The men seized their carbines and fired a volley of shots after them. "I directed Capt. Salazar to take a sufficient detail and follow the fugitives. He took six or seven men and proceeded up the road about 200 yards and came upon the bodies of Watts and Butch lying in the road. They were both dead. I ordered their bodies be covered with loose earth in order to prevent them from being disturbed by coyotes . . . I telephoned Lake Valley the fact of their death with the request that their bodies be sent for."

Eventually the cattle rustling ring was broken up, most of its members fleeing toward the Mexican border. Some were intercepted but most escaped. Thus ended rustling on a big scale in that section of New Mexico.

MOST REMAINING RELICS show a d o b e construction, fronted by whipsawed lumber; this one shows unique combination of adobe and stone. Adobe was not of prefabricated bricks as usual but extension of mortar.

HE BROUGHT LIGHT IN

Madrid, N.M.

Nobody thought a nice fellow like Lloyd, clerk at the Albuquerque and Cerrillos Coal Co., would ever be put in jail . . . and there was the sheriff going to the Cerrillos railroad station after somebody else. Well after all, this was Madrid, New Mexico, where anything might happen. It did, that night. They let Lloyd out of jail on the promise of a keg of beer, the sheriff brought Marjorie in and the miners threw a big party for the bride and groom.

Coal was found at Madrid as early as 1839 and probably used at the nearby Cerrillos gold mines. When Gen. Stephen Watts Kearney came through New Mexico in the 1840s he used Madrid coal for his army. And it is said that at one time ox teams hauled the coal all the way to St. Louis.

Legends grow more factual when the Madrid mines were opened by a subsidiary of the Santa Fe Railway in the early 1880s. In 1899 when the town had a population of 3,000 the Colorado Fuel and Iron Co. took control, later selling to the Albuquerque and Cerrillos Coal Co. In 1910 Oscar Huber went to work for the company, eventually

buying them out, the property still owned by his heirs in 1964.

Marjorie Lloyd came to the coal camp as a bride in 1913, she recalled in a *New Mexico Magazine* article. Her new husband was very much concerned about the charivari that might greet them when they arrived from Denver as bride and groom. He was employed in the camp as mine clerk and well aware of rowdy welcomes of the sort. He arranged to have the Madrid sheriff meet their train in Cerrillos, three miles distant, and spirit them into his home unobserved.

The miners however discovered why the clerk went to Denver and the next day through a ruse managed to lock him up in the town jail. Kept a prisoner until dinner time, Lloyd was glad to buy his freedom with a keg of beer and the traditional charivari was staged after all.

At that time, as now, the residential district consisted of four long, dreary rows of houses sadly in need of paint. They faced the company store, offices, tavern and other business, a row of shade trees bordering both sides of the main street. The population was about 3,000 and there were no vacant homes, the Lloyds being forced to live at one of the three boarding houses, the one having the only green lawn in Madrid.

The company employed one doctor, the entire medical facility for the town without hospital or nurses. Every man paid a dollar a month for any medical care he might need. When his wife had a baby he paid extra for the delivery. The town's water supply was a sometime thing. Railroad tank cars brought water from springs five miles away, siphoning it into a reservoir. Sometimes the supply became exhausted and pipes were dry for a whole day until another tank came in. Mrs. Lloyd wrote, "Dishes, laundry and baths just had to wait. If you got too thirsty the tavern wasn't too far away."

Electricity was unavailable for homes in 1913. Generated in a powerhouse the current was sufficient only for company houses. Families had to rely on kerosene lamps and candles. Cooking was done on coal fires, the fuel bought "reasonably" from the company. Sometimes a dynamite cap lost in the coal would liven things up in the stove.

CHRISTMAS CITY of New Mexico. Below are most of the buildings remaining in Madrid, all vacant. On hill at right still stands cross that centered electrically lit "replica" of Bethlehem with large cut-outs representing Biblical figures, display one of many completely surrounding town. Surmounting each of 12 hills on both sides of Madrid was huge Christmas "tree"—pine pole with iron bars for limbs, each generously strung with colored light bulbs. Tree in foreground alone remains erect.

Fire was always a hazard, some houses burned through the use of lamps and candles, the company finally wiring them for electricity but limiting them to a single bulb hanging naked from the ceiling, the "juice" turned on only at a given time after nightfall. In time daytime electricity was allowed, for ironing—one day a week.

The men made their living at the company mines and were expected to spend it in the company store. But the drygoods section offered little more than jumpers, overalls and a few women's house dresses. When wives ordered more frilly items from mail-order houses, they had to do it secretly and hope no company official would see her carrying the package home.

All this was before Oscar Huber. He changed everything, literally brought light to shine on Madrid. He became superintendent after working there for several years, bringing his wife and children from Albuquerque. Marjorie Lloyd says of him, "I used to enjoy watching him stride up the street each morning. You sensed in his quick decisive step that he was definitely going some place." Huber planted flower beds in his yard, the only

ones in town, and soon had a showplace, with flower boxes under the windows. When others admired the effect, he made available water flowing from one of the mine tunnels, piping a convenient supply to each section of houses. That summer there were splashes of color in almost every yard.

Huber had the main street paved and new houses built in all lots made vacant by fires. Then came a six-room hospital, first grade and high schools to replace old residences used by students. An employees' club was organized, baseball diamond and bleachers built, Madrid becoming famous for its ball team, the company paying its transportation to compete in other towns. Yet no change in the gloomy, soot-blackened town was as spectacular as allowing all residents unlimited use of electricity.

In the first winter after this innovation, Huber helped the people put on a Christmas display, the like of which had never been seen in New Mexico. Huge figures were created—of Mary, Joseph, the infant Christ, shepherds and wise men. Miners enthusiastically painted and wired them for electrical illumination. The nativity scene, utilizing

OLD CEMETERY on hill above Madrid contains many markers and enclosures individually hand-crafted from local materials. Not all graves are fenced, or wooden pickets have disappeared, many graves marked only by piles of stones.

CACTI "ask but little here below," growing happily on dirt roof of stone house. Plastered inside with mud, it is one of the oldest relics in Madrid, dating from days before large companies took over coal production.

COMPANY HOUSES—4 long lines of nearly identical units—presented dreary sight to residents but now of interest as ghost town relics. Originally standing in Kansas, houses were sawed in quarters, shipped to Madrid on Santa Fe Railroad. Reassembled they were plastered to make windproof but storms soon seeped through. Most had living room, kitchen on main floor, 3 bedrooms upstairs. Danger of fires was always present from overturned kerosene lamps or candles. In absence of water firemen dynamited burning buildings to prevent spread of flames.

live sheep, burros and oxen was set up on a hill overlooking the town, followed by a Bethlehem scene with central cross and many buildings. As each Christmas came, new ones were added until in a few years both sides of the canyon were covered with brilliantly lighted Biblical scenes. Every building in town displayed strings of colored lights and in the ball park was a display for children featuring Santa Claus and mechanically lighted toyland figures.

The magnificent pageant drew thousands of visitors from other parts of the state, the show of lights maintained from early December through

New Years. The program set in motion by Oscar Huber gave the miners initiative to organize choral clubs with many fine voices and during evenings of Christmas week various groups were stationed at strategic points, breaking into coordinated song with the words "Let There Be Light." At that instant the main switch was thrown on and the dark old coal town broke into a blaze of glory and glad voices.

In the '30s the town that shipped millions of tons of coal annually began to show signs of slowing down. Gradual conversion in railroading and industry to other fuels slackened coal production.

116

OLD BEDSTEAD and climbing vine offer composition on wall of old Madrid house.

COMPANY OFFICES near north end of city on road to Los Cerrillos and Santa Fe. Close inspection reveals strings of lights still clinging to structure.

World War II brought it up some temporarily, 20,000 tons going to Los Alamos to help build the first A-bombs. But Madrid's Christmas lights were turned on for the last time in 1941. When the switch was thrown off at the end, the choraleers sang "Auld Lang Syne" while almost everyone wept openly.

117

MAGDALENA, NEW MEXICO

Socorro is the town where one turns west for Magdalena and Kelly. The old shipping center isn't dead, though sleepy, and has a plaza authentically Mexican. The church of San Miguel is one of the oldest in the country. The town, during the old, wild days, was the current hangout of Russian Bill. Not actually a killer, Bill only liked to pose as one. He suffered from a compulsion to stay in the public eye and the only way he knew how to do it was to keep up a constant stream of practical jokes. The town's patience grew thin, and by one Christmas Eve, reached the breaking point. The main hotel boasted a card room as well as dining hall, and it was there Bill played his last game of poker. He got drunk, and bragged about his marksmanship, proving how good he was by expertly shooting one finger from the hand of one of the players. The rest of the gamblers grabbed him by the scruff of the neck, read a charge against him of "being a damn nuisance" and hanged him right then and there in the hotel dining room.

Some twenty-seven miles west is the old camp of Magdalena, still having life but showing its age in the many false fronts scattered through the town. Alice Morley Cleaveland in her book "No Life For A Lady" gives a vivid picture of her advent there. "We arrived in Magdalena in February, 1886. The town sprawled in the sun at the foot of Lady Magdalena Mountain, a bare and defiant monolith in the midst of her decently pine-clad sisters. . . Halfway up the mountainside, Lady Magdalena herself gazes into the blue sky resting upon far mountain peaks, her face turned away from the town. . . There is a legend that Lady Magdalena Mountain was a sanctuary respected by the Indians, where fugitives, whether deservedly or not, found refuge from pursuing enemies. The legend did not hold after the paleface came shooting his way into the land. Many a pursuer fell before his enemies in the streets of Magdalena.

" 'Please give us a room that is not directly over the barroom,' my mother stipulated to the hotel-keeper the night we arrived. 'I'm afraid those bullets will come through the floor.' It was years later before Magdalena gathered herself together and made it a misdemeanor to shoot within the city limits."

In the 1880's when Kelly was already a boom town, Magdalena was hardly more than a watering place at Pueblo Springs. There was a station of sorts there as a convenience of the stage line from Socorro to the western part of the Territory. There the cattlemen watered their stock on market drives and cowboys unlimbered their legs while they had the chance. The present town of Magdalena didn't occupy its present situation until '85 or so, when it began to grow into the place where "the lights were repeatedly shot out by ebullient buckaroos." It was then getting its water the hard way, hauling it from Pueblo Springs at a cost of ten cents a barrel. Kelly nourished the place by sending down her miners who wished to carouse but found insufficient space to spread out in the narrow confines of the canyon in which Kelly is cramped. On the plain there was room for saloons and dance halls of generous proportions and these promptly took shape. Other factors contributed to the economy, such as the railhead and the sheep and cattle ranches which sprang up in the surrounding ranges. The railroad's purpose was to serve the booming mining town of Kelly, up the steep canyon from Magdalena. One look at the canyon's grade, however, and the engineers gave up, saying in effect to the "city fathers" of Kelly, "If you want a train, come and get it." And this Kelly did, rolling its ore and bullion down the short but precipitous wagon road to the station.

When Kelly died, so did a large part of Magdalena, that part having to do with the shipping of supplies for a vast area of cattle ranches and sheep ranges, but days of the old reckless shootings on the main street are gone and the town drowses.

PYTHIAN HALL, BUILT IN 1907 at height of Magdalena's development, is one of New Mexico's best examples of architecture of the time. Decorations are ornate but lack gingerbread effect of other structure of period. Tiny building at right once housed newspaper office, served many later purposes. Eyebolts above door seem to indicate one time sign or awning. Magdalena's prosperity depended upon that of Kelly, mining camp two miles up canyon. Before railroad came to Magdalena, Kelly's ores were shipped 29 rough and rocky miles in ox-wagons over Blue Canyon road to Socorro. Closeness of railhead enormously amplified output made practical by easy disposal. Many mines in district had euphonious names, as Ambrosia, Cimmaron, Alhambra, Little Louella, Iron Mask, Legal Tender, reflecting literary, political or practical leanings.

119

MOGOLLON, NEW MEXICO

Young Sergeant James C. Cooney was one to keep his eyes open and his mouth shut. When, in 1870, on a scouting expedition out of Fort Bayard he found a rich ledge from gold bearing float was crumbling, he kept the discovery secret until his hitch was over. This feat is unparalleled in the history of most mining towns. Whiskey usually loosed the tongues of those finding gold.

As soon as Cooney was mustered, he confided in several men he could trust, among them Harry McAllister, forming a partnership to explore the possibilities of his find. The area was in the mountains called the Mogollons (pronounced muggy owns), thickly infested by hostile Apaches. Cooney's party was attacked by Indians so continually that, after establishing several locations, the prospectors retired to Silver City to nurse their wounds. Two years later, with augmented defenses and supplies, the men again set out for the claims. Two ox-drawn wagons carried their equipment and food.

The first place to be established as a camp in the Mogollons was Claremont but this one was short-lived. Then a camp in Cooney Canyon was started and flourished as a typical rough-and-ready camp for a brief period of glory.

Indians were a constant menace and on one occasion when it was rumored the redskins were about to attack the camp was evacuated as usual. A couple of miners named John Lambert and George Doyle were hiding in the bushes just above the houses when the Indians came down the trail. The white men had their little dog with them and he began to growl. Fearful of attracting attention, they choked the animal to death. The Indian party ransacked the house, one squaw coming out with a full length mirror tied to her back. She was followed by a retinue of delighted youngsters who vied for positions to see their reflections.

At about this same period nearby Alma was established and shared attacks by Apaches. In one of these, James Cooney was killed and his camp at Cooney taken over by his brother Captain Michael Cooney.

In the spring of '83 the Captain grubstaked a man named Turner. Rumors persisted that Turner found a bonanza but the man himself vanished. In '89 his body was found in Sycamore Canyon, waylaid by

PLANK PORCHES ALSO SERVED as sidewalks over stream bed, show wear and tear from use and weather. At about this point on one street of town, during Presidential election in fall of 1896, large picture of William McKinley was suspended from wire stretched across street by Republicans. Returns began to come in indicating candidate was losing. Portrait was lowered by Democrats, black cloth draped over it, and again elevated. Late evening stage came in with word that McKinley had won. Everyone, regardless of affiliation, got drunk, then went home to sleep it off.

ever-present Apaches. Captain Cooney determined to find the supposed wealth that was legally his if it existed. He started out in the fall; next spring *his* body was found where he had frozen to death, only about 100 yards from where that of Turner had been found.

In the meantime, the new camp of Mogollon had been started in the bottom of Silver Creek Canyon, a short distance from Claremont and Cooney. The first mines developed there were the Maude S., Deep Down, Little Fanny and Last Chance. It is the history of the Little Fanny that permeates the history of the camp itself.

Mr. Friolo was a resident of Mogollon all through its best years and still lives in the crumbling old camp, the only "bona fide" resident, the few others being summer campers. The old gentleman tells of how miner's consumption, so called, and "miner's con" in

his words, took a ghastly toll of men working in the Little Fanny. The jack-hammers used in breaking the quartz for removal from the mine made a cloud of gritty dust which affected the lungs, some miners lasted only three years or less. If they did not die outright they were relegated to lighter jobs, but even this did not save them. Water hoses were provided them by the company for wetting the rock to reduce or prevent the dust, but this procedure soaked the men too. They refused to work wet all the time, perferring the dust. Finally, in desperation, the company worked out a system where the water was squirted along with the air-pressure. From then on the toll from "miner's con" was cut down and the town's three physicians, Drs. Feel, Kern and Parm, had a respite.

At the time the Little Fanny was developed the population of the camp was about 2,000. That was in 1909. Two years later the number of people had

FACING J. P. HOLLAND GENERAL STORE is group of buildings constituting main business center of camp. At extreme left is tiny saloon, next is Mogollon Mercantile, then Annex to larger Holland store, specializing in furniture and "notions" after period as post office.. Large stone structure at extreme right was Howard's Drug Store, with doctor's offices above. Upper floor was gained by outside stairway, now smothered by "Trees of Heaven." Structure served as grocery store later, as town declined and adobe buildings disintegrated. Patch of mullein weeds in foreground is at edge of area once constituting red-light district.

IMPOSING ADOBE served Mogollon as roominghouse, was "respectable" since brothels were segregated, confined to flat at lower edge of town. Smaller "dobe" at left was grocery store. One road to mines wound up gulch back of buildings and many small cabins still perch along route.

expanded further and there were fourteen saloons, seven restaurants, five stores, two hotels and the usual brothels.

The sixth annual edition of "Mogollon Mines" pointed out that "there is room for and an absolute necessity for the establishment of a Society for the prevention of Cruelty to Animals in Mogollon. Scarcely a day passes but what a cruel and heartless driver abuses his animals. Whether in a team or a burro heavily laden with wood, both are subjected to knock-out blows with cordwood or loaded whips. It is not uncommon to see an animal devoid of one eye, and frequently this is in a bleeding condition, and the poor, suffering brute has no way to relieve itself of the constant annoyance of myriads of flies. . ."

By 1915 the camp's payroll was between $50,000 and $75,000 every month. Gold and silver bullion were shipped out regularly to Silver City. The distance was ninety miles and in bad weather the ore teams required ten days for the trip. Even in the most favorable weather, fifteen miles was a good day's average because of the frighteningly steep grades encountered. Ordinary harnesses were not used for the long line of 18-mule teams. A center chain ran the entire length, each team harnessed with hames and collars, belly bands, back bands and chain tugs, with the exception of the two wheel horses. Metal doubletrees were hooked to each section so the teams could pull. The teamster rode the right wheel horse with a saddle, and guided the teams with a jerk line which extended the entire length and was snapped to each team. On the steep curves the mules stepped right or left over the chain as it rubbed against their legs. Ordinary brakes were ineffectual. Rough locks with heavy timbers were dropped by a lever in front of the rear wheel of the train wagons. On the steepest grades the strings of wagons were separated into smaller groups.

The end of the haul at Silver City would see the 300-pound bars of gold and silver stacked in front of the Silver City National Bank, the return trip made with heavy loads of crude oil for the diesel engines at Mogollon. In 1912 when a flywheel weighing 12,400 pounds was hauled up to the Little Fanny, a 24-horse outfit was employed. The rigs were owned by W. A. Tenney, and operated from 1910 until the opening of World War I. Trucks took over but the camp was tired and beginning to drag its feet.

There was less and less of that famous "blossom rock" from which little nuggets could be shaken. What remained assayed poorly, was refractory and hardly paid costs of milling and refining. Several mines closed down entirely, others operated on a part-time basis. When the Little Fanny quit, so did the town. The Black Jack Gang, so belligerent at the turn of the century, was already long since tamed, holdups along the steep and rocky road to Alma and Silver City had become less frequent. Gunshots ceased to echo from Jimmy Johnson's saloon or the similar emporium of Pedro "Pete" Almeraz where the notorious Cosmo Zapata had been killed. Mogollon shriveled as people moved away, sighed and lay down to sleep.

PINOS ALTOS, NEW MEXICO

In the realm of legend is the story of a long vanished settlement on the site of the present town of Pinos Altos. Prior to known discoveries of gold in 1837 Mexicans were said to have found rich deposits of the metal in a stream at the foot of an enormous cottonwood tree. They erected an enclosure for protection against marauding bands of Indians, the barricade constructed of materials at hand — adobe, stone and logs, built in horseshoe shape. Men and animals were safely quartered inside at night while by day the men placered the gravels, the horses grazing on the hillside close by. In time all their rawhide panniers were filled with treasure and the decision must be made as to who was to take them to distant Chihuahua in Mexico. Here the men fell out. Everyone wanted to stay with the gold and return home. No one wanted to remain at the diggings and guard the stockade.

Here the tale becomes even more gossamer. There would seem to be two outcomes possible. The men all returned to their homes with the golden *chispas* or they fought among themselves and were overpowered by Indians.

Three items in this story are borne out by facts. There were running streams of water even though these flow now only in times of rain. Correlated is the fact that an ample stand of tall pines, *"pinos altos,"* existed before the slopes were wantonly logged off. Gone now is the forest and the streams of clear water once stored by a generous groundcover. Remaining are faint signs of horseshoe shaped ruins, outlined by enduring stones.

More substantial history begins in 1860, when a party of twelve scouts left Tucson for the Rio Grande. A long rest was taken at Mesilla, N. M. Here the men heard rumors, always flying, that there was gold in "them thar hills." Re-routing to Santa Rita they stopped again, this time to stock up on supplies and split into smaller parties. The group made up of three men named Hicks, Snively and Birch made their camp on the banks of Bear Creek and eagerly rushed to begin sifting the gravels of the creek bed. Birch is credited with having been the first to find a couple of nuggets, the *"chispas"* of earlier Mexicans. Frenzied search rewarded each man with a handful of gold. All found it hard to sleep that night and rose early for a council as to what was to be done. The obvious problem was to get provisions and tools if they were to stay

on. But how to keep the discovery a secret? It seemed wisest to go to Santa Rita, confide their secret to trusted friends who would purchase food and supplies so as to rouse no curiosity. The confidants were the Marston brothers and one Langston all of whom swore secrecy. The three discoverers then slipped unobstrusively back to their diggings.

Arising bright and early next morning to begin work, they made another discovery. They were not alone. A party of three Americans had crept in and staked several claims close by. All day and for weeks and months thereafter a motley assemblage of Mexicans, Americans, hard working miners, soft-handed gamblers and con artists streamed in to swell the population of the infant camp called at first Birchville.

The original discovery by Birch had been on May 18 and by September there were 700 men panning the streams. Santa Rita now boomed, supplying staple groceries, as did Mesilla the source for tools and clothing.

At first all gold recovery was done by panning and sluicing in the stream bed, but as rewards grew slimmer, the sources of loose dust and nuggets were found in rich lodes on the hillside. At first these needed only scraping, plenty of ore was easily obtained and crudely refined in primitive "arrastras." A low circular rock wall was built. About twenty feet across, it was centered by a short pole topped by a spike holding the end of a beam that reached outside the wall. A horse or mule, sometimes a burro for small outfits, was tied to the outer end to walk in a circle, dragging a heavy rock around inside the wall. Ore was dumped into the enclosure to be more or less pulverized. At intervals the larger, harder chunks were thrown out and the fine material treated as usual in rockers, Long Toms, sluices, or even in some small operations, panned out.

The town grew to the point where the Mesilla *Times* was running little news items about it. Some of these, gleaned by Dorothy Watson in her *"Pinos Altos Story,"* read: "Thomas J. Marston is pushing ahead his work of grinding quartz, although constantly annoyed by Indians." "The Pinos Altos Hotel serves bread and meals." "Samuel G. and Roy Bean (prominent in Law West of the Pecos) are dealers in merchandise and liquors, and have a fine billiard table." "Thomas Marston wants 200 quartz miners." Marston added that he was willing to pay top wages, up to two dollars a day.

Following this cozy period came a long spell of strife, involvement in the fringes of the Civil War and constant harassment by Apaches. When the Confederacy was established, the area including Pinos Altos was claimed by the South. On August 1st, 1861, Col. John R. Baylor, governor at Mesilla, proclaimed the area to be part of the Territory of Arizona. He then afforded some small protection from Apaches for the settlers and miners by sending Snively, now promoted to captain to help control Cochise's savages, and making another captain of Thomas Birch to watch over his mining camp. About the same time the Apaches made up their minds to get rid of the whites, once and for all. They gathered on September 14, for a concerted attack. Cochise as usual, was in the forefront with his warriors from Chiricahuas, and joined by Mangas Colorado and his band of Mimbrenos, led 400 yelling braves down upon the whites from the forested slopes of the continental divide upon which the camp lay straddled. The attack was begun at dawn and raged until afternoon. The toll of retreating Apaches was fifteen, one of these was killed by a dog belonging to a Mexican miner named Carlos Norero. Two Americans were killed outright and Marston was so severely wounded he died a few days later. He was buried beneath a juniper tree in the little Pinos Altos cemetery.

Although the Indian attack had been successfully repulsed, the miners compared the relative values of gold and their scalps, then decamped in large numbers to engage in what they thought might be the comparative safety of the Army. Some chose the Union side. Others were more in sympathy with the South. The remaining residents felt their numbers were so decimated as to make them targets for further attacks and screamed for help. Governor Baylor responded with a detachment of 100 men under Major E. Waller for their protection.

Even with this another Apache attack occurred in which forty miners were casualties. This one was executed in crafty manner, with a full understanding of the emotions lonely young men must be feeling after such a long time in camp without women. Mangas Colorado stationed a group of his more attractive young squaws on the hillside above the camp in full sight of the miners. The girls languidly combed their hair and otherwise displayed their feminine charms.

At last the men could stand it no longer and most of the shrunken male population made a mad rush up the hill. Apaches ambushed them on both sides and cut off any retreat. Other Indians united and drove off the horses. Additional parties of Apaches seized a number of whites who were hunting game in the hills. One of the hunters who escaped the terrible slaughter reported the hills "full of Indians."

Mangas Colorado had been subjected to many indignities and treacheries by the whites, blaming them as the reason for his continued attacks. General Carlton sent out word that Mangas Colorado must be captured "by any means deemed necessary." Captain Shirland and Jack Swilling located the chief in the Pinos Mountains and conveyed the message to him that the whites were anxious to negotiate and would guarantee his safety if he would accompany them to Fort McLane. In spite of all previous experiences with whites and "negotiations" with them, the chief went willingly and alone with the emissaries. On January 18, 1863, he was shot to death "while trying to escape." With the chief out of the way, the soldiers found courage to "capture" his wife who was taken to Pinos Altos and killed.

The last act of treachery on the part of the whites came in the summer of '64 when a partially successful treaty had established a certain amount of confidence on the part of the Indians, at least enough so that they came peacefully into camp for barter. One of the settlers owned a house larger than the rest. He asked some of the Indians to invite their friends to a sumptuous dinner he would serve them in celebration of the signing of the treaty. Some sixty guests responded. When all were seated the host opened fire on them, killing many, maiming many more. From then on it was not safe for a white to venture out of camp bounds alone or unarmed.

At the end of the war and with the return of most of the men, Indian harassments became less, though were never really absent for any length of time. A Navajo band drove off more than thirty yoke of oxen and were promptly pursued by about fifty men. In the ensuing clash thirteen Navajos were killed and a number taken prisoner.

After the establishment of several military forts in the vicinity in '69, such incidents were replaced by others of a more homely nature. A Sr. Ancheta, resident of Pinos Altos, made a visit to the hacienda of his old friend in Mexico. While there he fell in love with the wife of his host. He talked her into running away with him and as soon as the couple reached Pinos Altos, Ancheta made haste to reinforce the defenses and made port holes in the walls in case the bereft husband should pursue them.

Other men were content to take Indian or Mexican women as common law wives, to build log or adobe homes and start planting garden seeds. Orchards and vineyards were established and except for an occasional murder in the saloons or a miner being killed in a premature mine explosion or attacked by bears while hunting, life in the camp became almost prosaic.

Historian Dorothy Watson paints an idyllic picture of early day Pinos Altos. "They made of their homes a garden spot, there were fields of alfalfa, corn and beans, and smaller plots of garden truck and flowers. Besides his terraced grapevines and fruit trees Mr. Stanley had a rose garden. The Mexicans planted almond and peach trees around their homes and invariably had oleanders in tubs. During the summer they blossomed beside the doorways and somehow room was found for them in their small dwellings when frost came. They took fledgling mocking birds from nests, carefully tended and trained them. They were kept in large cages hanging outside on the walls where they called and exchanged confidences with the neighboring wild birds or complimented the guitar music. Each home had a small corral for a burro. Chickens and cows roamed at will and here and there goats would clamber over walls and roofs. Every day the yard was swept as clean as the mud packed earth floors of their dwellings. Peter Wagnor and John Simon brought wild roses from the canyon and planted hedges of them around their homes. Although the buildings were crude, the effect was pleasing."

The camp flourished for a long period but began to show signs of decay toward the turn of the century. Silver City had in the meantime come into prominence and in 1879 one newspaper there referred to Pinos Altos as "an abandoned camp in Silver City's back yard." The "abandoned" town had a population of 9,000 in the '80s and '90s, boasted a drug store, two hotels, barber shop, clothing stores and even a Turkish bath.

In spite of a downward trend there were several spurts forward, one in 1906 when the long dream of narrow gauge came into camp, enormously expediting the shipment of ores to Silver City. Excursionists were thrilled to ride on the tops of loaded ore cars. On one such trip, returning cars on the steep grade got away, failed to make a

sharp turn and landed in the gulch. After this no one but employees was allowed on the cars.

Great excitement was caused in 1911 when Ira Wright and James Bell struck rich deposits in their newly leased Pacific Mines. One lot of 1800 pounds of ore brought them $43,000. As was to be expected this set off a wave of high grading; miners were thought to have taken out as much for themselves as did the owners. All recipients were relieved of temptation when the shallow pocket gave out. Bell and Wright did not renew the lease, marking another downward step in the economy of the town.

During depression days idle men flocked to the diggings, scratching around once-rich shafts and tunnels, trying to eke out a living. Others were operating as many as seventy rockers in the stream beds so that the scene resembled the aspects of early days.

Altogether, The Bureau of Mines estimated, over $8,000,000 in gold, lead, silver and copper were produced in the camp once so blessed with tall pines and streams, now so barren and dry.

GOLD AVENUE METHODIST CHURCH w a s dedicated May 18, 1898. First Pastor was Rev. Henry Van Valkenburgh. Church was built on part of Good Enough Mining claim, the owners donating the site. Methodist ladies gave church suppers, basket socials to raise money for building fund. Phoebe Hurst, member of wealthy mine owner family, offered to help on condition reading room was provided. When edifice was completed it was found that separate room had not been provided, so front of church was stocked with magazines. 1942 picture shows bell surmounting frame tower at right. Earliest church activities were Catholic, diocese was in Mesilla. Priest visited parish, baptized children, blessed casual unions entered into since last visit, said Mass for those who had died.

TWO BOOMLETS FAILED

San Pedro, New Mexico

Just south of the mining camp of San Pedro are the ruins of an ancient Indian village called Paako, the language spoken there either Keres or Tewa. In 1598 the explorer Onate called the pueblo Tano. The houses were built of native rubble and generally two stories high. There were three kivas, those circular holes in the ground, paved with rock and used as places of worship. Early historians state the pueblo was still occupied as late as 1626 but by 1670 all Indian inhabitants had vanished.

With Spanish occupation a mission was established on the site in 1661 and named San Pedro de la Cuchilla after the patron saint. The University of New Mexico did some excavation at the site in 1936, uncovering traces of stone walls and kivas. Adjoining the remains on the north was the early mining camp also called San Pedro as was the huge Spanish land grant including Indian ruins, mission church and hundreds of acres of pasture land.

The exact date of gold discoveries at San Pedro camp is uncertain but in 1846 army Lt. J. W. Abert visited there. In his report to Congress he said, "In the evening we visited a town at the base of the principal mountains here, mingled with the houses were huge mounds of earth thrown out of the wells so that the village looks like a village of giant prairie dogs. Nearly all of the people were at their wells, and were drawing up bags of loose sand by means of windlasses. Around the pools men, women and children were grouped, intently pouring over their bags of loose sand, washing the earth in wooden platters or goat horns...."

The fevered days of washing and panning by hand did not last long because particles of gold had to be a little larger than "dust" to be discovered in sediments, specks smaller than flakes of coarse pepper usually going undiscovered. Also water had to be available where the gold was. Primitive hand panning was replaced in 1880 by big time hydraulic operations when the San Pedro and Canyon del Agua Company set up equipment. Overlooking the area is the now famed tourist attraction, Sandia Crest. Up there the company found ample water with a steep drop down to San Pedro.

Officials spent $500,000 for a pipeline to carry it into monitors or hydraulic nozzles that would wash whole hillsides into waiting sluices. While the pipeline was being constructed, the company made real estate hay by laying out a town for sales to credulous buyers who were told there would be a big city here. Then the company was beset by extensive litigation, pipeline and town building held up in the courts. Construction became so entangled the company was forced to quit. Again quiet settled over the San Pedro foothills.

A few years later another company moved in, putting up buildings on empty lots and in 1887 the *Golden Nine* was so optimistic as to proclaim, "Everybody is coming to San Pedro and the rest of the world will be used for pasturage," ... "Newcomers should bring a tent. There are no vacant houses here, there are families living even in the coke ovens...." But that boom died too. There were more recent spurts of activity, for a time during World War I some copper being taken out, but no big time mining has been done for years.

STONE COKE OVENS are only remaining tangible evidence of once roaring gold camp. Coal was hauled by ox team from Madrid to the north, roasted in ovens to drive off easily removed soot, smoke, leaving residue of highly efficient fuel for smelter. With roof already collapsed even this relic will soon become a mere pile of rubble.

SHAKESPEARE, NEW MEXICO

It was Christmas of 1882 in Shakespeare and the town was celebrating with a big community party. The tree was a symmetrical pine brought down from the mountains. It was lavishly decorated, most of the ornaments home-made but not the most conspicuous one. This was a doll, about two and a half feet tall with arms and legs of cloth, a sawdust body and head of china, the prized possession of eight-year-old Emma Marble. She had brought it from Virginia City, Nevada, when she came with her mother and sister to join her father who had established a home for them in the raw mining camp.

The doll was admired by everyone, especially little Jane, the daughter of Mr. and Mrs. Nick Hughes. Jane could not take her wide eyes from the china beauty and talked of it all the way home. Not long afterward she fell ill and in her delirium constantly called for the doll. Her sister Mary went to the Marble home and asked Emma if she could take the doll to Jane, offering a five dollar gold piece for the favor. It was gladly granted and Jane had her doll — for a few days. When she died she was placed in a simple board coffin and her arms tightly clutched the doll with the china head. The coffin was placed in the little cemetery already holding so many who had met tragic or violent death in the camp.

Two of the cemetery's occupants were Pony Express riders slain by renegade Indians under Cochise and Geronimo. The site of what would be Shakespeare was decided by the presence of a good spring a few miles from the site of Lordsburg. The Butterfield Stage Station called Barney had been nearby, failing when the Butterfield Lines met disaster from effects of the Civil War. As soon as it ended a new line called the National was established and John Evensen was sent out to refurbish the station, now called Pyramid after the nearby range of mountains. The next name change came when Evensen, impressed by the current popularity of General Grant, bestowed the officer's name on the tiny group of adobe buildings. A year later the county was also named Grant.

About this time a government survey party, of which one member was W. B. Brown, was working in the area. Brown was a prospector at heart, not vitally interested in surveying, so the rocky ground received more attention than did his transit with the result that he found a spectacular specimen crisscrossed with veins of silver. He deserted the survey party and rushed to San Francisco with the sample.

A believer in going straight to the top man, Brown obtained an interview with Bank or California magnate William C. Ralston simply by showing his chunk of silver ore. Although Ralston was fighting Adolph Sutro's attempts to bore a tunnel to the bottom of Virginia City's mines, he was not too absorbed to overlook a good thing in Brown's offer of a partnership in exchange for capital to develop the New Mexico silver property. The financier personally had the ore sample assayed and when results showed 12,000 ounces of silver to the ton he formed a company to stake out further claims and set up a mining district to be called the Virginia Mining District with the little stage station as its center. With the consequent influx of workers and drifters a town soon developed at the hub and was rechristened Ralston.

The company made a miserable attempt to recover values and quickly failed. Blame was placed partly on absentee ownership, Ralston being too busy with Bank of California interests in the fading Virginia City to pay much attention to a far

LOOKING DOWN AVON AVENUE from intersecting old stage road. Long unused branch line of Southern Pacific runs along middle of street. Tin version of "covered wagon" stands bereft of wheels at left. Behind is old saloon. Right is Grant House, then Stratford Hotel where George W. Hunt, late great Governor of Arizona waited table as youth. At right, on near side of street is General Store.

away New Mexico mine. Then Ralston's bank was forced to close its doors in the financial panic and Ralston resigned as officer of the bank. He went out for his customary swim in cold San Francisco Bay, was apparently seized with cramps and drowned, some sources claiming it was suicide. With this event the town and the nine-by-four mile mining district in the Pyramids took a new name, that of the new owners, the Shakespeare Co., a concession to a large block of British stockholders. One of the two little adobe hotels was also named Shakespeare and a most natural title of Stratford House settled on the other.

The town was subjected to many short booms and sharp declines, the result of over-promotion. An editorial in the MINING NEWS, July 26, 1881, said of the situation: "Work at Shakespeare is being pushed ahead systematically. Shakespeare has had no little to contend against. When the district was first opened up it was puffed and lauded to the skies by a series of mining speculators who wished to dispose of their claims before doing any work to show there was anything in them to warrant investment by capitalists. . . . The mine owners of this

camp have begun to realize this fact and have thrown aside the puffing policy and gone to work in earnest."

F. Stanley, New Mexico historian, gives a vivid picture of the place in his SHAKESPEARE STORY: "The houses were built of adobe. The walls were thick to withstand Indian attacks, the windows small so they could be boarded up in a hurry. Victorio and his warriors were still making the rounds during the early days of Shakespeare history. The town was unique among mining towns of New Mexico, if not the Southwest, for it boasted no plumbing, no club, no church, no school, no fraternal organization, no bank. Even the dance hall girls who came in from Deming and Lordsburg were permitted neither residence or domicile in Shakespeare. The same carriage that brought them also took them back the same night."

Later no doubt, when the town had reached its peak of about 3,000 people, such extreme restrictions on the girls' activities were relaxed with the opening of Roxy Jay's Saloon. Its bar ran the length of the building, the longest adobe in the area. Made of polished mahogany, it was brought from St. Louis,

DINING ROOM of Grant House, scene of hanging of Russian Bill and Sandy King. When management offered no such diversions as cutting down bodies, diners amused selves shooting at flies on wall.

part way by eighteen-mule freight wagon. Also freighted in, and even more precariously, was the wonder of the town, an enormous mirror for the back bar. It was held in such awe and respect by habituees that although the doors were so full of bullet holes "they look like lacework", the mirror was never hit by flying lead.

Although Shakespeare was considered to be an extremely "honest town", one prominent citizen known to keep as much as $30,000 in a baking powder can, there was no lack of excitement. Most deeds of violence were perpetrated by out of towners. Frequent raids and shooting scrapes occurred when such "prominent" personalities as Curly Bill, Johnny Ringo, Dave Rudabaugh, Sandy King and Russian Bill came to town. The activities of these gunmen were so frequent the nerves of citizens finally snapped into action. They organized the Shakespeare Guards which were recognized by the Territorial Government in 1879. The Guards summary treatment of two of the more persistent tor-

mentors was followed by several peaceful years.

One was Russian Bill, fugitive from Russia where, as Count Feador Telfrin, member of the Imperial Guards, he had been involved in some shady money deals. Fleeing to Arizona he went to work on the McLowery ranch and also became associated with the equally notorious Clantons. Finding himself without a horse near the Speer ranch one day, he took one, but was spotted by a ranch hand. Apprehended in Deming, Russian Bill was brought to Shakespeare's shiny new jail which had been heralded in the Santa Fe NEW MEXICAN on September 28, 1881: "Shakespeare is to have a substantial calaboose. Its cost is estimated to be about four hundred dollars."

Flung into this proud structure, Russian Bill found he was not in solitary. One Sandy King had the honor of being the jug's first guest. Sandy had refused to pay for a gaudy silk handkerchief in Smyth's haberdashery, then literally added injury to insult by whipping out his six-shooter and clipping off the index finger of the clerk's outstretched hand.

The NEW MEXICAN reported the events that followed: "You doubtless have heard of Russian Bill and Sandy King, two noted horse thieves and desperados. They were brought to Shakespeare a few days ago and lodged in jail. Yesterday they were loud and demonstrative against the citizens, declaring that the people of the town would have a chance to dance to their music in twenty-four days. During the small hours of the night the jail was visited by an armed force, the guard was overpowered and in an hour or so two pulseless bodies, stiff and cold, could be seen suspended by a cord to a girder in what was formerly the barroom of the old Shakespeare Hotel . . . Shakespeare is on its mettle and woe betide the unfortunate who raises the next row at this place. A coroner's jury ruled that the men met death by suicide."

Other reports fill in some details lacking in the newspaper statement. The reason the beam in the room was selected as a gallows was the scarcity of trees. The bodies were not cut down immediately. A large number of passengers was expected on the noon stage and it seemed a shame to deprive them of the edifying spectacle, so the bodies were left in place until after their arrival. One of the passengers offered to help carry the body of Russian Bill to the cemetery in exchange for the fine boots he wore. He said he thought they would fit him and they did. A final note was sounded by the NEW MEXICAN a few days later. "Shakespeare has not been annoyed by ruffians since the last necktie party. The friends of the two men who were lynched there a week or so ago have not avenged the death of their comrades as they threatened to. There is nothing that lessens the zeal of the average desperado than a conscientious vigilante committee." This story of Russian Bill's demise differs sharply from one credited to a member of the School of Mines at Socorro. (See GHOST TOWN ALBUM).

Then there was the affair involving the handsome "Arkansaw". Young Robert Black, who bore the nickname because he had come from that state, was carrying on an affair with the wife of a prominent citizen of the town, the outraged husband said, when he urged the vigilantes to action. They

GRANT HOUSE. Old stage station and dining room was named when whole town was called Grant for Civil War general. Windows were unusually large for day, more cheerful than most, but presented hazard in times of Indian attacks. Supply of rocks was kept piled inside under windows, stacked on sills in case of raid, providing protection from arrows, holes for extending rifles.

were reluctant but finally the wandering Romeo was caught and given the rope treatment. His feet had just left the ground when the saloon keeper, Roxy Jay, grieved at an obvious waste of an efficient mine worker, called out: "He's too good a man to hang. Let the woman and her husband get out of town."

Hangings and near hangings were interspersed with sporadic Indian raids, most of them without fatalities. At each alarm however, one of the women, Mrs. W. D. Griffith, would rush to the closet where she kept her treasured wig. She said that if and when she was scalped the Apache would get her "falsie" and not her own locks.

Ghosts have made their presence known in Shakespeare where in most deserted towns they remain secluded. Several spectres have become familiar through reported appearances, one preferring to attract attention to his sulphurous aroma. This one "lives" in the basement of the adobe residence of Mr. and Mrs. Frank Hill, used as a school about 1905. During a lunch hour the children amused themselves by digging in the dirt floor of the basement, unearthing a number of bones which the teacher identified as human and ordered them reburied immediately. Since then, at intervals of several months, the ghost comes upstairs, companionably emitting faint sulphur fumes "like the odor of a struck match."

"Be wary of the shadows!"

TYRONE, NEW MEXICO

The unprepared ghost town hunter, arriving in Tyrone, can hardly be blamed if he rubs his eyes in disbelief. Palaces in Spain must have been the models of the dazzling, rococo mansions and public buildings lining both sides of the street in opulent splendor. It is a dusty and deserted street. The ornate arches along shady corridors are crumbling and there are long cracks on the plastered walls of the depot. Patios and pavilions are centered by stone fountains long dry. Where emerald lawns bordered by flower beds once flourished, dry clumps of desert grasses and sage brush now share the courtyards with shriveled corpses of trees and shrubs. Behind these crumbling shells, once so splendid, the hill rises sharply then levels off just enough to give space for an impressive assemblage of imposing Mediterranian-style homes, stuccoed and tiled. Here again are the signs of ruin and crumbling decay, broken windows and fissured walls show that this is no lush resort on the Riviera. Tyrone is indeed unique among deserted towns.

When white men came to the Burro Mountains in the early '70s, they found a marvelous climate, beautiful scenery and Indians busily engaged in the mining of turquoise and copper. Winters in the valleys at the base of 8,035 foot Burro Peak are mild and sunny, summers are warm, there is just enough rain to nourish the typical desert vegetation consisting of juniper, pines, live-oaks and clumps of bear grass. June and July see the magnificent white plumes of "Our Lord's Candles" (yucca radiosa) rising ten or more feet above the valley floor.

But the early whites were interested only in mineral wealth. Their first burrowings were scattered all over the hills, in time became consolidated in larger mines as companies with capital took over. The major operation by 1904 was the Burro Mountain Copper Co. About this time the giant Phelps-Dodge Corporation became interested in the manifestly rich copper deposits in Tyrone and bought an interest in the Burro outfit. Pleased with the results produced under improved methods the Phelps-Dodge people infiltrated the workings until they were the major owners of the whole operation.

There had been two distinct settlements haphazardly growing up near the two main groups of diggings, Leopold and Tyrone. These now became one. Although there were good showings of zinc and lead, they were by-passed in favor of the more available copper. The fact that turquoise existed in the Burro seems to have been kept under wraps —nothing must interfere with King Copper. Ore had been shipped laboriously by wagon and ox team to Silver City where the smelters were, but now a railroad spur was extended from the Deming-Silver City line.

Up until this time Tyrone looked like any other mining camp of that day. The dream of making Tyrone the most beautiful mine town in the world was born in the brain of Mrs. Dodge. The New Tyrone would rise like Phoenix from ashes of the little frame buildings with typical false fronts that had been Tyrone. Her first step was to invite to this New Mexico wilderness the famed architect Bertram Goodhue from his home on the French Riviera. Goodhue also designed the famous buildings of the Panama-Pacific Exposition, San Diego, in 1915. The same fundamental plan was worked out for Tyrone with long arcades along the main boulevard. These were actually covered walkways giving access to stores and public buildings. Mrs. Dodge envisioned a resort town with a large steady population, augmented by a huge influx of tourists in the delightful winters of the valley. The T. S. Parker Hospital was constructed on a rise above the "downtown section," it was amply large and well equipped to take care of several hundred patients. The depot would handle a large volume of traffic and the stores were to carry the largest and most modern line of merchandise to be found anywhere in all New Mexico.

The principal buildings beside the hospital and depot were four large commercial structures, a handsome school with ample capacity, a Catholic church and an office building for the company headquarters. All these structures were planned and built on the grand scale, with no consideration of expense.

A large residential section was laid out on the bluff above the town and filled with handsome homes, many of them imposing two story structures, all in the same old world style. They made a brave and colorful showing in pink, cream, blue, tan and white, each with a tiled roof of red.

More than a million dollars had been spent building the new town and now in 1915 all was ready for occupation. But something was obviously wrong. While a few people bought houses on the

hill and others rented several of them there was no influx. There were alarming rumors being circulated that the rich copper deposits were not so rich as before, and some mines were frankly depleted. Rumors became established facts and no one wanted to move to a failing operation. Added to these calamities was the depression following the war, and in 1921, only six years after Tyrone was completed, the mines closed down and everyone moved away. Everyone, that is, except a skeleton crew in the now shrunken office of the Phelps-Dodge Co.

Tyrone's palatial buildings have been crumbling for more than forty years and have long since ceased to be useful or safe for occupancy. At intervals tiles come tumbling down from the roofs, chunks of masonry or stucco break off from the walls to come crashing down on the paved but cracking walks. Because of the extreme danger, visitors, while welcome to look from the safety of the road, are forbidden access to the buildings. Some of the houses on the heights are occupied by summer vacationers, rentals range from $17.50 per month to a top of $35.00 for the most luxurious homes. There is abundant water and electricity. Tyrone harbors the thought that its ghostly aspect would disappear if it were near a big city.

"PORTALES" — COVERED WALK — ceilinged by exposed beams—"vigas"—runs along entire length of two-story, imposing building planned to house general store, other commercial establishments. Street is at left, view looks toward railway depot.

WATROUS, NEW MEXICO

Soldiering "Out West" was all right, except for the twenty-four hour leaves. Most of the time all you had to do was see you didn't sleep next to a rattlesnake or let some Apache get close enough to put a hole in your ear. It was those floozies in town that put your foot in the gopher hole.

Soldiers on leave from old Fort Union were offered a choice in places for hell raising. Las Vegas had more kinds of bordellos but it was twenty miles farther than Watrous. The correspondent in that town contributed this item in the Las Vegas OPTIC of November 28.

"One of the soldier boys from Fort Union came to our town to have the pleasures of gambling his money at our saloons. After four or five hours he came out without much success, and insisted on our citizens to loan him money, which they did, and after having success on borrowed money failed to divide up, after which harsh words ensued between parties and causing our soldier to receive one eye loss. Our doctor claims the eye is ruined. We feel sorry for his losing his eye, and also his money. Would not consider it a safe and pleasant place for boys to come and spend their money."

When the boys wore out their welcome in Watrous, they turned to even smaller Loma Parda which soon got tired of roistering soldiers, boarded up all business places and closed up. Then back to Watrous went the soldiers and back in the news they came, just after Christmas. "On Christmas Day," wrote the OPTIC correspondent, "there was horse racing at Watrous as well as at Tiptonville. The school children went from Watrous to Tiptonville (where the Mission school was located) to sing Christmas carols. All was quiet until the body of a soldier from Fort Union was found in the Mora

TWO WELLS about six feet apart showing water table was near surface and well digging easy. Watrous was built on point of land at junction of Mora and Sapello Rivers, first settlement called La Juncta de los Rios. Well nearest camera served cabin behind photographer, house shown one of group built in earliest days of town, all fashioned of logs, brush, anything available, then covered with thick layer of "stucco"—hard-setting native clay.

River. Since the excitement caused by the visit of four drunken soldiers and the finding of the dead body of one of them in the Mora River a few days afterwards, nothing has happened to disturb the quietness of our town until last Sunday. On that day a rumor reached us that soldiers from Fort Union were coming to raid our town in revenge for their comrades. But they didn't come which was fortunate for them as our citizens were prepared for anything of the kind and any visitors on any such errand will meet with a hearty reception, and find they have not got another Loma Parda to deal with. It is but justice to state that the better class of soldiers at the fort, together with the officers, condemn any such demonstrations, and the perpetrators of the last outrages will be severely dealt with."

In the early days Watrous was known to Indians and Mexicans as La Juncta de los Rios, the name describing the location of the village at the junction of the Mora and Sapello Rivers. Originally a meeting and barter place for pueblo and plains Indians, it became the gathering area for sheep herders from Las Vegas, Mora, Abiquiu, La Questa, Antonchico, Albuquerque and Manzano. Nearby were camps of transient comancheros, Comanches, Utes, Kiowas, Cheyennes, Arapahoes, Navajos and Apaches.

By 1801 the spot was where mule trains of all sorts stopped, most of them carrying cargo valuable in a land where comforts of civilization were few. They attracted bandits who could sell stolen tobacco, jewelry, furs and other luxury items. Yet in spite of constant depredations, the beauty of the locality with ample water supply and extensive green pastures for stock was so appealing many merchants — drivers tarried and even settled down to stay.

New Mexico was still under Spanish control for not until 1821 did it become independent, then a province of Mexico and in 1848 a part of the United States. It was the age of land grants and Governor Armijo was known to be generous in bestowing vast acreages upon prospective settlers. At Juncta de los Rios a group of farmers banded together, drawing up a formal petition to Armijo for the surrounding lands. While legalities were pending, raids by

STONE HOUSE, walls covered with clay mud, then finished with finer clay and painted. Long unused, building served many purposes — saloon, dance hall, store. During '80s it was remodeled for livery stable, blacksmith shop. Many other original buildings remain in Watrous.

marauding Jicarilla Apaches discouraged some petitioners but the steadfast were eventually rewarded with deeds to the property.

When Samuel B. Watrous arrived on the scene he was footloose and fancy free, not interested in land grants. When he did decide to settle down he was too late for the free land deal and was forced to buy his farm from one of the original grantees. Born in Connecticut, orphaned at an early age, Sam was sent to live with an uncle in Vermont. The boy resented what he thought was undue discipline imposed by the uncle together with very early rising, before breakfast chores and day long hard labor. He fled, joined a wagon train heading west, arrived in Taos, New Mexico, to work as clerk in a store. Young Sam quickly caught the popular fever and headed up the Rio Grande with a gold pan at every chance. The virus hung on and he gave up the clerking job for the booming placer mines of San Pedro. The good ground was all taken and finally discouraged with mining, he married and went back to storekeeping, this time on his own, in the village of San Norios.

In a few years he fell ill and forced outdoors by doctor's warnings, he left wife Josephine to run the store and took off for the hills. He spent much time with various Indian tribes and acquired knowledge of their ways which was to prove valuable in later years of frequent clashes with raiding Apaches.

Now the wanderer made up his mind to earn his living on a farm and cast his eye on part of the parcel called La Juncta de los Rios. After years of legal delay, title was finally cleared and in May, 1846, Sam Watrous bought out Richard Dallam's interest in the grant. Josephine joined her husband, the farm and business affairs of Samuel Watrous flourished and he became a leading member of the community.

One of the larger enterprises was the general mercantile, operated by partners Watrous, Thomas Rice and Sam's son-in-law, William Tipton. This was broken up in 1865, Sam's son Joseph becoming the new partner, the store operating as S. B. Watrous & Son. It was about this time the Watrous herds and flocks pastured near Tucumcari were being repeatedly run off by Comanches and Kiowas, Watrous' locally good relations with Indians apparently not extending to that area.

Then in 1879 came news that the Santa Fe Railroad would build through La Juncta de los Rios and public spirited Sam and son promptly donated land for right-of-way, station and yards.

But Sam was most surprised of all to see WATROUS on the new depot's name board. Officials told him it was the least they could do and moreover there was already one station named La Juncta de los Rios in Colorado.

S. B. Watrous & Son also donated land for a park, fenced it, planted trees, all providing if and when the county seat came to Watrous, the courthouse would be erected on it. When neighboring Mora got the prize the Watrous interests did not sulk but set about getting a fine new school house, donating land and initiating a campaign for building funds. At first the project seemed to be a success but it fell through when pledged money failed to materialize. The disappointment to Watrous was all the more bitter because the upstart neighbor Tipton, which did get the school, was founded by son-in-law William Tipton, Sam's ex-partner.

There might have been biological reasons for the school going to Tipton. Its founder also started a population explosion sufficient to fill it. A roster of pupils in 1881 shows two Watrous descendants, Charles and Rose, followed by Lizzie Tipton, Susan Tipton, Martin Tipton, Louise Tipton, W. B. Tipton, Tom Tipton, Charles Tipton, Ella Tipton and several less numerous representatives of other pioneer families.

Another newspaper item, this one dated February, 1888, shows that life at Watrous and environs continued to be as interesting as in earlier days. "James Lafer, who was arrested at Watrous, was wanted for a murder he committed in Olean, New York in 1882, for which his twin brother served two years imprisonment but was pardoned when he turned out to be the wrong man. This Lafer was run out of Las Vegas as a bad character. He worked as a cowboy and was known as a rustler. He would shoot on the slightest provocation. On more than one occasion he cleaned out the town of Watrous, riding in and terrorizing the people by firing revolvers promiscuously through the streets. He once rode into Fort Union in the middle of the night and tried to assault the sentry who was walking post but was captured and slightly wounded in the melee. In Loma Parda he is still remembered as the man who picked up a New Mexican woman in the street, placed her across the horse in front of him, and rode into the saloon, making the bartender set up drinks for the whole party, and because his horse would not drink, he shot him through the head, lifted the woman from the saddle before the horse fell, and walked out, leaving the horse dead on the floor."

WHITE OAKS, NEW MEXICO

John J. Baxter was a disenchanted '49er. For every one who got rich in Calaveras county and other gold diggings in the Mother Lode, a thousand got only broken picks. Many of them left California for the glitter of other fields and Baxter was one of them, wandering eastward into the territory ruled by the Spanish and Mexican military. He found natives from San Antonio, Luis Lopez, San Marcial, Valverde and Socorro escaping the watchful eye of soldiers from the presidios and searching for gold. And there were rumors that some of them found it.

Baxter was curious and vigilant. He tracked one of the peons down a gulch, part of the shallow canyon running east from a mountain to the arroyo which later would form the western boundary of White Oaks. Having had experience with the rigors of solitary digging, washing and panning, Baxter took into his confidence John H. Wilson and John Winters and proceeded to the spot with whatever primitive equipment they could scrape up without creating too much attention.

They did find gold there—lots of it. What they did not find was water. The camp had to be two and a half miles away where the springs were. There were two flows, generous ones for so dry an area, surrounded by a grove of white oak trees. In the morning after breakfast, the men would set out for work at the diggings taking as much water as possible on the backs of several mules. This they would use as sparingly as possible to wash their pans of gravel. At night the process was reversed, pay dirt went home with them and was washed where the water was.

Hard work paid off. Even little nuggets turning up to cheer the laborers. News of their find got around and when the summer was nearly over they had a visitor. He offered no information except his name was also Wilson. Some said he was from Arizona, others Texas. Most agreed, judging from his furtive manner, he must have a price on his head and wouldn't tarry long. The miners put him up for the night and fixed him a lunch for the next day.

Instead of going along with them to the gravel bed, the new Wilson set out for a walk up Baxter mountain to survey the country. While resting and eating his lunch he idly chipped off some interesting rock and put it in his pocket. He then took a good look around from his vantage point and returned to camp. At supper time when all were assembled, the chips were displayed. Excitement grew as the more experienced miners confirmed what Wilson had only guessed. The whole group hurriedly took lanterns and retraced Wilson's steps, finding the spot without too much trouble.

Early next day stakes were set out and Wilson was asked how much he wanted for his share. He said that gold was of no use to him, he'd have to go, and whatever the others wanted to give him would be all right. He took the offered $40 in washings, $2 in silver, a pistol and another lunch and was on his way, disappearing from the pages of White Oaks history. The others realized $300,000 apiece not much later when the mine was sold as the Homestake. The original claim returned a total of more than $3,000,000 during its useful life.

The early days of gold discoveries in White Oaks were somewhat frenzied even allowing for the florid style of reporting in the newspapers. The *Albuquerque Journal* for April 6, 1881 touches on some of the finds. "One pocket being found from which in one day there was taken by the men over three hundred dollars. For several weeks thirty dollars was average for each man . . . on March 1 was struck another body of ore with gold visible to the naked eye all through the rock . . . An assay of a piece of ore from the last find, showed no free gold, was made on March 24, resulting $17,000 per ton, flour gold. Surprise to relate, the float from this vein, on the side of the hill and the bottom of the canyon, near where the last gold was found on the last soil being washed from it, shows free gold sticking to it on all sides and on breaking gold appears all through the rock. . . The Old Abe seems to be an immense deposit of gold bearing rock. The deposit is about a hundred feet in width."

The town itself grew up on a flat of about 160 acres beside the stream bed. The founding date was August 15, 1879—a tent city growing up even before saw mills could be built or lumber freighted in over almost non-existent roads. Tents gradually gave way to shacks. The first real house was completed July 17, 1880 and occasioned a big celebration. Population in the camp was then about 800 (it was later to grow to 4,000). The growth was so rapid the burgeoning town was splitting its seams, it couldn't absorb all elements in orderly fashion and some sections acquired cognomens of their own. There was Hide Town where buffalo hunters spread their odoriferous wares for curing and tanning. Hogtown was composed of cantinas, gambling dens, brothels, dance halls and like places where the miner could be parted from his money.

The camp was a fertile breeding ground for newspapers, some of which lasted a while, others got out one or two issues. First to come out was the little sheet modestly titled *The White Oaks Golden Era.* A year later partners Fenn and Morse

EXCHANGE BANK OF WHITE OAKS — l a s t survivor on main avenue. Town had 213 houses in 1885. First President of bank was editor of White Oaks Eagle, John Y. Hewitt, whose crumbling mansion also still stands. One historian calls city "attorney ridden" because of plethora of lawsuits over ownership and profits of cattle, horses and mines. Total list of lawyers is long, those having offices over bank were Hewitt himself, W. C. McDonald, later first Governor of New Mexico under Statehood, and H. B. Ferguson, later delegate to Congress.

planned a new paper, *The White Oaks Scorpion*, but this one never even got going. Then came *The Lincoln County Leader, The Old Abe Eagle* and the *New Mexico Interpreter*. Each lasted several years. An ad in the *Interpreter* extolled the qualities of a commodity strange in a rough mining camp—Ah Nues Song Birds, "The best in the country, and his cages the most beautiful. Those desiring a lovely singer should give him a call. His prices are very low."

The water problem was solved by the discovery that the moisture table was only about fifty feet down. For more serious drinking "the cantinas supplied various brands of gutrot at fifty cents although quality stuff was higher. After you drank enough of the putrid liquid that had been mellowed by dead rodents, snakes and birds, the quality stuff tasted like poison."

Then there was the more enterprising drinking establishment which put on stag shows in its enlarged building and booked traveling companies such as the famed "Wallace Sisters." The place was called the Starr, after a popular prospector of that name. Not all troupes made a killing at the new Opera House. Sometimes performers were compelled to remain for further shows to get sufficient funds to move on to Socorro.

The least excuse called for a celebration in White Oaks, and such occasions as Independence Day necessitated a real rip-snorter. The whole town turned out to eat at a table "130 feet long, loaded with all the good things of life." Beer and liquor flowed freely and the usual quarrels flared up, though with not too many casualties.

Outlaws of every description left their mark on the town. Among these were Dave Rudabaugh, Joel Fowler, Jim Greathouse, Toppy Johnson and Billy the Kid, attracted to the camp's larger saloons, better entertainment and fancier women. Tall tales of cattle rustling centered in White Oaks. Those episodes in which Billy the Kid and his pal Rudabaugh were involved are bloody episodes in the history of White Oaks. These two had their hang-out at the livery stable belonging to West and Dedrick; many of their depredations stemmed from there. The Kid's contact man in White Oaks for the sale of stolen horses was a man named Wheeler. He was caught trying to handle too large a job, the disposal of thirty head turned over to him by the Kid and Rudabaugh.

JUNIPER-RINGED SCHOOL is imposing structure, best preserved in town, cost community $10,000. Teacher of earlier, smaller school was Mrs. McCinnis, who took over as principal when more elegant structure was completed.

SILVER TONGUED SALESMAN made pitch for Singer Sewing Machine during week's stay in White Oaks, left most homes equipped with gadgets. House is built of adobe with annex of hand-adzed timbers with plenty of adobe mortar. Building materials, native to site were used in construction of many structures in camp like bistro where Jose Leal was master of ceremonies. On one occasion when *baille* was in progress there, Jose M. Ribera, full blooded Yaqui Indian crashed party. Guard had been posted at entrance for just such contingencies, attempted to stop Ribera, was succeeding when intruder was reinforced by friend Justo Salas. Indian entered, one shooting six-gun, other brandishing knife. General melee developed, ending with cracked skulls for several participants, death for Leal, Ribera and Salas. Mass funeral was celebrated next day.

Short time later Salcedo, full of White Oaks' special brand of rot-gut threw wild shot at M. Leecher in latter's home. Leecher picked up club, k n o c k e d weapon from attacker's hand, dispatched Salcedo with gun. Rash of killings continued, avoided in such smug items as story in New Mexico Interpreter for June 24, 1887. "There is no more orderly city west of the Allegheny than White Oaks . . . Our Supreme Court, M. H. Bellomy held a session on Wed. and Thurs. White Oaks is too peaceable to make this court a financial success and we hope it may continue."

In 1887 clamor for a railroad grew more intense. The *Interpreter* stated that "White Oaks is bound to be one of the best towns in the Territory. It has the precious metals and immense beds of coal right at its own doors and when the railroad reaches that portion of the country, White Oaks will grow rapidly." In 1888 rumors flew thick and fast, "it is generally understood that the Sante Fe road will . . . push from Socorro to White Oaks . . . The Kansas City, El Paso and Mexican Railway known as the White Oaks Line is being pushed with great vigor."

Property owners were called for a special meeting to allocate land for the anticipated right-of-way and station. Instead of making things easy for the railroad company, however, the town's business men decided that since the road "had to build into the city" they would make a killing and put a stiff price on the property, making no concessions of any kind. To their dismay, rails were laid through Carrizozo instead. Although the local worthies begged the company to come on any terms, it was too late. White Oaks had cut its own throat. The effects of this fiasco were far reaching; the town actually died of disappointment, at least it started downhill then and never came back. Family after family moved away and the remaining ones began to tear down vacated houses for fuel. Whole stretches of store and business buildings became empty and roofs fell in. White Oaks was on its way to becoming the ghost town it is today.

SOME ADOBE HOUSES in Lajitas were repaired, covered with new tin roofs during small uranium boom, others exposed to infrequent but heavy downpours, are already melting away. Adobe bricks vary from place to place in binders, extenders, but all have two common characteristics: basic material is native clay and bricks are unfired except by sun. Usually mixed with clay are stones (as here), chopped straw, weeds. These hoed into mixture with water, packed into wooden forms much larger than fired-brick shapes. Partial drying shrinks adobe enough to allow removal of form for further "baking." Adobe building stands solidly as long as roof is intact, walls weathering in rain only slightly. Once roof goes entire building melts rapidly away.

140

Texas

A BANDIT LIVENED IT UP

Lajitas, Texas

He was said to be a peaceful lad until he killed an official who raped his sister. Then the teenager Arango took another name and started a career of banditry and revolution. He made many raids on the Texas side of the border, some of them from the easy crossing at Lajitas, and set the state on edge, the army on point. This was Mexico's colorful bandit, Doroteo Aranga, better known as Francisco (Pancho) Villa.

It was naturally, before Pancho Villa, a peaceful village, lying on the Rio Grande River where it flows tranquilly in shallow reaches over easily crossed sand bars just before it plunges into the spectacular Santa Elena Canyon. Aborigines traveling the old Comanche War Trail stopped to rest or camp here overnight, water not being so readily available for many miles farther on. Perhaps some stayed longer, built adobe houses and planted gardens. Vegetables thrived in this region of mild winters, warm summers and plenty of water from the river. Spanish and Anglo explorers found Lajitas (meaning "little flagstones") a village of Indian and Mexican farmers and goat herders drowsing peacefully on the banks of the Rio Grande.

Although on a dirt road Lajitas was a port of entry and the United States took the precaution of sending army troops to protect the rich mining camps of the Big Bend area, by far the largest being Shafter and Lajitas. Gen. John J. Pershing and Lt. Gen. George Patton were there, their tenure just before the advent of World War I. Villa was murdered in July of 1923, his death ending a period of prosperity of sorts for Lajitas.

It sprang to some activity as the main importation point of a plant growing in abundance on the Mexican side, useful in the manufacture of chewing gum. Locally called "candelia cactus," it was the source of a wax which supplied 45% of Wrigley's

CRACKED, FALLING PLASTER makes pattern on old adobe wall. Finishing plaster coating is simple mud, water mix, smoothed on and often whitewashed. Area in upper left of photo shows detail of brick and same-material mortar construction.

141

NATURE WRITER Donald Culross Peattie once said of those easterners who starved in western deserts, "These courageous greenhorns, these corn and beef fed farmers, these small townsmen whose food came out of barrels, sacks and boxes—how could they guess that the Lord had appointed any manna in the valley and shadow of death?"

Peattie was referring specifically to Bennet-Manley party in desperate circumstances, lost in Death Valley in 1849, but point could apply to thousands of pioneers who went hungry while succulent, sweet and nourishing pods of Mesquite bushes hung over their heads. "Mesquite" comes from Nahuatl Indian **mizquitl**, most common species in southwest **Prosopis juliflora.**

Bean pods of plant growing as shrub or small tree can be eaten in green state or ripe seeds can be ground into flour. Roots hold soil, trunk makes good fuel, fence posts, blossoms making excellent honey. Against these are vicious thorns, aggressive takeover of forage lands. Thorn shown here, upper left, explains why careless treatment of thicket is likely to draw blood.

need. Actually a relative of the Christmas time poinsettia and properly *Euphorbia antisyphilitica,* the plant has slender, rodlike branches about three feet high, almost leafless and growing vertically. Around 1949 there was a big boom in candelia but it ended when Mexico placed a ban of exportation of it.

Then came the atom bomb and the frantic search for uranium. Believing a fortune could be found in the Big Bend country, prospectors bought their supplies in Lajitas. The climate tended to dry their throats so the bistros there flourished. With dreams of uranium fortunes fading, the prospectors

drifted away and Lajitas was quiet again.

The near ghost town is situated in Brewster County, largest in Texas and one of the most thinly populated. The community was without electricity until 1964 when all of fifteen meters were put into service. Lajitas has the reputation of being several degrees hotter than Presidio which often reports the highest summer temperatures in the United States. Spring, fall and winter months are the best time to explore the Big Bend country, preferably February to June. Even in summer months many high-elevation foot-and-horse trails in the Chisos offer cool comfort.

SILVER IN BANDIT COUNTRY

Shafter, Texas

The sun was good to John Spencer. He probably cursed the glaring, dazzling spot in the sky all day as its heat burned into his back and bounced up from the stony cover to blind him. Water was little solace as it disappeared so fast and his thoughts dwelt so bitterly on the damn foolishness of a Rio Grande rancher to go prospecting when he ought to go to town and get food for his kitchen. He was just about to quit and go back to camp when he saw, glinting in the dusty shafts of the near-setting sun, a shiny streak in a rock. It was nearly pure silver.

He looked around and found other pieces of float, deciding he had surely enough located a projecting lead of silver. Pocketing the sample he strolled back to his camp where "tame" Apaches were preparing supper, saying nothing of his find. The party got an early start for Fort Davis where Spencer purchased his supplies.

Some historians say John Spencer was one of the "original settlers" in the area but there is proof of white men being in that part of Texas in 1571. While some of these first Spaniards were "explorers," some remained to live along the Rio Grande, then called Rio Bravo del Norte. And before that

SEVERAL FAMILIES still live in few adobe cottages remaining more or less intact. Senora Lupe Munoz is lady alcalde of old mining camp, operating store, only business here. She attends to twice daily mail call at post office a block away. Spanish is prevailing language in village, only few of about 20 residents understanding English. Rocky foothills of Chinati Mts. seem entirely barren but support wealth of plants appearing exotic to northern strangers—many kinds of agaves, more cacti species than most southwest sections.

an advanced Indian civilization flourished there as long ago as 8,000 B.C.

Until Fort Davis was established in 1854, Milton Faver was the only Anglo-American to settle in the Big Bend country. Fluent in several languages, Faver was thought to have fatally wounded a man in one of the southern states and escaping to Mexico, joined a cattle train traveling north on the very long established Chihuahua trail. Crossing the Rio Grande at Ojinaga he dropped out to set up a ranch-fort at a point later called Cibolo. At that time the water table was much higher than now, creeks flowing abundantly and steadily to make a lush growth of grass. Faver ran cattle on his ranch and later at other nearby locations, Cienaga and El Morita. It was generally supposed to be impossible for a white man to hold out against marauding Apaches for any length of time but Faver did and others were encouraged to follow. Some lost their lives in Indian attacks but one who lived to thrive was John Spencer, his ranch a few miles from Cibolo as was the place of his silver find.

Adjacent to the military establishment of Fort Davis was the little town of the same name. As Spencer suspected, the assay office there reported

OLD SHAFTER CEMETERY lacks softening influence of green grass, shrubs, trees, is typical of burial grounds in arid sections. Area at right rear is "populated" by descendants of earliest settler Milton Faver. He died in 1890s, is buried on his Cibolo ranch, now inaccessible. His son Juan had daughter Francisca who married Ira Cline and still lives at Shafter, giving this reporter much of mining town story. "Many victims of mine accidents rest under those stones in cemetery," she said in Spanish. Identifying descriptions on wooden crosses are completely weathered away.

his sample to be heavily laden with silver but he kept his secret well. He was not known as a prospector, simply a rancher laying food supplies.

At the time there was an outburst of the always smouldering hatred between the original dwellers on the land encompassed by the Big Bend of the Rio Grande and the white settlers. Ranches were pillaged, buildings burned, women carried off. Could Spencer, in the face of widely scattered attacks, safely start and carry on a mining operation? To make sure he could Spencer shared his secret with Major Shafter, in charge of cavalry, and Indian fighter Lt. John L. Bullis.

Major Shafter, later made full general, must have been something of a financial genius. In San Francisco he raised enough capital to start the Presidio Mining Co., then joined his cavalry with the Seminole-Negro scouts of Lt. Bullis. Although the Chinati Mountains were teeming with lurking Apaches they had little chance against a concerted attack by trained soldiers and were soon all killed

or put in full retreat. That left the field clear to start mining.

Everything needed for it was hard to come by being so far away from source of supplies. Machinery was at first shipped from the east by Southern Pacific to the rail crossing of the ancient Chihuahua Trail, thence to camp by freight wagon and assembled at the mill site on Cibolo Creek where there was an ample water supply. Furnace fuel was delivered on contract by a wood-cutting firm which stripped the fine oak and sycamore groves along water courses and pines from high elevations—which have never regrown due to lack of water.

Mexicans from both sides of the border nearby were employed as laborers, most of them honest and reliable. One who was not caused a small scale riot in Shafter a few years after the town was started. Always a drinker, he spent a good share of his payday dollars in one of the several cantinas and then declared he wanted a woman. Si, si—he

RUINED BUILDING is near mill site, was likely residence or office of mine, mill officials. Photo shows structure in brilliant, head-on morning sunshine. Accompanying photo shows building in late afternoon light with near-setting making star pattern in door opening.

could have one of those handy at the *burdel* on a back street but he wanted class. On the main pike he openly propositioned every senora and senorita he met and then attempted to rape a girl in the middle of the street. Free and easy citizens thought this edging beyond good reason and had the local constabulary grab the miscreant and tie him to a tree until he could be taken to the nearest jail, in Marfa.

During the night several miners untied the man, took him out of town and shot him to death. Fearing further trouble the company called in the Texas Rangers. The famous early law men arrived, quieted all outward signs of violence and departed without the actual culprits being identified. At a dance held soon afterward a quarrel broke out between those who sympathized with the lynch mob and those who favored the law. Gunfire and stabbings caused authorities to call the Rangers back which neither faction liked as they felt they could settle their own squabbles. Joining forces all gathered in a barricaded building and when the Rangers approached they were met by a blast of rifle fire which killed one and wounded several. The Rangers returned some fire, inflicting casualties on the rebels inside and held them trapped. Reinforcements arrived and they surrendered, allowed to return to their jobs after a short cooling off period.

All wood supplies for mill furnaces were exhausted by 1910 but oil was then available and hauled in by truck from Marfa. Mine shafts penetrated the limestone to pockets of silver at depths of 700 feet. Writing for *True West*, Robert Graham says some of the silver concentrations yielded as much as $500 per ton of ore. By 1913 mules used to haul ore from mine to mill were replaced by tram and in 1914 came the exciting period of the Mexican Revolution and Pancho Villa.

Villa, deeply involved in the revolution that deposed dictator Don Porfirio Diaz and installed as president Francisco Madero, retired on funds supplied by Madero. He went to live in Juarez, El Paso on this side of the border not offering the luxuries he wanted, but leisure was not Villa's "kind of country." When President Madero was assassinated by Don Victoriano Huerta, Villa planned a coup against Huerta. He had friends in Ojinaga, Mexico, but could not go there safely with Huerta in power, so he looped around by way of El Paso, Valentine and Shafter. He rested at the mining camp and went on to the border, marshalling willing forces at Ojinaga.

At once Villa set out to attack his bitter enemy Gen. Orozco who had once sentenced the bandit to death for horse stealing, a fate escaped through help from Madero. Orozco and forces were routed, fleeing into Texas, a flagrant violation of neutrality laws. According to common rumors he knew the area around Shafter, had in 1913 escorted Gen. Luiz Tarrazas to an abandoned mine shaft there to conceal a fortune in gold and silver the absconding general had spirited across the Rio Grande. And this time Orozco was carrying some $80,000 in bills of large denomination.

Encountering a party of Americans he exchanged gunfire with them, hurriedly buried his loot somewhere on Eagle Mountain and slipped into Shafter to hide out with old friends. According to the tale once the heat was off, Orozco retrieved his fortune and added it to the hoard in the mine tunnel. Then he recrossed the Rio Grande, hoping to return eventually and secure his treasure to live the life of leisure in Mexico. What he had not counted on was the implacable hatred of Pancho Villa who was hot on his trail. He died while still running from the bandit without revealing the location of his cache of riches.

At its peak operation there were 4,000 people in Shafter, 500 men in the silver mines, prosperity for town and company lasting until 1931 when the price of silver dropped to 25c an ounce which brought mining to a grinding halt. During Pres. Roosevelt's time silver values rose to reactivate it.

In WPA days Shafter was said to have a population of 300. "It is a far cry," says the Texas Writers' Program, *Guide to the Lone Star State*, "from urban luxuries to this village of adobe houses tucked away in this mountain wilderness. Hidden trails to the south are still frequented by smugglers and raids by Mexican bandits occur. Life is often lonely for officials of the mines. Free barbecues are a favorite pastime, but owing to the difficulty at times of freighting in sufficient refreshments for the guests, invitations for such festivities have borne the initials B.Y.O.B. (bring your own beer)." This level of activity lasted until 1942 when mines were again closed, this time the machinery removed which seemed to ring the death knell.

But in 1954 the few people left in town were thrilled to see surveyors and prospectors employed by Anaconda Lead and Silver Co. working in town and the surrounding Chinatis. Rumors circulated that the firm would resume mine operations, that ore would be hauled to Marfa for refining since no water existed in Cibolo Creek except in unpredictable floods. Anaconda said only that its men had located vast reserves of high grade lead and silver in the Chinatis, but their men went away and never came back.

Today Shafter is very quiet industrially. There is no grind of tramway cables or noise of revolving ball mills, and there are no Mexican mine workers singing ballads in their homes in the evening. Yet an inspiring medley of sounds does reward the ghost town scout who camps overnight in some thicket of mesquite trees on a deserted back street. Morning brings cascading bird songs and calls unequalled in the west. Chirps, trills and cadenzas are linked together by the varied overtones of mocking birds, more numerous than any other. Not too intrusive is an occasional challenging rooster crow from the yard of one of the ten families remaining to remember a lively past.

ARID SOUTHWEST AREA generally is lacking in timber. Early builders here erected structures of material available, the earth underfoot. Clay was mixed with water, often combined with straw, weeds or other binder, then shaped into large bricks and laid in hot sun to dry. Walls made of adobe blocks were almost proof against heat and cold, but vulnerable to rain, lasting until protection of roof failed, then slowly succumbing to weather.

ADJACENT TO OLD HOSTELRY were stables, "parking places" for wagons. Study Butte has had minimum amount of vandalism, possibly because old store was more or less continuously occupied.

GENERAL VIEW of Study Butte shows company offices in foreground, stables in middle distance left, still operating store near center. Fringes of hills, mountains in background, lie across Rio Grande in Mexico. Photo was sent author by Texas State Highway Dept. with information, "Considerable activity has recently been noted at Study Butte, but information as to nature is unavailable and property is now posted. Assumption is that quicksilver mining will be resumed soon."

SIMMERING in one of U.S. hottest spots are ruins of adobe buildings that housed company offices at Study Butte. With protective coating of plaster gone historic building is not long for this world.

THREE TONGUES — THREE TOWNS

Terlingua, Texas

Old Terlingua was situated at the junction of 50 mile long Terlingua Creek and the Rio Grande. When the first Spanish speaking travelers arrived there well before 1800 they found a village of adobe huts and corrals built of spiny ocotillo canes. The natives were peaceable Indians but savage Apache tribes attacked at intervals, driving out both Mexicans and Indians. The natives invariably returned to find homes destroyed, domestic animals driven off or killed for food.

About 1859 a troop of U.S. Cavalry arrived with supplies on backs of mules and camels. They did not remain permanently but the threat of unexpected return had a restraining influence on the raiders. Yet the menace of them was not removed until 1880. The name Terlingua almost certainly corrupted from the Spanish *tres lenguas* but what were they, the three languages? Originally the name referred to a tiny Indian village on the banks of the Rio Grande just above its plunge into the narrow-walled Santa Elena Canyon. Early Spanish explorers are said to have found the Indian inhabitants of Terlingua speaking three distinct idioms. Another theory is that after some Spanish and later Americans settled in the area, the three languages were Indian, Spanish and English.

When cinnabar was discovered in the hills just

IMPOSING MANSION on hill was placed to allow superintendent's observation of entire town and mine workings. Built by owner Howard Perry but not used continuously by him. He spent most of his time in Chicago after Terlingua mines were well established. Smaller adjoining structure at far right served first as stable, later as garage.
During period when Pancho Villa was raiding border towns, Perry made hurried visit to Terlingua, ordered superintendent to sandbag and barricade parapets of house, keep guards posted with order to fire on any suspicious strangers. "Constable" Bob Cartledge soothed excited owner, argued that constant presence of U.S. troops not far away would be enough protection.

LONG, BRICK-PAVED CORRIDOR follows entire east length of house. View here to southeast shows old store framed in second arch from left. Barren Hills at rear are still in Texas, those at extreme right part of Sierra Mulato, Chihuahua, Mexico. Mansion has no inner hallway, all offices and first floor rooms opening on walk. Each has fireplace and wall-recessed shrine.

above the old village, the town growing up around the mines was also called Terlingua, or Terlingua-Chisos, the name of the largest and oldest mine. In further complication, when these mines were flooded out underground in 1942, what was left of operations went near the still-producing Mariposa mine, a post office named Terlingua established there. So there were three towns of the name too.

Just who found the first cinnabar in the area? There is no record but a modest amount of the brilliant red, softish, mercury-yielding rock was mined around old Terlingua. The cattle wranglers, Devine McKinney and Jess Parker, who accidentally found a red outcropping while rounding up some stray cows were not aware of its potential value. They secured the cows and went back to do enough digging to believe the deposit was extensive and perhaps worth claiming.

Discreet inquiry revealed the property had recently been acquired by a man completely unknown in the area, Howard E. Perry. McKinney and Parker learned he was in the lumber business in Portland, Maine, and wrote to ask if he would sell his Texas property. Not hearing for several months they wrote again and still heard nothing.

There was a reason. Perry was thinking. Described by Texas historian Ed Syers as "tight-fisted, close-mouthed," he suspected a reason behind the unusual interest and hired lawyer Wingfall Van Sickle of Alpine, 90 miles distant, to get the facts. Van Sickle rode a horse to the Indian village, pronounced the reason as cinnabar and by urgent message advised Perry to secure title to the property firmly and start mining. Perry heeded the advice, went to Terlingua, set up full scale operations and hired experienced Robert Lee Cartledge of Austin to manage the property.

The quicksilver operations started under extremely primitive conditions. All equipment was hauled the 90 miles from Alpine over a sandy trail in the river washes, wagons of the old Studebaker freighting type hauled by twelve Spanish mules used to profanity. And the finished product, mercury, was shipped north by the same means.

While sometimes found in the pure state the metal is almost always combined with sulphur to form cinnabar, mercuric sulphide. The Terlingua area ore is brilliant vermilion, soft enough to rub off on the hands and for use by Indians as war paint. Piles of ore, ready to be roasted for separation of quicksilver, still stand near the old Rainbow mine at Study Butte near Terlingua, appearing like heaps of glowing coals in the hot sunshine.

Terlingua was always plagued by water trouble—too little above ground, too much in the lower levels of the mines. For a long time a tiny spring was piped downhill to a town tank, the precious liquid rationed at two pailsful per day per family. These were carried uphill by shoulder yoke to some tiny tin-roof adobe or ocotillo cane, mud-plastered shack. Or if the family owned a burro a carreta could be hauled to the Rio Grande for a full cask of that kind of water. Most of the time it was as said, "Too thick to drink, too thin to plow." Later, when ground water became a menace to the mines,

HEADFRAME in background. Built of bolted 12x12s, structure supported cable system operating two cages allowing continuous up and down traffic. Shaft drops 600', laterals at 50' intervals. Horizontal tunnels, interlacing, connecting total 50 miles in length, some reaching under old cemetery where miners killed in accidents were buried. At left background is waste dump, comparatively small due to richness of Terlingua ore. Rock houses, now roofless, were homes of better-paid miners, some officials. Ordinary laborers lived in tin or adobe shacks.

it was pumped out for the mills and domestic use.

The town was strictly company owned, right down to the little jail with iron rings in the floor. An industrious Mexican laborer could earn up to $2 a day and whether he spent it for food at the company store or tequilla at the company cantina, Howard Perry got it in the end. If an over-thirsty peon got drunk and was thrown in the company's own *carcel*, he could bail out with a fine. The company "court" got this too.

Ed Syers, author of *Off the Beaten Trail*, asked Bob Cartledge, retired in Austin, about the jail's leg irons. "We didn't use them," Cartledge said. "Just the sentence, 'report to jail on Saturday!' If he had a sick wife he could come when convenient." "Constable" Cartledge may possibly have forgotten

a few disagreeable incidents in Terlingua's history. The rings in the floor show signs of some use.

Perry's Chisos and Terlingua Mining Companies hardly paid their way at first. The demand for mercury fluctuates to an extreme. Gold discoveries in California in the late 1840s and '50s created a sudden need for the liquid metal used in gold amalgamation, mercury later driven off as steam, cooled and saved. At that time the only source was Spain, shipping a near impossibility. Luckily cinnabar was found in California at just the right time. In Terlingua the demand for mercury was moderate over the years, prices generally low, until World War I started when the demand boosted the town's economy to the point where $2,000

SEVERE BUILDING, strictly utilitarian, served as assay offices where steady stream of core samples drilled from deep-down bedrock were analyzed. Fading or expanding values in cores controlled direction of penetration in rock. Short distance from photographer is yawning shaft opening, many hundreds of feet deep, no head structure or barricade to warn of danger. In background is rear of officers' quarters.

REFINERY MILL, one of several almost open to the sky. Cinnabar, mercury ore, composed of metal combined with various sulphur compounds, was roasted for separation. While both mercury and sulphur are volatile, latter vaporizes first, is driven off without opportunity to cool, solidify. Quicksilver follows at slightly higher temperatures, (357°C - 675°F) is vapor-cooled and condensed into normal liquid form.

Finished mercury, named for speedy Greek god, was packaged in "flasks", steel cylinders. Threaded at one end, when filled they were sealed tight by steel screw-in plug. Fit must be perfect, quicksilver making way through tiniest opening, as hairlike tube in thermometer, and no sealing compound could be used for stopper because of danger of contaminating product. Flask weighed fraction over 76 pounds, equalling weight of pottery containers Romans used for mercury. They called heft **quintal**, 100 libre. Quart of heavy liquid would weigh 28 pounds.

was rolling in every day. These were Terlingua's golden years.

During this period the Chisos Company greatly expanded all facilities including the store. A six-pew church was built, brick factory, large hotel, several cafes, even an adobe movie house. Local baseball and basketball teams were said to equal all rivals in the area. About this time a company of infantry in the Texas State Guard, says Texas historian Dick King, was made up entirely of Terlingua men.

The decline that followed the end of the war brought panic to Terlingua. Perry over-extended his Chisos operations in a desperate attempt to maintain war-time prosperity, and lost all he owned. The property stood idle for a few years and some families remained in hope things would

pick up, most of these gradually moving away to leave but a half dozen houses occupied. In 1946 all residents were ordered out, homes dismantled and all valuable mill machinery removed, Terlingua becoming a deserted city.

Today it is a fascinating ghost, completely deserted except for a caretaker at the old store making welcome the few visitors who reach this remote area. A sign, posted conspicuously near the open gate, warns sternly of open, dangerous shafts. The warning is not over-emphasized. Everywhere there are yawning holes where a person could drop hundreds of feet. Running children and pets should be confined to the car. Summers are likely to be hot, with temperatures often highest in the nation, but a dry atmosphere relieves oppression.

NEVADA
GHOST TOWNS

IN THE 70's STEADY STREAMS of customers poured though doors of Unionville "Emporium." Stone is local and varied in color, making beautiful effect.

AURORA, NEVADA

Angus McLeod crossed the plains in 1856-57. The journey lasted six months and included his helping to drive 1200 head of cattle from Dover, Arkansas, working in the California placer mines, farming, clerking in a Genoa, Nevada, store. After this devious circuit he settled on land near Yerington, Nevada, in 1862.

The land extended a mile and a half along the Walker River and he was hardly established before trouble began. Three men — Lee, Mills and Greely — built a flour mill just below the McLeod land, constructing a stout dam and digging a ditch to convey water to power the mill wheel.

As water rose behind the new dam it flooded the land above to a depth of several feet, Angus McLeod's ranch included. Determined to avoid it being turned into a lake, he cut an outlet for the river water to flow around the dam and drain his land. This resulted in the mill ditch running dry and filling with sand.

Lee, Mills and Greely were blazing mad, bringing suit and a year-long legal hassle. The first skirmish ended in success for the mill men but at the conclusion of the trial, McLeod was the victor. Both sides however were drained of cash. Angus leased the ranch to Charles Martin and with his wife went up to the roaring camp of Aurora. He owned an interest in the big Wingate Hotel which had stores and lodge hall on the ground level, and he also owned a lumber yard and the toll road extending from Wellington.

Aurora had sprung up almost overnight. In August, 1860, a prospecting party composed of J. M. Corey, James N. Braley and E. R. Hicks stopped to let their horses forage in a grassy little gulch well watered by Antelope Creek which came out of nut pine covered hills. All three men took their picks to the surrounding rock outthrusts. Braley and Corey had come over the Sierra from San Jose, California, had looked over the ground at Virginia City where they met Hicks. They were too late at the Comstock but not on Antelope Creek. Hicks, a part Cherokee, chipped off the first piece of glittering rock near the top of the hill. Corey found his treasure about the same time and in a day or so the three had located four claims. Next morning when the rising sun colored the entire eastern sky in a blaze of glory, the imaginative Corey tossed out the name of the location — "Aurora, Goddess of the Dawn."

The three founders of the lofty camp did not stay long. Corey and Braley made 357 mining claims, selling them in two months for $30,000, then departed for California to plant fruit trees near Santa Clara. On his departure for home in Arkansas, Hicks carried $10,000 in his poke.

When the three waved goodby to the town they did not leave it deserted. It was already populated with a motley crowd that had rushed in at the first news of the strikes. Almost before these men could start working their claims they had to have shelter and threw together whatever was at hand fast, for at that altitude of 7,741 feet, winter came early and snow sifted down among the pines. Houses were first mostly dugouts with stone fronts, roofed with brush and mud. The first business establishment, owned by one Pat Hickey, was fabricated of "sticks, stones, shakes, canvas and mud." Crude as they

OLD ETCHING OF EXCHANGE HOTEL from "History of Nevada" by Thompson and West. This is same building which Angus McLeod bought about 1880 and was later burned by revengeful arsonists. Front, facing Antelope Street, was fancy, 1910 photo showing plain side and rear.

RARE PICTURE OF AURORA made by "Scotty" McLeod about 1910 while on prospecting trip. Town has nostalgic memories for him, being born in Dunlap house at far end of Antelope Street which angles across lower left in photo. House has dormer, is trimmed white. Road leads right to workings of Esmeralda Lode, discovered on afternoon of Aug. 25, 1860, by J. M. Corey. Below mine is small group of mine buildings, one of which is only brick structure remaining. In central foreground on Antelope Street is burned out shell of Exchange Hotel, that street continuing on down through old Chinese quarter to become road to Bodie, Calif. Route is no longer passable, only entry at left through Fletcher, which road passes Aurora cemetery at top of hill.

were, stores and saloons were well patronized by thirsty miners. A few slugs of Aurora Lightning and nobody worried what the walls were made of as long as they stayed still.

Every bit of food, every pound of explosives, in fact every item necessary to work or life itself, had to come in over rough trails on the backs of mules. Even after a semblance of a road came in from Bodie, wagons were sure to break a wheel on a rock or get mired in deep mud. Prices for everything were sky high and the estimated keep for a mule $3 a day.

The Angus McLeod family first lived at the Dunlap House at the upper end of Antelope Street and later on, April 29, 1878 their son Charles was born there. Now, at 86, Charles or "Scotty" as he is affectionately known all over Nevada, lives in Yerington. He is alert, witty and after a lifetime of mining activity is a mine of information and anecdotes about the state's boisterous early days.

"We lived in the Dunlap House only a short time," Scotty relates, "and then father bought the Exchange Hotel farther down the street where we lived in upper floor rooms. I was little more than a baby then. One of the roomers had three canary birds, a novelty in that rough town, and went on a short vacation, leaving the birds in mother's care. She went in to feed them once and found me there. Two of the little things were already dead on the floor and I had the third in my fist, squeezing the life out of it. When mother asked me what in the world I was doing, I told her: "I'm making them sing, mama." Scotty proves this with the old hotel ledger. Item in column of expense, dated Dec. 21, 1881 — "Three birds, $30."

Meanwhile the three losers in the lawsuit against Angus McLeod were still smarting with resentment. Charles noticed one day that his friend the Chinese cook for the hotel was missing, a strange white man in his place. That night the family was awakened with the Exchange Hotel in flames. All occupants escaped in time, most of the men in their underwear, leaving six-shooters and ammunition behind. As all stood outside watching flames engulf the

160

hotel, bullets in guns and cartridge boxes began to explode, the air full of flying lead.

Investigation later showed that the Lee brothers and Greely had arranged the substitution of cooks, the new man pouring "coal oil" over the floors and igniting it. The hotel was completely gutted and never entirely rebuilt. The McLeod family moved again, this time to the toll house at the end of the road where Charles' brother Neil was born. The road in those days came in from the notorious Bodie, California, passing through Del Monte on the way and where it entered Aurora at the lower end of Antelope Street was a Chinese section. Asked if it contained the usual joss and gambling houses, Scotty replied: "Oh, no. They were all very fine people, industrious vegetable growers. Of course they may have had those things in another section of town but if so, I was too young to know about them."

Prowling about a shed at the toll house one day, young Charles found a box of dynamite percussion caps on a shelf. He dislodged them with a stick and the box fell to the floor, scattering the caps in all directions.

In playing with them he heard the call to lunch and popped one into his mouth as he ran. When he climbed up in the high chair he spit the cap out on the floor. The hired girl, Josie Hernleben, picked it up took a pin out of her blouse and poked at the white percussion dot in the bottom of the lethal cap. "There was a terrific explosion," Scotty said. "Josie's thumb and forefinger were blown off and stuck to the ceiling. No one ate much lunch that day."

When Charles was a little over eight years old the family moved down to the ranch, remaining there many years. As the boy grew up he followed the prospector's trail as did many other young fellows of the day. One of his buddies was J. C. Bray, with whom he later made the first claims in what was to be the fabulous camp of Rawhide.

Aurora was destined to suffer a long time from a unique problem. It wasn't sure just where it was. No one knew if the town lay completely in California, or in the Territory of Utah or whether it straddled the line. During the first winter a petition was presented to the California legislature, asking for the creation of a new county just for Aurora, so as to "release us from the hated laws and restrictions of Utah." By spring the California authorities concluded that since nobody knew just where the line was, they would arbitrarily include the new county, which held out such juicy prospects for taxes, in the state. Mono County was created in March, 1861, with Aurora as the county seat, a full set of county officials installed.

By April as weather improved, the real rush for the new camp set in and by June the residential total was 1,400 and increasing each day. When not a year old, town lots were selling for as much as $1,500. Four brickyards were started in the canyon and one of the first brick buildings was a schoolhouse, there being eighty children. That summer the first stamp mill was built, replacing several Mexican arrastras. By 1864 there were eighteen mills.

The summer of 1862 saw several outbreaks of Civil War antagonism. Southern sympathizers gathered in "underground" meeting places while Union organizations were more open, forming two groups— Esmeralda Rangers and Hooker Rifles. The fledgling city also had a newspaper, the ESMERALDA STAR and on August 23, 1862 it reported: "The Dixie group made a complete pandemonium of our town and continued their hideous orgies until late on Saturday morning, cheering Jeff Davis, Stonewall Jackson and the Southern Confederacy." The town was definitely on the Union side however. When the telegraph brought the astounding news of the assassination of President Lincoln, the whole town was "wrapped in gloom and tears rushed from the eyes of young men and old."

One dissenter, A. G. Judeigh, was so bold as to assert—"Lincoln was a tyrant and ought to have been dead long ago." Unfortunately for him the remark was carried to Captain Kelly who asked the Esmeralda Rangers to arrest Judeigh. He was placed in confinement with the immediate prospect of being taken to "Fort Churchill to carry sand." Under this threat he recanted, took the oath of allegiance and was discharged. He made a wise decision as he would have had to carry a fifty pound sack of sand on his back, marching up and down the parade ground in front of a soldier who would have corrected any loitering with the jab of a bayonet.

And all the time the ferment of Aurora's position went on. Far from settling the trouble, the California action only added fire to the dispute. A new group called Esmeralda Union Club spoke openly of being "California secessionists" and fought to get Aurora over the line into what was by this time Nevada, that Territory having been sliced off Utah. The solution of the wrangle caused a situation unlike any other known. Aurora, the seat of Mono

161

County, California, now became the seat of Esmeralda County, Nevada, as well. Mining affairs were delegated to Nevada courts, litigations connected with franchises on roads and utilities were handled under California jurisdiction. Private quarrels could, at the discretion of those involved, be taken either to Esmeralda's Judge Turner or Mono County's Judge Baldwin.

Soon after this dual arrangement was put into effect, a general election was held and Aurora citizens had a choice. A resident could be registered in California or Nevada or both. He could vote the Republican ticket at one polling place (for California, the police station) and the Democratic at the Nevada end of town (City Armory) or vice versa, or vote the same ticket at both places. The situation suggests a Roman holiday with twenty-two stops along the way where a man could refresh himself. It was remarked the town's bistros did their biggest business that election day, a fact apparently more important than being able to vote for a state and territory at the same time.

The situation, amusing to some, intolerable to others, was brought to an end by a survey party in September, 1863, when Aurora was irrevocably placed on the Nevada side with a good three miles to spare. Bodie remained securely in California by a five-mile margin. Finally convinced that their position was now untenable, Mono officials in Aurora packed their things and departed for Bridgeport, which replaced Aurora as the county seat. With them went all money collected and left behind were all outstanding warrants for some $20,000 indebtedness.

Aurora was still behaving like a mining camp. During the halcyon days of heavy gold production, bullion was shipped out on stages, duly recorded as loaded. Even to this day skeptics maintain that the return stage brought back the same gold to be re-

loaded and rerecorded. If this were so, it was done by sharp design. High records of production from certain mines boosted the value of stock. Express company records list shipments in 1869, for example, as $27 million. This could have been accurate but whatever the figure, there was a lot of bullion on the move—certainly enough to rouse desire on the part of highwaymen. Holdups were frequent and occasionally a stage driver was killed.

There was even a "crime boss" in town, one John Daley, secure in his position as the head of a gang of thugs. Not knowing any better, W. R. Johnson, a vegetable grower on the Walker River, shot and killed one of Daley's men, James Sears, for stealing a horse from him. It is not entirely clear whether Johnson himself did the shooting or sent one of his hands, John Rogers, to do it. But the thief was dead and Johnson was responsible. Daley was not the type to overlook the incident and vowed to get Johnson.

His opportunity came soon, when Johnson came into town with a load of vegetables. Daley gathered his henchmen and waylaid the farmer in a dark alley. First, Daley knocked Johnson down, then shot him. Gangster William cut his throat and "Three Fingered" Jack went through the victim's pockets while James Masterson poured kerosene over him and set his clothes on fire. By this time Johnson's mistake was definitely paid for.

But the executioner had overdone it this time. Aurora was already a little touchy about its record of twenty-seven unpunished murderers and this last atrocity was enough to trigger reaction. Some 350 citizens gathered in a hall in the Wingate Hotel, organized a vigilante committee which quickly gathered in Daley and his crowd. All were thrown into jail and guarded closely while a coroner's jury deliberated. It was over like that. The four were found guilty and sentenced to death on the gallows.

All saloons were closed for the affair, mines were shut down and stamp mills ceased to chatter, the gallows was ready and execution only an hour away. Someone decided Governor Nye ought to know what was going on and so informed him by wire. The governor immediately responded that there must be no violence, that law and order must be preserved. Laconic was the telegraphed message to Governor Nye. "All quiet and orderly. Four men to be hung in half an hour." And they were. All the gallery had the help of brandy to sustain them, two being so well sustained they had to be held up. After that day, Aurora was somewhat more peaceful for a few months.

It was reported at one time that Aurora had "seven hundred and sixty-one houses of which sixty-four are brick". In 1864 there were 6,000 people living in the town, the top population a few years later said to be 10,000. There was a fine brick courthouse, the ESMERALDA STAR was joined by another newspaper, the AURORA TIMES, many hotels, rooming houses and stores, almost all built of brick or stone. The first structures used bricks imported from as far as Sacramento, it was reported. Scotty McLeod says that after that a kiln was built and "bricks were baked right there in the canyon."

And Scotty settles another question, was the "Mark Twain" cabin which was sent to Idlewild Park in Reno actually the one occupied by the famous humorist during his short stay in Aurora? He says: "The Dunlap House where I was born still stands at the upper end of Antelope Street. Directly across from it was the Mark Twain cabin. I often played in it as a child before it was removed to Idlewild Park." The defense rests.

When Aurora began to decline it went fast. Golden bonanzas had been genuine enough but shallow. Mines never went very deep, less than a hundred feet. The $30 million in gold and silver had been scraped off by the 70's. Though mining continued after that in desultory fashion, the glory that was Aurora's had faded. The tenure of the McLeod's just covered the waning period for when the family returned to the ranch almost everyone else left too.

Scotty furnishes another bit about the use of brick in Aurora. His friends Vic and James Bernard, whose family had lived in the town, recently visited there and found an opening to the old sewer lines. They were built entirely of brick, arched at the top which was high enough to allow a man to stand up. Unused for years, the lines ran for miles and the "inspectors" concluded many brick masons must have worked on the job at tremendous cost.

For years Aurora was a magnificent ghost town, intact except for some frame buildings lost by fire. But later the blocks of brick buildings, many still holding their contents, were wantonly razed for their bricks. Mrs. Ella Cain, who with her husband, owns most of Bodie and Aurora, told this author a few years ago: "We couldn't keep up the taxes on all those buildings and gave permission for removal of enough bricks to reduce the building valuations. Vandals came in and removed almost everything, entirely wrecking the town."

Today there are barely enough remains to give some vague outlines — foundations, shapeless piles of brick, an iron door. The streets can be seen though overgrown with sage brush. There is exactly one brick building intact and why that was left is a mystery.

"SCOTTY" McLEOD hauls first baby carriage to Rawhide in first rush of 1907. Note bale of hay, bed spring, barrel of flour, box of china and high chair. Of pair engaged in horse play, man at left is Charles B. Holman who named town Rawhide in fit of pique over rebuffs in self-sufficient camp of Buckskin.

TOWNS OF THE CREAKING DOOR

AUSTIN, NEVADA

Austin is one of those historic old mining camps that would be a true Ghost Town but for the highway running through it.

Old brick buildings with collapsed walls and ruins of adobe structures alternate along the street with small stores and gambling houses. The "one-armed bandits" have replaced the real thing in Austin, and probably receive a much larger "take."

The history of Austin began when, in 1862, a horse kicked up a piece of quartz, laced with gold. The owner of the horse was W. H. Talbott and he sent the specimen to Virginia City for assay. Finding that there was silver as well as gold in it, he staked out his claim, others followed, and a silver rush was on.

The locality was inaccessible, but miners and would-be claim owners helped build a road, receiving city lots in exchange.

A brick courthouse was built in 1869, Austin having become the county seat in September of 1863, when some 10,000 people swarmed the town. Already a lumber mill was going full tilt and more than four hundred houses had been built. By the time the courthouse was in use there were many other "permanent" structures including schools, three churches, several hotels, stores and the usual quota of saloons and red light houses.

Austin was composed of so many brick and adobe buildings, clay being more plentiful than lumber, that it suffered somewhat less from fires than did other camps. But floods, especially those of 1868 and 1874, ravaged it.

By 1880 Austin had started the downhill slide and most of its total of $50,000,000 in ore was an accomplished fact.

The railroad, result of so much hard work to acquire, was abandoned in 1938, and this really was the finish of the town as a mining center.

Austin, once so hard to reach, now one of the most accessible of the old camps, is comparatively unspoiled and well worth the study of those interested in the bonanza day of the Old West.

BELMONT, NEVADA

Belmont's history was hectic and brief, with only about twenty frenzied years allotted as the life span for the city. In that time Belmont became the seat of Nye County and produced $15,000,000 worth of lead and silver ore. There were spasmodic bursts of enthusiasm at intervals after the boom period was ended in 1885. Discovery of turquoise in 1909 caused a flurry, but this was short lived. A 100-ton flotation mill was built in 1914 with bright hopes and almost the entire resources of its promoters, but after a couple of years it failed. Another stamp mill was built in 1921 but suffered the same fate in less time.

The Nye County Courthouse, built in 1867 dominates the town, an interesting and picturesque structure. A few feet from the imposing front door is a small stream meandering across the grass-grown street.

In common with other early day mining camps the place saw its difficulties between miners, owners and the unions. Two of the union organizers found such a complete lack of welcome that they were forced to flee. Unfortunately they didn't go far enough, holing up in a mine tunnel near town. Here they were caught, dragged into town and hanged on the main street. One was only a boy of 15.

Across the street from the spot where this brutal episode took place stands one of the most interesting of old-time buildings, the Music Hall, and across the front in old-style lettering is its name, fading but brave, the "Cosmopolitan." Once garishly red and green, time has subdued the brilliance of its paint, and warped its boards to curls. Flagstones, split from nearby rocks, pave its outdoor foyer, under the extending balcony. Remains of fancy lace curtains hang from glass upstairs windows and weeds and sage grow in the doorway. An iron ring to which the driver tied his horse while the star stepped from her carriage, still hangs on one of the posts supporting the balcony.

DESERTED MAIN STREET sees little traffic now, but once was busy parade of buggies, ore wagons and people in costumes of period from 60's and through gay 90's.

MONITOR-BELMONT MILL is almost gone but stack of smelter stands as monument.

CENTER OF ALL PUBLIC entertainment in bustling era of Belmont's heyday was "Cosmopolitan." Music hall dominated street.

LIFE OF IMPOSING NYE County Courthouse extended from 1867 to 1905. Building had no "central heating"; rooms were heated by stoves connected to many chimneys. Even jail at rear had its own.

ACROSS FROM "COSMOPOLITAN" stands group of typical mining camp buildings. Here were hanged labor organizer and youthful companion. Street becomes road leading down hill to Monitor-Belmont Mill.

ONCE "IMPREGNABLE" JAIL, now open-air affair, is extension of courthouse.

BERLIN & UNION, NEVADA

The past of this ghost town goes back some 100 million years, not to gold but to the amphibious animals, *Ichthyosaurs*. Berlin had gold but along with it the fossil remains of these "fish lizards" or more accurately water creatures akin to whales. Harold and Dorothy Newman will explain them successfully. They are the only residents of Berlin and are responsible for the preservation of the relics.

Berlin is easy to find. Unlike many ghost towns, hidden away in some brush-grown gulch, adobe or rock walls melting into the mother earth from which they sprang, Berlin's bones are gaunt frame structures, worn and weathered but defiantly erect and stand out boldly in a substantial group conspicuous for miles. Further dramatizing the old camp is the backdrop of Mt. Berlin rising to a height of 9,081 feet above sea level. Set high on the flank of the Shoshone Range and seen from a distance of several miles across a flat, dusty basin the dead town seems still pulsing with robust blood of yesterday. But it isn't. The buildings are only hollow shells without doors, the windows staring without glass. Only these and the Newmans.

The agatized remains of the marine creatures were interesting to the more knowledgeable prospectors from 1860 on. Possibly the first printed mention of the fossil finds appeared in the July 29, 1865 issue of the NYE COUNTY NEWS, published in

PARTS OF SKELETON of huge ichthyosaur, turned to agate-like substance after millions of years of burial, are exposed but left in place by student paleontologists directed by Dr. Charles L. Camp of University of California during four year period following spring of 1953. In foreground are pelvic bones; extreme left is fetus; left center, vertebrae. Tail of twenty-five foot amphibian stretches into background. Altogether nineteen large ichthyosaurs have been uncovered in limey shale. Guardian of deposits, Harold Newman, when asked about future excavations said they are uncertain because of short political tenure of interested officials. "By the time they learn to pronounce 'ichthyosaur' they're out of office."

BUNK HOUSE for Berlin mine workers seems to have been dropped on the ground. In many early mining camps violence often erupted in bunkhouses where drinking and gambling was carried on in evenings, but Berlin seems to have no records of murder or lynching at camp.

Ione, a short distance from Berlin. "Several of the boys have been bringing in to this editor some strange specimens for this country so far from the ocean. They are enough to make one think that perhaps this whole area was once covered with water, even to the mountain tops where the shells were found. They are indeed objects of study for the curious."

It was not until 1928 that the stony bones received official recognition, when a faculty member of Leland Stanford University made public their importance. Later Geologist Margaret Wheat exposed more fossils with simple hand tools. She interested Dr. Charles L. Camp, distinguished paleontologist in the possibilities of an on-site exhibit. The Museum of Paleontology, University of California, carried on delicate but extensive excavation work from 1953 to 1957 and Dr. Camp was successful in

getting the State of Nevada to designate the area a state park.

The name ichthyosaur translates "fish lizard" but the animal was neither. One miner-historian describes the geneology as a "cross between a shark and a whale", a biological impossibility. Actually the animals were entirely warm blooded with some of the characteristics of the modern whales and porpoises, and except for whales and some forms of prehistoric dinosaurs, were the largest form of life known, reaching a length of sixty feet. They swam in warm waters which once filled the great basin, having their existence in the beginning of the "age of reptiles", the Middle Triassic, some 200 million years ago.

The particular group whose petrified remains came to light near Berlin seems to have suffered the same fate of whales today. They were beached and since the animals had a lightly constructed rib cage

SHELL OF COOK HOUSE stands next to mine dumps at Berlin. Large wood burning stove was carried out years ago, possibly to permit other use for building. While photo was being taken Newman's retriever entertained by flushing and chasing dozens of large jackrabbits which bounded back and forth in front of camera as though feeling spirit of game.

and not able to protect the lungs out of water, their enormous weight caused collapse and death. They sank into deep primordial ooze, flesh decaying and bones becoming fossilized. About 60 million years ago the whole area was covered by volcanic flows, then much later the protective stratum split and erosion began, exposing some of the bones.

The deposits lie on a bench directly above a canyon holding other remains —those of the once thriving mining camp of Union, about two miles south and east of Berlin. Union owed its origin to P. A. Haven's discoveries as did Ione, Grantsville and Berlin in 1863. In common also with its sister towns, Union had an initial boom of all too brief a duration, then several spurts of energy equally short.

An item from the NYE COUNTY NEWS of Ione, July 8, 1865, said: "The first lot of bullion from the Union district amounting to about 200 pounds was shipped from the Pioneer Mills. We hope next week to give a larger figure." Next week's issue failed to carry any figure at all but there was a pat on the back for Union, a generous gesture considering the traditional rivalry between the two camps. "There is much doing at Union. It promises to rival our town. We congratulate the Union boys upon their prosperity."

About a year after Union's beginning, a Mr. Shobe, while prospecting the area, came across a large deposit of clay. Shobe could see an indirect glitter of "gold" in the material, found where there

169

ADOBE BUILDING only substantial ruin at Union. Roof has preserved it from complete deterioration, will soon give way. Search up and down long canyon revealed many fragmentary signs of occupation by hundreds of miners and store keepers.

was no lumber which was always a fire hazard. He abandoned all further prospecting, took a claim on the site and set about getting capital to build a large kiln. His first big job was not for house building material, though, as the NEWS stated: "Mr. Shobe of Union has taken the contract to burn 100,000 bricks for the Atlantic and Pacific Construction Co. to be used in constructing a large roasting furnace for their mill." Several brick buildings using Shobe's product remain at Grantsville, including the school house and mess halls at the mill.

Just below the enclosure containing the ichthyosaur exhibits is the camp set up by excavation crews composed mostly of men students interested in the

work. It took advantage of several old buildings remaining from Union's lusty days and added a few ingenious improvements. Coming in from work, covered with dust and perspiration, the men used a unique bathing arrangement. Water from an icy cold spring was conveyed to a metal tank near quarters, the sun heating it during the day to usable temperature. Immediately below the tank a bath tub was placed and connected to the tank. It is included in the park camp grounds and campers are free to use it, if privacy is not required. This fact usually confines the use to small fry whose mothers are glad to remove a few layers of road dust from the young hides.

BROKEN HILLS, NEVADA

Joseph Arthur just stood there staring. He could hardly believe in the reality of the gleaming rock there on the ground, glinting with bright streaks of metallic silver. When he picked it up and turned it over and over, he found he was talking to himself. "This is it! This is it!" And indeed the chunk of float proved to be a fair sample of the wealth soon unearthed in the sagebrush covered Broken Hills.

The discovery was not a haphazard stroke of luck. No burro's frisking heels uncovered it, nor any dying vulture's thrashing wings. It was the just reward of a long conducted search. In fact when Joe Arthur was only a small boy he had stood on a hill with his father who had brought him to Eastern Nevada. He looked out over the vast panorama to the west and asked: "What's over there, dad?" The answer: "Many ranges of mountains with many valleys between. That's where prospectors go looking for gold and silver." Little Joe considered that as he traced the outlines of the ranges sharply defined in the desert air. "That's what I'm going to do," he said with conviction, "when I grow up".

The Arthur family, father, mother, sister and Joe — had come to the new raw country from England. Mr. Arthur got a job in the Ruby mines and on Sundays preached in momentarily quiet saloons and gambling houses. As soon as Joe was old enough to work he too got a job in the mines, all the while listening to talk and reading about mining, metallurgy and prospecting for his own education. As soon as he could he headed out into the mountains — and learned a hard lesson. The first few years he met nothing but discouragement but he learned how to persevere. He kept on prospecting and working in the mines when he had to for money to keep on prospecting.

The gods were on his side for in the same vicinity another Englishman, James M. Stratford was looking for something better to happen. Stratford had made one fairly good strike in the Desatoyas, a few miles north of where the modern day town of Gabbs is. A moderate rush had poured in around the claim and a little town named for him. But the mineral wealth proved to be confined to his claim only and was very modest at that. So the camp melted away and left Stratford to eke out a meager living. Now Joe Arthur came along to check on a claim he had filed in the Stratford area. He found no metal but did find a kindred spirit in Jim Stratford. The two joined forces and that fall headed into the hills together.

They worked all winter and into spring, systematically pecking at ledges, cracking pieces of float, panning samples of gravel in streams. Results? Nothing but discouragement. On the evening of

STORES and other places of business in Broken Hills were modest, this one including living quarters at left. Storage shelter for food supplies is dugout, partly showing at rear corner.

GRAVE OF MATT COSTELLO is lonely one on top of knoll. After life of grinding poverty miner made good strike, sold claim for $1,500. Few days later he was found dead, sitting at his table. Friends buried him near cabin all traces of which have vanished.

April 12 as the two were preparing supper, Jim breathed his discontent. "I'd sure like a cup of coffee when it's ready. Joe — let's call it quits." We'll never find anything this way." Joe nodded — but he hadn't forgotten the lesson he'd learned, keep on trying. "Let's look around just one more day, Jim. If nothing shows up by tomorrow evening, I'll be ready to give up."

The next morning the men separated so as to cover as much ground as possible, Jim taking the ridge, Joe the gully. In the first half hour Joe found several small pieces of promising material and followed the trail, growing more excited by the foot. He kept picking up more fragments until he saw the large, glittering rock.

He had been almost afraid to let himself believe the signs but now he let his feelings break loose and was shaking all over. As soon as he could get settled down he piled rocks to mark the outcropping from which his silvery find had come, then systematically staked out three claims — the Belmont, Grand Prize and Butler. With his own "grand prize" in his hands he went back to camp and waited anxiously. A pot of coffee was waiting for Jim when he returned dejectedly. "I didn't find a thing. How about you?" In dramatic silence Joe held out the silvery rock.

SMALL, SCRUBBY DESERT GROWTHS persisting in dry gravel cast long shadows as another long, lonely day ends for Broken Hills. Town's life was lively but short, only strike of value being that of man who founded town. Main street was curving gravel road at right. Facing buildings here are a few more across road.

Partners Arthur and Stratford were able to raise money for equipment and supplies to start operation by simply showing some of the ore so rich in gold and silver. Others flocked in, scraping away sagebrush to start a little one street town called Broken Hills. One of the men, Maury Stromer, long afterward told Nell Murbarger, author of "Ghosts of the Glory Trail"; "It was a nice little town, good, decent folks — decent and law abiding. Sure, we had a few saloons, bawdy houses and gambling halls, but they didn't dominate the place."

Joe and Jim stayed with it for five years by which time they had taken out $60,000. They then sold out to George Graham Rice, notorious promoter of Rawhide, for $75,000. Joseph Arthur, still only forty-three, retired to Reno to live with his wife Zua, and Stratford, ten years older, also retired.

In 1921 there was a substantial hotel in Broken Hills operated by partners Daniels and Ross of Yerington, Nevada. "Scotty" McLeod of the latter place tells of the tragedy that took place there. Ross had a beautiful daughter, an accomplished pianist. A single man was greatly attracted to her but the girl did not return his feelings. The man made strenuous advances one evening when they were alone in the kitchen. Repulsed, he raged out of the hotel, first emptying a kerosene lamp on the floor in the hallway and setting it on fire. Neither Daniels nor the girl's father was in the building and first learned of the disaster when they saw the flames. Ross tore himself from restraining arms, dashed into the inferno to find his daughter on her knees in a corner of the kitchen "with her hands folded as if she were praying."

Her father dragged her to the door where he collapsed. "His ears were burned clear off and the flesh fell from his hands," Scotty says. Ross soon died in agony and a double funeral was held in Yerington. "My wife and I went to both service and mass the next morning. It was the saddest thing we ever knew."

Broken Hills was a waterless place. Every drop had to be hauled several miles across the desert from Lodi Tanks, natural reservoirs. Lodi had been a booming camp in the '70s with hotel, saloons, etc. but it died early, leaving only the water. When Rawhide flared into lusty life in 1907, miners had a need for water though despising it for drinking purposes. So Lodi Tanks came to life again and had spurts of activity every time another camp sprang up. It was a spasmodic sort of existence but Lodi

PRICKLY "DESERT POPPY" blooms profusely in lone streets, is properly called Argemone. Various parts of showy annual plant have emetic, narcotic properties. White petals have crinkled, satiny look, are centered by cluster of yellow stamens, flower being about six inches across.

had nothing else. When Broken Hills came begging for water, Lodi was willing to provide it. It was free at the source but by the time it was hauled to Broken Hills by wagon it cost $2.50 a barrel. Later Maury Stromer obtained a truck and hauled the water for $1.

Arthur and Stratford left a 6,000 ton pile of inferior ore on their dump to be worked when and if a suitable mill was erected. It was this potential added to the mines that interested George Graham Rice. His interest was not quite the same as the original owners. He was a promoter only, his methods in Goldfield and later Rawhide only a bare jump ahead of the law. Before he acquired the Arthur-Stratford mine he sent geologist Arthur Perry Thompson to check out the possible wealth in Broken Hills at $60 a day. This was to appear in a fancy prospectus and sometimes a geologist at $60 a day could make things appear very glossy. Sure enough the reports from Broken Hills were very enthusiastic. Cracker Jack, Black Dog, Grand Prize, Belmont, Go-Between and the Broken Hills claims were all of "unusual merit, fully deserving of future development". Governor Emmett D. Boyle, himself a veteran mining man, also seemed to see a rosy future for the camp — "The best potential I've seen in any new Nevada territory for many years." Analyzed, the ambiguous statements did not mean the prospects were good but who wanted to doubt anything that sounded like they wanted it to sound. Much property changed hands and the Arthur and Stratford holdings were paid for by Rice — with, of course, his stockholders' money.

As it happened the new owners of the claims could not get going, though now and then they did send in a small shipment of reasonably good ore, enough to keep the share holders from screaming too loudly. Altogether production under the new management amounted to a paltry 35 tons worth some $7,000. When some investors compared this with the $75,000 dropped in the mine shafts, they put the glasses on Mr. Rice. His activities led to a full scale investigation and his confinement in the penitentiary.

Smaller operators took over at Broken Hills, the town barely existing. There was a minor burst of activity during the depression years and figures show a production of $197,195 between 1935 and 1940. As people returned to their former jobs, Broken Hills faded away entirely, except for Maury Stromer. He continued to work his mine, the Badger, the hard way, descending to dig ore, loading it in the bucket, hauling it back up. He made about $5 a day at this backbreaking work.

Winters are raw with snow in Broken Hills and Maury finally took some holidays with his daughter in Paso Robles, California. He was taken ill in March, 1956, and died in the hospital. Burial was in his beloved Nevada at Reno. That left Broken Hills, a place deserted except for jackrabbits bounding among the sagebrush and pack rats making homes in the empty shacks.

"HIS" AND "HERS", built straddling worthless mine shaft, offering some hazards as supports barely touch crumbling edges of deep hole. Incidental is beauty of desert —etched wood showing grains and textures.

WRAITHS OF THE WAILING WINDS

CANDELARIA, NEVADA

"Patrick O'Leary, Native of Ireland, Age 25 yrs." So reads an old headboard in the desolate cemetery on a sunbaked knoll above Candelaria.

Patrick sleeps in a setting far different from his cool, green Emerald Isle. There is no grass; no trees shade the little plot filled only with leaning headboards, blistering rocks and rattlesnakes.

Candelaria never had a Chamber of Commerce to boost it as a good place to live. It wouldn't have done any good, anyway. There were several livery stables with big piles of horse manure in back. The flies multiplied by millions and had free access to screenless windows of houses, hotels and boardinghouses.

All water was hauled from a spring nine miles away and cost those who used the stuff a dollar a gallon; whiskey was cheaper!

Even the stampmill dispensed with water in the crushers and the resultant pall of dust settled in the lungs of the miners, who died by dozens of "miner's consumption." Perhaps poor young Patrick O'Leary was one of those.

Mexicans had found silver ore here in 1864, but siesta prevailed until 1879, when a polyglot population of Germans, Slavonians and others, mostly foreign born, took over and built a boom town. Construction was largely of adobe and stone. At this time the big producer was the Northern Belle, credited with a $15,000,000 production in silver.

A narrow-gauge railroad, the Carson and Colorado, connected Candelaria to Keeler on the shores of Owens Lake (which once lay at the foot of Mt. Whitney) and to Mina. Other small towns sprang up along the line; Sodaville, Belleville, and more, but these are nearly gone by now.

After the first big silver boom the town nearly died, breathing only fitfully until about the turn of the century when it revived to the tune of some $1,000,000 worth of gold, lead and copper, along with more silver.

FORTRESS-LIKE STONE STRUCTURE had varied career. It served as a bank, was almost impregnable during raids by bandits and holdup men. Stores, saloons and other business ventures shared quarters at different times. Interior seems dark in contrast to glare of outdoors, windows were purposely omitted as offering weak spots to attack.

HOT SUN SIMMERS GRAVEYARD. Grave enclosures were common in early cemeteries. Ornamentation differed on each. In this picture the one at left protects the grave of Patrick O'Leary. Main street of Candelaria extends beyond. Extensive stamp mills were at point where road curves to left in distance. Most mines were on hill at left, just out of camera range.

DAYTON, NEVADA

Adolph Sutro was a "man with a dream" who conceived the idea of a horizontal tunnel so as to haul out the ore and drain off the water from the deepest shafts of the Comstock, whose mouths opened up near the top of Mt. Davidson, the site of Virginia City.

Almost insurmountable obstacles were placed in his way, especially financial ones. The big mining companies agreed to put up the huge sum of $5,000,000 and the money was eventually forthcoming in the shape of royalties of $2.00 per ton, the water to be free.

Delays stalled completion for thirteen years, so long that the heyday of the Comstock was over. Ore removal continued for years, however, and in 1880, as a sample year, the 20,489 feet of tunnel delivered two billion gallons of water; water almost impossible to remove vertically, which flooded mining operations and was so hot it steamed.

Dayton now has a charming old-time atmosphere with a good many of the original buildings standing here and there. It is not quite dead, however. Complete demise is impossible for any town on a highway. There will, at least, be filling stations and taverns.

YEARS HAVE PASSED since services were held in little church in Dayton. Graceful architecture is evident in doorway. Old church is separated from center of town which offers a typical group of early-day buildings.

EUREKA, NEVADA

Eureka, in 1864, was all set for the explosive rush and boom of other mining camps. Certainly the discovery of lead-silver deposits was as spectacular and important as most, and one of the first big finds of the bi-metallic ore in the country. But expansion of the infant settlement was slowed by the refractory qualities of the material. New methods of smelting had to be devised. The first plant built in 1869 was a failure. Another was erected with different, hitherto unknown grinders and baking methods. This was more successful and pointed the way to still better ways of extracting the metal. Then the boom began in earnest and by 1880 Eureka's population had reached nearly 10,000. But then production began to fall off and things looked bad for the young town. About this time several Comstock-made millionaires built a railroad into Eureka, and because of its central position in the state, the town became a railhead for the whole area.

But the mining boom was over, to revive weakly at intervals, in 1905, during the first world war and in the 30's. The smelters, established under such difficulties, had been closed since 1891. Stamp mills, cyanide plants, refineries and smelters have always meant as much to the economy of these early camps as the actual mining operations. Their end means slow strangulation and such was the case for Eureka. However, there is still life here, partly due to the fact that a paved highway with its tourists passes through. Eureka deserves a day or so of looking around, for it is full of historic buildings, ruins of smelters and mementos of the days when it produced $40,000,000 in silver, $20,000,000 in gold and 225,000 pounds of lead.

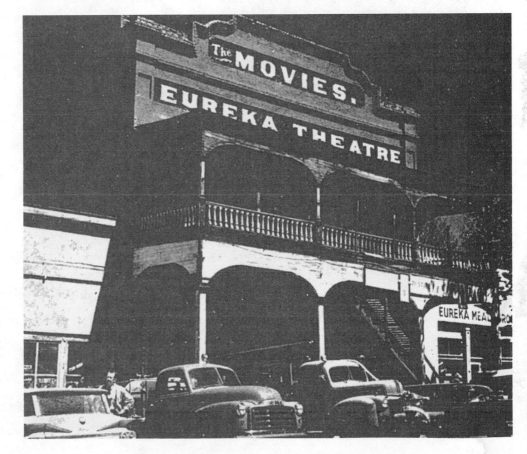

OBVIOUSLY NOT A "DEAD" ghost town, Eureka is a museum of mining history. The Main Street, coinciding with the highway, is lively with stores, fire department and other establishments. Balcony of theatre offered cooling breezes during intermissions, was not so popular in winter.

FAIRVIEW, NEVADA

Fairview did not want to stay put; it pulled up stakes twice. The first location was no doubt settled upon because of unlimited level ground on which to build. The view from the site is a magnificent, endless expanse of desert backed up by equally arid mountains. One of these, nearer than the others, has two humps on its low summit. Naturally, the mine gouged out on its side was called "The Dromedary."

The most imposing structure built on site No. 1 was the bank, which included a solid stone and concrete vault. That there were many streets of houses and buildings to shelter and serve the 2,000 people who lived there, is attested by rows of cellars open to the skies. It seems the populace grew weary of commuting so far to the mines and mills, so they moved everything except the bank vault to a spot in the narrow canyon a couple of miles nearer the working area. The ancient vault, standing as the only monument to mark the abandoned location, can easily be seen from the highway.

After a few years in the constricted defile of porphyry rock, the new town again grew restive. Not finding enough space for expansion it was getting longer and longer with the width limited to one block.

So the third and final move was to gather around the mill, and here remain the vestiges of Fairview, its perambulations now long ended.

RAMBLING LITTLE "MAIN STREET" is remaining nucleus of once extensive town. Building at lower right once housed nice flock of chickens, but food for them proved difficult to provide. Buildings at left hold variety of ancient cars. Sagebrush on hills is almost evenly spaced, limited by scarcity of moisture.

GALENA, NEVADA

What remains of this once bustling gold camp forms a satisfying ghostly remnant. Complete desertion is the lot of Galena, where once the population surpassed that of the nearby metropolis, Battle Mountain.

It was laid out in 1869 and in a couple of years had burgeoned into a boom town complete with a park, a rarity in a day when more thought was given to roistering than to the beauties of nature. The most conspicuous feature of Galena, though, was the smelter built to extract silver and lead from the rough material produced by the Dutch Creek Mine. This amounted to some $5,000,000.

The mill itself has long since disappeared, but its site is marked by extensive tailings dumps. These are constituted of flour-fine material which has solidified into piles of something like hard clay. Above these are dumps of waste rock, each heap a different color, the native material being so varied from place to place.

The cemetery is quite large. The earlier dates still discernible on the old headboards are in the 70's. It is close to town, the equivalent of a couple of blocks, and those who died with their boots on were simply carried over and buried with little ceremony. A bottle was passed around afterward, and that was that.

IF THIS WAS "PUBLIC SQUARE," perhaps tiny band played Sousa here on summer evenings, as was the custom in so many towns of era.

MAIN STREET IS SPARSELY fringed by scattered structures. Upper, with fancy railing likely was boardinghouse. Rock in street is mostly galena ore, some glittering with silver, lead.

GENOA, NEVADA

"Fighting" Sam Brown of Virginia City was pure bully, although he bragged he had filled a graveyard singlehanded. For a time he ran things in the mining camp on Mount Davidson and it was at the height of his ascendancy that one of his young henchmen was caught holding up a stage and was taken to the then county seat of Douglas County, Genoa, for trial.

Sam stormed down to the picturesque Mormon town at the base of the Sierra to attend the trial, fully prepared to bluster the judge and jury into intimidation and thereby, free his cohort.

What Sam didn't know was that the county had a new District Attorney, Bill Stewart, and that young Stewart had been informed of what he might expect of the witness. Testimony at the trial had been going against the stage robber, and when it came time for Sam to testify he was boiling mad. Storming up to the stand he was fully primed with the best liquor Genoa had to offer and was prepared to bluster that young lawyer into submission. The edge of his resolution was considerable dulled when he found himself facing the muzzle of a gun held in the steady hand of the man who would one day be U.S. Senator from Nevada. Cowed, Sam gave tistimony at best not calculated to help the case of his friend, who was soon convicted.

As soon as he got out of the courtroom and away from the end of Stewart's six-shooter, Sam, regaining his courage, raging at his failure, and returning to the Comstock, took it out on an innocent Dutch farmer who lived near the road, firing several shots in his direction. His aim being as bad as his disposition, Sam missed the Dutchman, who now understandably got *his* dander up, and with considerably better aim, cut short the career of "Fighting" Sam Brown. A coroner's jury held that "Brown came to his end by the dispensation of a Divine Providence." Van Sickle, once more phlegmatic, paid little attention, having returned to his again placid fields.

Those Argonauts heading for the California gold fields that preferred going overland to an even more dangerous sea voyage again had several choices of route. Some sought to shorten the distance by crossing the terrible Salt Lake Desert to reach the Humboldt. More headed for Fort Hall and Soda Spring, thence south to the river. Some went north around the main part of the great desert, avoiding the greater part of it though still suffering their full share of hardships.

For the first few years of overland travel pioneers could count on shooting game for a food supply. As travel increased, all living creatures soon were exterminated over a wide band adjacent to the route. Those depending on the bounty of the land found themselves hungry to the point of starvation by the time they reached the Humboldt, many had even eaten their dairy cows and some of the beasts hauling the wagons.

It was only natural, therefore, that trading posts would soon be established along the Humboldt Road as the wall of the Sierra grew nearer, the travelers sometimes still having a little cash, not having had any opportunity to spend it. A small settlement grew up beside the first of these establishments. Weary, dirty families often took the rest stop as an opportunity to wash out all clothing still serviceable, hanging the tattered remnants on surrounding bushes to dry. And so "Ragtown" came into being, the name later was changed to Leeteville.

For a time this was the last settlement, then, in June of 1849 Col. John Reese, a trader sent out by Brigham Young, built a log stockade, corrals and a cabin or two at the very foot of the Sierra. At first the place was called, simply, Mormon Station, that being exactly what it was. As others became established this one needed a more identyfying cognomen and a settler with an Italian background called it Genoa. Since the earlier Ragtown never became a permanent fixture, Genoa was the first real town in the state of Nevada, although that state didn't exist at the time of Genoa's founding. For those who fol-

lowed every tenet of Brigham Young it was the state of Deseret. In 1850 the United States Government declared the area to be part of the Territory of Utah, the southern part of what is now Nevada going into the Territory of New Mexico.

An interesting sidelight on the story of Genoa is that when the first gold-hungry men who were heading for the Mother Lode and Northern Mines stopped beside the Carson River near Genoa they panned the stream and actually did find a little gold, but were too filled with dreams of the other side of the Sierra to pay much attention. Later, when the big Washoe Boom hit the Nevada side many of those same adventurers, disappointed in what they found in California rushed back again, proving once again that the grass is always greener on the other side of the fence.

The Sierra was a formidable barrier between east and west travel. Placerville, the fastest growing boom town of the gold rush on the western slope, was the terminus of a rude "road," little more than a path. Genoa was at the eastern end, exactly at the point

STORE DATES FROM EARLIEST DAYS in Genoa. Colonel John Reese, his brother Enoch, and Steven A. Kinsey were among first builders of Mormon town. First lady settler was Eliza Ann Meddangh Mott, the wife of Israel Mott. Their daughter Sarah was the first native, she grew up here and married a Mr. Hawkins.

OLD SIGN ON GROCERY is protected from elements by canopy, has withstood ravages of time. Last item, "Queen's Ware" is flooded by direct sunlight, overexposed in picture.

"SNOWSHOE" THOMSON LIES AT FOOT of beloved Sierra in pioneer cemetery at Genoa. Snow-covered hills rising sharply in background are first easy step in what becomes giant barrier rising to over 14,000 feet at highest elevations, passes over which Thomson hiked averaged 7,400 feet. Thomson's "snowshoes" actually were skis, the first ever seen in West, when the word ski was unknown. Thomson's name is spelled "Thompson" in all available historical references. In face of evidence on stone and fact that Norwegians mostly spell the name without "P," we here follow them.

where the wildly rugged route suddenly flattened out into the desert. Situated as it was, the town could hardly help growing. By 1858 the place even had a newspaper, the first in the Territory. The few inhabitants of the whole area, still less than a thousand, were so hungry for news that a few "newspapers," really only hand-written sheets, had already been attempted. The *Scorpion* and *Gold Canyon Switch* were among these and had a tiny circulation in 1854. So a real, printed paper was an impressive and eagerly accepted innovation. It was called the *Territorial Enterprise*.

The infant paper remained a single sheeter for a time, then when the Washoe Bubble swelled the paper burgeoned into four-sheet size. It soon outgrew Genoa and as population expanded in Carson City the paper moved itself and equipment there. Then came the soaring expansion of Virginia City and the *Enterprise* again moved to what proved to be its permanent home, becoming a daily September 24, 1861.

The at first strictly Mormon settlement of Genoa began to be infiltrated by residents of other faiths in

a few years and among these was a sizable group of adherents to the Catholic faith. These managed to co-exist with the Mormons, but were unable to celebrate masses, confess or participate in any of the rites of the Church except in unconsecrated structures. Then in 1860 with the arrival of Father H. P. Gallagher a simple church was built and consecrated, the first Catholic one in Nevada.

Genoa has an interesting old cemetery with many ornate monuments, some enclosed by elaborate wrought iron fences. A more simple marble stone marks the grave of a Norwegian who was certainly the most remarkable mail carrier known to history. John A. Thomson, born 1827, traveled to the United States with his parents when he was ten years old. The family started farming in Illinois, then moved around through other midwestern states until John was twenty-four. This was in 1851 at a time when the whole country was filled with stories of fantastic gold discoveries in California. The young farmer was so taken with the idea of making a quick fortune he headed for the El Dorado. Arriving at Genoa he climbed over the Sierra along with hundreds of other goldseekers, coming out at Placerville on the California side. He didn't know it then, but the hardy Scandinavian was to retrace this route many times, and more, by himself with a heavy packful of mail on his back.

John worked in the Coon Hollow and Kelsey's Diggings near Placerville for a while, but with poor results. Becoming disgusted with mining he decided to try farming and bought a small place on Putah Creek in the Sacramento Valley. In 1856 he heard about the difficulties the government was having in getting the mail over the mountains in winter when deep snows clogged the high passes and this got Thomson to thinking. He loved the mountains, he had a strong physique and couldn't get lost, having "something in my head that keeps me right."

So he went out to his woodlot, cut a live oak down. He chose a good, nearly straight section about eight feet long and split the stubborn-grained wood into sections. Of the two most even ones he fashioned a pair of skis such as he had seen in Norway, full-sized versions of the small ones he had worn as a boy. They weighed twenty-five pounds. Then came an improvised balance pole. John took his new equipment up to the mountains and practiced on the snowy slopes. Then he showed up at the post office in Placerville and said he'd carry the mail over the snowy mountains, just like that. And carry the mail he did for twelve years, begining in January of 1856.

At first it took him four days to cover the ninety miles between Placerville and Carson Valley, but he soon pared off a day. His pack of mail often weighed

MAIN SECTION OF ORIGINAL TOWN of Genoa shows grocery at right flanked at left by newer, presently used grocery and filling station. At extreme left is inevitable tavern, housed in brick building dating back to 1860s.

eighty pounds so he carried little to eat, a few dried sausages and crackers, and no blankets. When forced to rest, he set fire to a dead pine stump, cut a few boughs and napped with his feet to the fire.

He often played the role of Good Samaritan as well. On one trip, he found a James Sisson half dead and with frozen feet in a cabin on the Nevada slope but nearer Placerville. After making Sisson as comfortable as possible, he returned to Placerville, persuaded several men to don makeshift skis, return to

the cabin with him and take Sisson down to Carson on a sledge. There a doctor decided Sisson's feet would have to be amputated but no chloroform was available. So Thomson retuned over the Sierra to Placerville where he got the precious stuff and again crossed the divide to get the anesthetic to the suffering man in Carson.

After a dozen years of this, the railroad was completed over the pass and Snowshoe Thomson was no longer needed. All this time he'd had no pay and, feeling he should have a little something for his efforts, applied to the post office. There he was told he'd have to go to Washington and make personal application for an appropriation, and this he did. There he got glowing promises of adequate reward, returning home well content. But nothing happened. Later, more promises came along.

He had established another farm in the upper Carson Valley barely on the California side and here he settled down to agriculture again to await his pay. It never came. Although of the most robust constitution Thomson had suffered much in his snowy journeys, losing so much resistance to infection that when an illness attacked him May of 1876 he lasted only four days. His body was taken down to Genoa and buried there.

IN SHADE OF GIANT LOCUST TREES is restoration of old Mormon Station. Here, on June 10, 1851, Colonel James Reese arrived with 18 men, ten wagons full of supplies, received warm welcome from Hampden S. Beattie, who, with small contingent, had established waystop two years earlier. Combined force built original log Station headquarters, destroyed by fire in 1910. Reconstruction was done of historic building and completed in 1947 by Nevada State Planning Board in cooperation with Genoa Fort Committee.

"HANG ON TO IT, SANDY"

Gold Hill, Nevada

You could say "Old Virginia" Finney had two loves—his home state of Virginia and Forty-rod whiskey. He deserted the first but fell hard for the amber lightning. Once he stumbled at his desert camp, breaking the flask of whiskey in his hip pocket. He gazed ruefully at the dark spot on the ground and decided some use should be made of it. Scattering broken glass over the stain he intoned, "I christen this spot Virginia."

John Bishop's modest discovery of gold up the canyon from Johntown sparked the larger exploration of Nevada which was to some extent still unknown to man. Without Gold Canyon, Nevada's vast stores of mineral wealth might have remained under the ground for many years. Certainly the "fine dust" Bishop saw in the bottom of his pan eventually led to the later discoveries farther up the hill and the founding of Virginia City, most fabulous mining camp of all time, largely instrumental in saving the Civil War for the Union.

Old Johntown, long since utterly vanished, was a cluster of saloons, honky-tonks and shacks near the mouth of Gold Canyon and not far from where Dayton was later established. It was a hangout for prospectors and drifters of all kinds. In the summer of 1859 men were swarming all over the surrounding hills, including Sun Peak (later Mt. Davidson). No spectacular discoveries were made but enough to warrant further search. Autumn brought a heavy freeze followed by continuous cold, all streams freezing solid, stopping all pan-

GOLD HILL BAR AND HOTEL flourished with mine production, ups and downs reflected in patronage, gambling tables. Sustained prosperity was maintained for 20 years, 1868-88. Records show Yellow Jacket mine poured forth $14 million, Crown King $11, adjoining Belcher $15,397,200 in dividends. Old stone and brick structure is still solid. Turned balusters on balcony are originals. Much plaster has fallen from walls, exposing field stone.

ning and sluicing attempts. Everybody retired to Johntown to spend the winter.

Toward the end of January there was a general thaw that sent water running in all the gulches. Men suffering from cabin fever and satiated with the pleasures of the flesh headed up Gold Canyon, the party that included John Bishop having a certain place in mind, a rocky knoll on the west side just north of where Gold Hill would be established.

Bishop later wrote, "Where Gold Hill now stands I had noticed indications of a ledge and had got a little color. I spoke to 'Old Virginia' about it and he said he remembered the locality, that he had often noticed it when out hunting for deer and antelope. He also said he had seen any quantity of quartz, so he joined our party and Comstock also followed along. When we got to the ground I took a pan and filled it with dirt with my foot as I had no shovel or spade." Bishop took the pan to a cluster of willows on the creek. "There was considerable gold left in the bottom, very fine, like flour," he said. "Old Virginia decided that it was a good place to begin work."

The immediate problem was water enough to wash the gold dust and Old Virginia Finney appointed himself the one to go look. He set off up the canyon while, as Bishop told it, "I and my partner meantime had a talk together, and decided to put the others of our party in the middle of the good ground." When Finney returned with the news he had located ample water and learned he had been omitted from these plans he was under-

standably irked. He made some bitter remarks and added, "Well, if you boys are going to hog it all go ahead. I'm going to make my own strike." However he must have changed his mind for when the claims were laid out to be staked, he took his along with the rest. When the men conferred on a name all at first favored Gold Canyon but since the strike was on a hill, the name would be Gold Hill.

Other prospectors sniffed at Bishop's find. The dust was so fine it was hardly worth bothering with, they said. But when the dirt was worked up to a point where a rotted ledge of quartz was uncovered it became evident the boys had a bonanza, foreseen by the astute Bishop. Johntown unbelievers widened their eyes when Gold Hill takes grew from $5 a day per man to $15, then $25. Then came the rush with the men camping under small trees all along the canyon, then in shanties and then log houses. Gold Hill could now be called a reality.

Another celebrated personality of Gold Hill was Allison "Eilley" Orrum Hunter Cowan Bowers who had progressed from her native Scotland to the camp by a devious route. When Eilley reached her fifteenth birthday she became a Mormon convert at the urging of Stephen Hunter who was proselyting in the old country. It turned out Hunter had more in mind than converting the attractive lassie. He ran off with her to Nauvoo, Illinois, the Mormon stronghold in America, and married her in the church.

GOLD HILL city fathers were once so optimistic as to introduce act in Territorial Legislature to put up state capital building on level spot near town. Prosperity in mining camps was largely gauged by price of drinks in saloons. 10-cent shot indicated camp of small respect and when bars in Gold Hill began charging "two bits" for slug of redeye, high rating of town was acknowledged.

Fires periodically ravaged thriving camp, one in Yellow Jacket mine erupting April 7, 1869, most sombre day in town's history. Combined fire fighting forces of communities failed over flames roaring thru underground tunnels. 33 men died, only 27 bodies recovered. Some fires smoldered 3 years.

Another fire in 1873 killed 4, injured 11. These ruins were left when ground level flames gutted interior. Though then doing little business post office managed to operate until Feb. 27, 1943. Years before that drinks in saloons were reduced to 10 cents, Gold Hill News editor remarking, "With nothing but ten cent saloons in town we might as well suspend," and did just that.

All went well with the romance until Hunter took a second wife under the policy of bigamy. Eilley's was an independent spirit not tolerating a second woman in her husband's bed and during preparations for the epic Mormon migration to Utah, the ex-Mrs. Hunter met and married young Alexander Cowan.

The Cowans had barely settled themselves in Salt Lake when they were sent still farther west to help colonize the valleys near Mormon Genoa in Nevada. Then once again plans were interrupted. The United States threatened to send troops against the Mormons and Brigham Young called back all scattered settlers in far flung places. Eilley's new husband was eager to respond but not his Scottish spouse. She was sick of repeated expeditions forced by the church and bade her second husband goodbye. She remained in Nevada.

In Johntown Eilley started a boarding house that was successful from the start because of her good Scotch cooking. She followed the mass evacuation to Gold Hill and set up her business there. Among the boarders was young Sandy Bowers who attracted her despite his being fourteen years younger and she began showing him favors of several varieties, eventually marrying him. It was gossiped about by other boarders that Sandy had run up a big board bill and was vulnerable to the lady's proposal. His present to the bride was a strip of "dirt" alongside his own early established claim.

Married life was just under way when the diggings began to fail generally with the result that the more easily discouraged sold out. Mrs. Bowers persuaded Sandy not to capitulate but rather buy some of the now cheap claims. The rest is history. While others lost their holdings the Bowers sud-

BANK OF CALIFORNIA was branch of main office in Virginia City, short distance above on Sun Mountain. Intense rivalry existed between towns. To escape being overwhelmed by larger VC thru greedy operators who wished to grab Gold Hill's support for building sidewalks, gas, sewers, street lights, other improvements in VC without benefit to GH, it incorporated Dec. 17, 1862 gaining victory over faction in legislature featuring its annexation to VC.
Boundaries were described as "on the north by the southern boundary of Virginia City; on the east and south by the boundary line between Storey and Lyon (Counties); on the west by the boundary between Storey and Washoe." Apparently Gold Hill was ever optimistic about wealth underground, permanence of then booming town.

HUGE BOWERS MANSION was built in 1862 at cost of $300,000, largely furnished with expensive appointments bought by the Bowers on triumphal tour of Europe. On return of new-wealthy pair, Sandy Bowers felt uneasy in luxurious aspect, preferred saloons, housekeeping rooms at Gold Hill. When he died there at 35, members of Gold Hill Masonic Lodge conducted his funeral at Fraternal Hall, and in accordance with last wishes to "Follow me as far as you can," population formed procession on horses, in carriages and wagons extending almost solidly down to Bowers' mansion. Sandy Bowers was laid to rest on hill few yards behind great house he disdained. Later he was joined in death by adopted daughter Persia. Many years later when owner of Bower house heard of Eilley Bowers' death he had her body brought home, placed beside kin. Graves are in brushy area of high fire danger, access denied by authorities.

denly began to take in thousands of dollars a day from their united claims which hit a bonanza. In a few months Eilley and Sandy were millionaires.

With huge wealth now at her disposal Eilley resolved to build a castle that would put to shame anything previously built in Nevada, an easy thing to do since few miners, even fabulously rich ones, wanted permanent homes there. And Eilley dreamed of a grand tour of Europe staging as a finale audience with Queen Victoria.

The great mansion was erected down on the level land near Washoe City (see *Ghost Town*

Album). And off to Europe she and Sandy went, buying splendid furnishings for the great house at every stop, the starry-eyed Mrs. Bowers paying any price asked. She would show those old fogeys in Scotland who had objected to her romance with Hunter what was what, even though Hunter had little to do with her present affluence. The tour was a shining success until she came up against British protocol. Queen Victoria refused to see Eilley, a divorcee.

After two years the Bowers returned home, following a steady stream of marble mantles, gilded French furniture and plush fixtures that had to be shipped around the Horn, then freighted over the High Sierra.

But all this was Eilley's dream come true, not Sandy's. He refused to live permanently in the mansion so lavishly appointed, caring nothing for the glossy society Eilley hoped to gather around her, and rejoined his old cronies in the Gold Hill saloons. Being nothing like astute he allowed his business affairs to become hopelessly muddled and suddenly died in 1868. He was thirty-five years old.

Sadly enough Eilley realized little from the claims when sold due to litigation and accumulated debts, although the properties were potentially very valuable. The widow, once so natively canny, became strangely trustful and careless. Before long it was necessary to mortgage the immense house and retire from public entertaining and ostentatious display. Too late she reversed her spending, making one last extravagant gesture—the purchase of a large crystal ball.

Acting on advice from the sphere she attempted to run the mansion as an elegant resort which involved cook and maid services for the paying guests. When there was no money left to pay them, they left and Eilley reverted to her former status as cook, maid and laundress. When she could talk her guests into it she told their fortunes with the aid of her crystal ball.

Apparently by not interpreting her advice correctly, one man lost a fortune in selling a claim that soon proved an El Dorado. The incident did much to undermine any reputation Mrs. Bowers retained. The activity of seeress and other sources of income fell off to nothing, the one-time millionairess was left broke and starving. She sold the house to a wealthy man who pitied her enough to allow her to stay as scullery maid and janitress, but Eilley was unable to scrub floors any more. She was discharged and drifted away to die in 1903, a ragged, lonely old woman.

BOWERS MANSION had advantage of high-priced architects, builders. Stone cutters were likely Cornish "Cousin Jacks" rightly reputed to be best in world. Stone blocks were so well trimmed little or no mortar was necessary. Cracks shown here were caused by severe earthquake that shook down magnificent ruin of Withington Hotel in ghost town of Hamilton (see **Western Ghost Towns**).

In 1873 State of Nevada had chance to buy Bowers house and surrounding 120 acres for $20,000, contemplating use as insane asylum but deal failed. Much later house and grounds became county park, with picnic area, swimming pool. In 1967 facilities were enlarged. Fortunately mansion itself remains intact, visitors conducted thru faded splendors for small fee.

GOLDFIELD, NEVADA

In the center of Goldfield is a large hotel. Although all its doors are padlocked, in the lobby there is a grand piano surrounded by leather "settees," and luxurious chairs.

In the dining room everything is set up for a normal, busy dinner hour. Leather-backed chairs are drawn up to the tables spread with linen covers. Silver, glasses and sugar bowl await the diner. Only the heavy mantle of dust gives evidence that these tables had been set up long ago for a repast never served.

Goldfield is dead. This is a city once boasting a population of 30,000 where, in the boom of 1906, lots sold for $45,000. Originally called "Grandpa" when Billy March and Harry Stimler staked out their claim in 1902, the name was changed when "jewelry rock" running $50 to $100 a pound was found.

There were plenty of labor troubles, strikes and disorders of all sorts. Several times State Police troops had to be called in to restore order, an uneasy quiet at best. High grading was common and almost unsuppressed. Miners put rich blosssom rocks heavily laced with gold in their pockets and lunch boxes, peddling them to waiting fences at night.

Uncounted saloons flourished in Goldfield, the most famous one, Tex Rickard's Northern, had a bar so long 80 tenders were necessary.

Tex Rickard made his fortune in the Klondike, lost it in California, and came to Goldfield with the gold strike. His first big promotion was the champion prize fight between Gans and Nelson in 1906. That fight lasted 42 rounds, and put Gans up as the world lightweight champion.

The all-time high in production was $11,000,000, but this phenomenal figure dropped to $5,000,000 by 1912, and those who recognized the signs began to pull out. In 1918 the mines put out only $1,500,000 and this was cut in half the next year. The next three together saw only $150,000 produced. Then even this dwindled and Goldfield joined the ranks of has-beens, but probably few Ghost Towns put on such an impressive front of buildings standing and in good repair. It takes a second look to discern the boarded-up windows, the bars across the doors, the padlocks and nails barring the way into once-busy buildings and stores. The corpse "looks so natural."

GOLDFIELD HOTEL puts up brave front but shelters no guests.

GOLD POINT, NEVADA

The town really boasts only one group of store buildings dating from the earliest days, the typical tiny structures huddling together, putting on a brave show of false fronts and gingerbread. A couple of blocks above is the Post Office, apparently abandoned. A sign, once hung over it, is now on its side on the porch; it reads *"Gold Point, Nevada live population (so far) 28. Ghost unlimited. Altitude 5,800. Taxes very low."* At *this* date 28 would be a high estimate, less than half that number still live in the Gold Point area.

Originally christened "Hornsilver," it went along with the title until 1929. At that time silver had so languished that investors decided that "Gold Point" would have more value as a name.

Two thousand people once thronged the streets, which provided the usual saloons, hotels and stores, now dwindled to our forlorn little huddle and some scattered shacks.

Poor milling processes in those days which lost most of the values in the tailings, together with constant litigation over rights of the mill to operate, killed the town. It slumbers now, awaiting the resurrection.

GOLD POINT NEARS END of yet another day. Desert landscape stretches beyond, its Joshua trees and buttes soon to merge into darkness.

GOODSPRINGS, NEVADA

"Things are quiet here," Sam McClanahan said, "if people keep on moving away this ain't going to be nothing but a damned Ghost Town."

He had seen the early boom days when Goodsprings was a lusty young camp producing not only gold but a wealth of other minerals, silver, platinum and vanadium.

These are still to be found and, if their recovery could be accomplished cheaply enough, would pay off. But the old mill, an extensive one, is a collapsed mass of ruined ovens, walls and machinery. Sam told the same old story of frozen gold prices, advanced labor and machinery costs. Fondling his ancient gold pan he surmised that "some day, we'll get going again, when gold advances." He showed me some pieces of tufa, a light, foamy type of rock which he had found in the nearby hills. With capital, he said, he could build motels of this material which would provide insulation, "and those tourists in Las Vegas could come up here and get away from the heat."

But old Sam didn't really feel all this would come to pass. Like many other gnarled old-timers of the western Ghost Towns, he was just reluctant to admit that the town he had lived with so long will soon join the ranks of those decaying remnants of another day.

WHERE TIME STANDS STILL and there is no "progress," outdoor "conveniences" are still prominent feature. Even such lowly structure exhibits beautiful textures of weathered wood.

ONE OF EARLIEST RESIDENCES has remaining stone wall propped. Door opens only into more open s p a c e. Goodsprings is center of highly mineralized area, azurite, chrysocolla, malachite, cinnabar are among many prized specimens found on dumps of mines in past. Sources are nearly depleted now.

GRANTSVILLE, NEVADA

On a cold and snowy day in February 1881, a frightened Mexican miner sat in a tunnel shivering. The tunnel was one dug into the mountains at the mining camp of Grantsville which had proved barren of gold and made useful as a jail. It was cold in the tunnel but the Mexican was trembling for another reason. He was charged with the murder of a fellow worker the night before and he was afraid Grantsville citizens, fired up with Shoshone Mountain hooch, would not wait for legal justice.

He was right. The heavy tunnel door crashed in and the roaring mob of miners made for him, the lead man carrying a rope. Pedro was hustled off to the stamp mill, hoisted up on a massive timber, the rope thrown over a higher one, noose slipped over his head. One push and the luckless man was swinging in the wind.

A coroner's jury next day named several persons thought guilty of the lynching. When questioned by the sheriff, the spokesman gave their reason for the

DWELLING IS BUILT of native, uncut stone. Some pains were taken to place flattened side outward for neater effect. Roof was of usual brush construction over poles, thick layer of mud plastered overall. "Airtight" tin heater in center of single room provided heat and cooking surface. Fuel was brush and pine wood.

LITTLE RED BRICK SCHOOLHOUSE supposedly had capacity of sixty pupils, but for this number interior seems cramped. Elegantly proportioned fireplace occupies left end. When supply of pupils dwindled, building was converted into boarding house, with kitchen at left, sleeping space gained by addition of shed at right.

action. The previous August another murderer had been arrested and tried in a legal manner. He was judged guilty but instead of the death sentence he was sent to the state prison where he was serving out an ordinary life sentence. The Mexican had been lynched to avoid his receiving similar soft treatment. The explanation was accepted and the incident forgotten.

The discoverer of gold in Grantsville was P. A. Haven, the same prospector who had located the first vein in Ione. Here he immediately organized a mining district and laid out a town. When eager miners came in droves, Haven was ready for them, selling them lots from $50 to $500. Whatever made the difference in the price, it was not the view, for all the lots had that if nothing else. "Grantsville is laid out," read an early description, "in a beautiful canyon" — a gross understatement. The steep canyon walls were covered with a heavy growth of nut pine trees, the predominant forest cover of the area and altitude. Later all the trees were cut down for fuel, shoring and charcoal.

Haven seemed to be more interested in discovering potential wealth and promoting it than in making any development. His original claim was worked out soon after he left and the place languished almost to a ghost town before it was ever well established. In September 1877, a representative of the Alexander Company, a big mining firm, traveled the seventy dusty miles from Austin and had a look around. He acquired the property for the company, set to work to develop it and Grantsville soon began to look like the town it had started out to be.

There were two general merchandise stores, hardware and tin shop, a livery stable, blacksmith shop, two barber shops and a jewelry store. The town also boasted of two assay offices, a bank, furniture store, two drug stores and a fine restaurant. As usual, saloons outnumbered all others — twelve. Not mentioned in the factual report were bawdy houses but the camp would not have been unique in this respect.

Three weekly newspapers spoke for the area, a succession starting with the NYE COUNTY NEWS in

1867. It made out for about two years, was supplanted by the GRANTSVILLE SUN which lasted only one year when replaced by the GRANTSVILLE BONANZA.

The gold and silver in the Grantsville mining district were found in veins of porphyry, limestone and quartz running northwest to southeast, dipping into the earth at an angle. Other metals were there in variety, such as lead, antimony and copper. Milling was done by crushing and roasting according to information dated 1881, but other methods came in later as is evidenced by old flotation and paddle vats still in the ruins of one mill.

There was plenty of wood, a heavy stand of nut pine trees being ravished for fuel, and plenty of water the year around from several good springs.

All food and supplies were freighted in from Austin at a cost of $40 a ton. Most perishable foods were not obtainable in hot weather because of spoilage or in winter when roads were impassable. Some butter and milk were obtained from Ione where there was a dairy. Occasionally someone would attempt to keep chickens but imported grain was too expensive to make this practical. Also hen houses had to have some heat in winter, otherwise eggs froze in the nest, as did chickens' feet on the roosts at night.

Although Grantsville held tighter to prosperity than did her sister Ione, her death was complete when it came. The town has been deserted for many years, is today one of Nevada's loneliest ghost towns.

EXTENSIVE RUINS of mining operations remain in Grantsville. In extreme foreground is up-ended two-holer. Behind is mess hall for miners and mill workers, with kitchen attached at left. At right of, and behind mess hall, are ruins of stamp mill. Extending upwards are various sections of mill. Recovery here was done at least in part by floatation, vats still in lower section. Principal mines were Alexander which had shaft 1200 feet deep and Brooklyn. Young pines make gallant attempt to reforest denuded hills but progress is slow in short growing season.

"Alone? No!
...there was something else!"

HAMILTON, NEVADA

Hardly a more wind-swept, storm-raked, altogether desolate landscape could be imagined than the one on the slope of White Pine Mountain in 1865. The only living things were the rabbits, squirrels, snakes, owls and other desert creatures.

In that year a group of prospectors from Austin found rich silver deposits there. They banded together with other Austin men of more wealth to form the Monte Cristo Mining Company. The whole thing was kept as quiet as possible and for several years not much happened.

Then, on a bitter cold, stormy day in January 1868 a nearly solid silver deposit was found on Treasure Hill, just across the bowl-shaped hollow in which lay the beginnings of Hamilton. This set off one of those fabulous "rushes" during which people of every sort and description poured into the snowy, inhospitable town which burgeoned till it burst at the seams. Jerry-built and substantial structures rose side by side. A new county was created, "White Pine," a courthouse rose almost overnight. This was used largely as a place to settle constant litigation over conflicting claims.

By now the rabbits were displaced by 25,000 humans scattered over the several ridges contiguous to Hamilton. These people ran the gamut from respectable, hard-working men down to the ever present hangers-on, the sharpies and prostitutes. Several houses for the latter lined a short street near the edge of town.

At 8,000 feet elevation the climate was rigorous, there was no local water, food had to be freighted in from Elko and bandits waylaid the lines of stages and pack mules going out. But the dream of El Dorado sustained the populace. Wasn't the silver lying around in almost pure chunks?

One of the largest and most imposing buildings erected was the Withington Hotel, built of sandstone and Oregon pine and indeed a structure to endure forever.

Then from here and there in small, quiet voices began to come doubts that the silver went very deep, that when the shining surface deposits were scraped off, the future of Hamilton would be something less than the rosy picture painted by the newspapers of the town.

And these voices of gloom were right; the silver was all on top. By 1873 there was a noticeable drop in output. There was a leveling-off process of a few years with small spurts upward, bigger ones downward. In spite of all the glittering prophecies in the early years, 1887 saw the end of the big-scale production. By then there had been shipped out a total of some $22,000,000 in bullion.

RUINS OF Withington hotel dominate Hamilton.

People moved away almost as fast as they had poured in. The "birds of prey" went first to fatten in other, newer camps.

Before many years the town was completely deserted, the buildings fell into disrepair, then ruin. There were two disastrous fires. Stone structures crumbled.

About twenty frame and stone stores and houses remain pitifully scattered about the hollow. Traces of wooden sidewalks partly connect some of them.

DOORWAY OF WITH-INGTON HOTEL laid open to elements frames group of houses almost isolated by past fires.

IONE, NEVADA

"An Ione father who had passed incalculable sleepless nights has immortalized himself by discovering a method of keeping babies quiet. The modus operandi is as follows: set it up, propped by a pillow if it can not set alone and smear its fingers liberally with thick molasses. Then put a dozen feathers into its hands. It will then continue to pick the feathers from one hand to another until it falls asleep. As soon as it awakens again, more molasses and more feathers. In place of the nerve wracking yells there will be silence and enjoyment unspeakable."

Such heart-warming hints as this in the weekly NYE COUNTY NEWS were rarely needed to fill space for things were never very dull in Ione. In the early, flamboyant hectic days one rich discoverer followed another after the first one in April, 1863, by a disappointed Comstocker, P. A. Haven. His strike was made near the center of the Shoshone Range, a string of mountains running north and south as do most of Nevada's ranges. When the camp began to need a name, one erudite miner thought of Ione, the heroine in Bulwer Lytton's novel, "The Last Days of Pompeii".

In only a few short months enough hopeful prospectors had trekked up the Reese River from Austin to make a real town with all the trappings—saloons, stores, and many cabins, all thrown together with adobe, stone, brush or anything handy.

This motley collection grew and the citizens began clamoring to the legislature to have their town made the county seat. The authorities were willing but first had to create a new county for Ione to sit in. This was done by major surgery on two existing ones, Lander, and Esmeralda, carving hefty chunks from each to make the new Nye county. The august and liberal body of lawmakers even made available $800 for a courthouse.

The NYE COUNTY NEWS, published weekly in Ione during the summer of the following year, was a worker for progress in the mountain community. It ran a plug for a new stage line to Austin along Reese River: "The line is well stocked and has accommodating drivers and carries passengers and packages at a reasonable rate. It is not yet definitely settled as to what day it will run. We hope to carry an advertisement next week when we will tell all we know." The line came through with the ad next week. "STAGE FOR AUSTIN. The stage for Austin will leave at an early hour tomorrow, Sunday morning. Passengers, in order to secure a seat should book their names today." The next week, another item. "The stage has established its office at the Bellrude store. It will leave at its usual early hour tomorrow."

Then the lively weekly turned its efforts to securing a bank and assay office for Ione. "A GOOD OPENING" was the headline, and the editorial:

PRIMITIVE CONSTRUCTION dates from 1860s in many Ione buildings. These walls are two feet thick, cracks between roughly cut stones chinked with mud. Roof was covered with clay, mud and layer of gravel.

RAFTERS OF PRECIOUS SAWN LUMBER support heavy horizontal layer of lighter brush which is in turn covered with a thick layer of mud and gravel. Interior was once neatly lined with muslin, vestiges of which interfered with picture taking. Photographer moved aside ancient cloth and got heavy shower of dust on camera and face. Available light came from tiny, deep-set windows and small open door.

"Now that our town is making such rapid strides toward prosperity, we would suggest to some enterprising individual the start of a small banking house in connection with an assay office. There appears to be plenty of money in this community but a scarcity of change, and as work progresses in the various mines rich discoveries are made, which for lack of a competent assay office, their capacity is unknown." And the happy note was sounded two weeks later:

"LONG AWAITED ASSAY OFFICE OPENS by Thomas Cahill, five years assayer in San Francisco mint. We welcome him in our town, having waited a long time for something of this kind. Bring in your specimens!"

There was always room for one more saloon and the newspaper held out the glad hand. "NEW SALOON. W. A. Brophy, Esquire, one of the old settlers returned to our place yesterday with a large stock of liquor. He proposes opening a saloon in the old stand formerly occupied by the Fashion Saloon, next door to the News office. We shall be around, Billy, and 'sample'." And the next week's spread: "INTERNATIONAL SALOON OPENS — BIG FANFARE — FREE DRINKS."

The editor, having accepted payment for this ad in trade, was incapacitated for several days but rose valiantly to announce: "To Mrs. Michael Kelly we are under obligations for a plate of nice, fresh butter. We carried it to our cabin and our better ? half pronounced it A No. 1. Mrs. Kelly keeps a large dairy and furnishes our citizens with fresh milk and butter. We are glad to learn that she has a large custom."

And then the enterprising editor got apple hungry. "Grocer Bellrude says he has a large stock of fresh apples but as we have not seen any around the office, we have to take his word for it." Apparently Mr. Bellrude was properly rebuked for, a few weeks later came the enlightening information: "Happening into Bellrude's store yesterday we observed a large amount of flour, sugar and such like stowed away as if he was laying in a good winter's supply."

Theatrical news was not neglected. "The beautiful comedy, 'The Swiss Cottage', and a laughable farce, 'The Cobbler and the Lord', will be presented at the Ione Theater. Open 7½ o'clock, start 8, adm. 50c." And always among these lively notes was mining news. "On Saturday last the men engaged in sinking a shaft upon the Olive Ledge discovered a large deposit of gold-bearing quartz which

SOME EARLY CABINS were built of logs formed from nut pine trees and junipers dragged down from higher elevations. Trees are of small size and gnarly growth, logs short and knotty. Chimney is of roughly fired brick, possibly done in hot bonfire. By 1865 commercial kiln was established at nearby Union. Some claim this structure was first courthouse.

will realize $8,000 to $9,000 a ton. The outfit is called the Knickerbocker Mining Co."

The hard working editor evidently took time out occasionally to view the passing parade and voice his observations: "There are many strange faces on the street and it is not unusual to have them pointed out as capitalists" . . . "Emigrant trains still through our town, bound for California. A large train from Davis Cy, Iowa, passed through last night. They are headed for Sonoma Cy. California. They report a very pleasant trip, although there were some delays due to Indian attacks." . . . "Everyone in the city is hard at work. There are no idle men and the streets seem almost deserted in the daytime." . . .

"IONE LIVELY — from the number of teams seen on our streets during the week several times we have blinked our eyes and imagined ourselves on C Street in Virginia before the San Francisco bears got control of the mines." . . . "EVERYBODY COMING, to look at the mines. So many make plans to remain permanently Ione sees a brilliant future ahead."

But it was not to be. Ione's gold proved to be shallow, was soon exhausted and the town with the classic name was just another flash in the pan, as were so many other Nevada mining camps. It had been in the spring of 1863 that the first discovery was made, the spring of 1864 when Ione was made the county seat and the spring of 1867 when that honor was taken away and bestowed on an upstart fifty miles away — Belmont. What really hurt was Belmont's being populated largely with Ione people, miners and prospectors who had defected to the new strike on the old theory that gold is always shinier in the other fellow's claim.

Ione was slow to accept the inevitable. The newspaper of April 6, 1867, reported the county official would complete removal of county records to the new seat at Belmont "as soon as the citizens have reconciled themselves to the fact that they have lost the county seat fight."

Although staggered by the blow, and much shriveled in population, Ione managed to keep from dying entirely, even to the present day. Some small or large discovery has at intervals revivified it enough to hold a few people there. Up to 1880 the mines turned out a million dollars in gold and silver, a small figure compared to the production in the few big years.

One development kept things going for a few years. In 1907 a ledge of cinnabar was discovered in the hills just east of town. Its bright red color should have attracted attention years before but in those days gold was all anyone could see. Silver was recognized grudgingly later, it being so much harder to extract than free gold.

Immediately, upon finding the cinnabar, horizontal roasting furnaces were constructed to melt the mercury or "quicksilver" out of the ore. Fuel was mostly fast burning but plentiful sage brush. More substantial pine was brought down from high elevations after most of the brush had been cleared from slopes nearby. In the several years of operation, some 11,000 flasks of mercury were produced.

Today the town is very quiet, only a few residents hanging on, barely enough to keep up Ione's resolve to "never say die" — and they do miss the old editor.

MANY OLD BUGGIES AND WAGONS indicate remoteness of Ione. In old camps of more convenient access, such relics have been taken by vandals, wheels removed and carried off. Backlighting here brings out details of sagebrush and wheels.

Nevada

SAGA OF THE "LOST BREYFOGLE"

Johnnie, Nevada

Prospector Breyfogle lost a mine he never had. More accurately he could not find the place where he picked up the rich chunk of gold. He made many searches, all to no avail, and broken in health and spirit, he died in the desert. But at least ten rich mines east and north of Death Valley have been identified as the "Lost Breyfogle." Was the real one the Johnnie?

The road up to the large Labbe mine is rough but passable and old time Nevada miner Charles Labbe has been studying the Breyfogle story for many years. He believes he knows about what happened to Jacob (or Louis Jacob or C. C. Jacob or Byron W.) Breyfogle, the events before and after his death.

He says that around 1861 Breyfogle brought a fantastically rich chunk of ore into the thriving mining center of Austin, Nevada. He was barely alive, desiccated and near starvation but was able to say he found the sample somewhere in or near the eastern edge of Death Valley. As soon as he was able to eat and walk he started the first of many searches.

In 1865 a party was following the old Spanish Trail from California to Salt Lake. At a camping ground called Stump Springs, not far from where Johnnie would later be established, they came upon Breyfogle who had barely survived an attack by Indians. He was taken on to Salt Lake where he was nursed by one "Pony" Duncan. He regained a measure of health and took Duncan as partner on another hunt for gold. They had hardly made a good beginning when Breyfogle died, first confiding all he knew of his lost "mine" to Duncan. Later Duncan met the Montgomery brothers who were also looking for it and they pooled information.

In 1890 George and Robert Montgomery were camped at Indian Spring Ranch when they hired Indian Johnnie as guide. The Paiute took them almost directly to some veins with exposed gleams of gold. Excited at first, the Montgomerys cooled down when they found the gold in view was all of it, not enough to warrant the hauling of supplies and equipment to the remote spot. Then Indian Johnnie said something like, "Well all right then, I'll take you about four miles south of here where there is a quartz ledge really loaded with gold." About an hour later the party stood before what Charles Labbe says, "was either the Breyfogle or at least what was the nearest among many versions of the lost mine."

Robert Montgomery later reported the gold in the decomposed surface of quartz was like "plums in a pudding." It was this display of nuggets that gave the location the name "Chispas," literally Spanish for "sparks" or "diamonds," but locally meaning gold nuggets. The mine was rich enough, producing some $250,000 by 1899 when the ledge pinched out. In the meantime another, richer and longer lasting, find was made on the steep hill to

DECAYING HOUSES in Johnnie. Photo made from porch of one directly below, for a few months occupied by Kathryn and Bob West. Tangled remains of chicken wire was once neatly stretched, bore blooming annual vines that gave shade, color to bleak cabins.

the east. The town growing up near the Chispas and the new mine as well were named for the Indian guide. To avoid confusion the village became Johnnie Town, active workings above Johnnie mine.

After treating a hundred tons of ore at the new mine it was evident more equipment would be justified, so a 10-stamp mill was erected, its boilers at first fired by yucca stems. During those first months all machinery and supplies had to be hauled over desert roads 140 miles from Daggett. Later a railroad came to Barnwell, 100 miles to the southeast, a stage line starting from there.

Historian Harvey Hardy writes that sometime around 1900 the Johnnie mining claim was leased by a company with headquarters in Salt Lake City,

the officials mostly Mormons. When their lease ran out, the Montgomery manager whose name Hardy remembers as McArthur, refused an extension. Jerry Langford, manager for the Salt Lake concern, was determined to retain the mine against all comers, including the legal owners.

While armed guards protected them, Langford's miners continued to take out rich ore. One night a force was assembled by McArthur on the hill directly above the mine, among it such gunfighters as Phil Foote and Jack Longstreet. In the early morning light, before guards were stationed, McArthur's men opened fire on the miners going to work, routing and scattering them in every direction as long as it was downhill.

The legal owners then moved in and immediately

MAIN STREET of Johnnie mine looking up slope in approximately southerly direction.

began mining operations. When several days passed without incident, the gunmen relaxed vigilance and all guards were taken off. This was the signal for the enemy to take over the same hill from which they had been evicted and start shooting. In the reversed situation McArthur's men ran to the hoist house for cover. After suffering several casualties they were ready to give up but for a time were unable to find something to serve as a flag of surrender. Then the squaw of Jack Longstreet was found among the beleaguered and her white petticoat was tied to a rifle and effective in putting an end to hostilities.

Most seriously wounded among McArthur's men was Phil Foote who was suffering much pain. A man was sent to Johnnie Town to get morphine and after a record trip returned with storekeeper Sam Yount who administered the drug. The suffering man went to sleep, "permanently," as Hardy recalls.

According to this account, the Mormons con-

tinued to operate the Johnnie mine for some years, then ran into financial difficulties. Miners were not paid regularly and threatened to quit. With bills for services and supplies mounting the officials sent to headquarters for help.

From Salt Lake City came a man named Gillespie with money to settle outstanding debts which was totally inadequate and in the hassle as to who would get what money there was, Gillespie was killed by a shotgun blast. The town blacksmith was accused and taken to Belmont, Nye County seat, for trial but released for lack of evidence.

Charles Labbe's account of the trouble is terse. "The leasers wanted to jump the claim for themselves and all hell broke loose. Two men, Phil Foote and a man named Gillespie were killed, the mill burned down and office blown up. I picked up the safe, minus the door, 200 feet away." He recalls the dead were buried at Pahrump, not far away and that no trial was ever held.

In 1905 a Los Angeles concern took over the

207

Johnnie mine and production continued moderately until 1908. The "Happy Hunch" whose real name was Ed Overfield, hailing from Goldfield, led an exploratory drilling operation nearby that uncovered a vein three feet wide and assaying $30,000 in gold to the ton. Reporters from Salt Lake's *Mining Review* looked and hurried back to spread the sensational news. Labbe says he saw one chunk from the vein from which $20 gold pieces could be cut. Unfortunately the lead soon ran into Johnnie mine ground and operations ceased.

The Johnnie ran along on an extension of a "pocket zone" until 1940 when the owner died. In a year or so there was further activity by another Los Angeles promoter but when drilling produced no substantial leads, quiet again settled down on the old camp (see *Tales the Western Tombstones Tell*).

JOHNNIE MINE saw several alternating periods of desertion, activity. In 1941 two Hollywood, Calif. men, Joe De Grazier and Walter Knott, promoted reopening of mine with money "invested" for wealthy widow of movie capital. They hired mining expert Robert West, several other knowledgeable men to clean out shaft. "Bob" West and wife Kathryn set up housekeeping in old building still in fair condition. Activity was feverish for 3 months until authorities discovered De Grazier, Knott had mismanaged funds, depleted almost all before actual mining could start. Without waiting for outcome of shady affair, West quit, left for home. Promoters later received jail sentences. Photo of then active post office was made with old Eastman folding Kodak by Kathryn West. After closure office was moved to Pahrump in valley.

MANHATTAN, NEVADA

The town called Manhattan Gulch in early days lay almost on the slopes of Bald Mountain at an altitude of nearly 7,000 feet. This means heavy snows for a long winter, and Manhattan really had them. The ground was out of sight for many months, most winters, with hot summers between.

This sort of climate didn't prevent a hectic boom in the period from 1900 to 1905.

Nearly forgotten is the earlier period of activity there in the 60's. That first stage in the camp's growth was short, and from about 1890 until John C. Humphrey came upon his dazzling chunk of "Jewelry Ore," the town had slumbered. The few people still there awoke with a start at this discovery and so did a lot of opportunists throughout Nevada.

When Charles Phillips, now of Portland, was born there in 1910, Manhattan was a busy place, with about 500 people. Charles was only ten years old when he left with his parents, going to Goldfield, but he has many memories of the town in the Gulch.

"WE WENT TO RIPPY'S Grocery for almost everything, besides food. We went in by door on the corner, I remember." Native of Manhattan, Charles Phillips, says proprietor and family lived upstairs. Route to "outhouse" went down, then up.

"There were several mines going strong in that period," he recalled. "The largest was the White Caps, with its stamp mill and cyanide plant. The La Verde and Big Four also milled their own ore, all of it gold. I remember the White Caps pumped its seepage water into the gulch, water so full of arsenic it was useless. Too bad, since water was so scarce.

"Some of the main buildings along the main street were Oliver Giannini's Saloon, Ziegler's Butcher Shop, Ferguson's Drugstore and Butler's Livery Stable. The jail was close to the stone post office.

"The mule skinners used to throw whatever came handy at their refractory animals, and these missiles were often 'high grade.' I've heard since, that during the depression days, a man and his wife harvested these chunks and sold them for a tidy sum. Those were mostly $5.00 rocks!

"I remember a character who made his living at 'dry placering,' a process using air instead of water. He was called 'Dry Wash Wilson' and had the largest feet ever seen in that part of Nevada. He realized a dream of many years when he bought a 1910 Model T Ford. But his happiness turned to gloom when he found he couldn't put his foot on just one pedal at a time.

The town now can hardly muster up 20 people, some remain from the small-sized resurgence in the 30's. Most are about ready to admit theirs is a Ghost Town, with small hopes for revival. A few feel that if the price of gold would advance, "something good might happen to Manhattan!"

CATHOLIC CHURCH commands imposing position on hill above town. Interior is empty except for altar rail and confessional.

POST OFFICE WAS FOCAL point of all activity; when mail came into town, everybody picked up his own. Jail stood almost against building and was usually well filled with drunks sobering up.

MIDAS, NEVADA

When the populace petitioned for a Post Office in 1908 the desired name was "Gold Circle." The powers that be, however, looked on this name with about as much favor as they had for Raw Dog, Oregon, but for different reasons. There were already too many Gold this and Gold thats in Nevada, so how about "Midas" which, after all, did have a golden touch?

Original discoveries had been made the year before and the town became a reality shortly after. It grew apace, though not with the resounding boom that was being enjoyed at the same time by Goldfield and others. Estimates of peak population vary from 5,000 to 20,000. This will allow a safe margin for errors. There was a Chamber of Commerce, city water system, a newspaper, four big general stores and several hotels and rooming houses. In addition, there existed the usual shady area, dotted at night with red lights, and numerous saloons.

The big mine in Midas was the Elko Prince. About 1910, miners were forced to accept part of their wages in stock, times were so hard, but some sold later for as much as 500 per cent gain.

The Post Office, always a barometer of a town's population closed in 1942 along with the gold mines, the school in 1952, lacking the three pupils required by law to keep it going.

PEACEFUL IS THE WORD now for Main Street in Midas. Little store at right carried everything from corsets to kerosene.

"Branches as bare as bones . . . as white, too!"

NATIONAL, NEVADA

CABIN HAS LONG LACKED human tenants but birds have made themselves at home.

What is left of National is in the Humboldt National Forest. The area was classed, in a time of rich bonanzas, as one of the richest. Its ores contained many "jewelry store specimens," a term used to describe chunks of quartz in which gleamed solid nuggets of gold. The National mine alone produced more than $8 million.

National had a short life but a merry one. Ignored by prospectors in Nevada's early gold discovery period, it did not come into its own until the period called "automobile prospecting days." As evidence that the time of the burro had passed, two of the places named around National were Auto Hill and Radiator Hill.

Soon after the first discoveries of gold on the site by J. L. Workman, blocks of land were leased and the place became a beehive of real estate activity as well as the essential mining. In 1909 the Stall brothers ran into the National vein 40 feet down. Much of the ore removed from it assayed out at $75 per pound, the bulk of the shipped ore $24 per pound and tons were discarded with a value of $2 per pound.

With ore so rich "high grading" was carried on by many of the miners. It is estimated the National alone lost more than a million to these thieves. The worst of it was the citizens seemed to regard the

**WORKINGS OF OLD NA-
TIONAL MINE** are perched
high on mountain above plain,
visible in distance. Ore carts
ran on rails spiked to ties now
only fragments. Hill in background is typically clothed with
sagebrush, one in foreground
made up of tailings and dump-
ings of mine.

practice of smuggling out "blossom rock" as being
quite legitimate. The company had a hard time
prosecuting the occasional miner who was caught
at it, public sympathy being with the culprit. Dis-
charging the guilty one only resulted in reprisals
by the other miners, sometimes known to blast a
tunnel after their safe exit. Even though lunch
boxes were searched nuggets were often concealed
in body cavities.

During the period of greatest activity the only
law in National was that of the company which
played searchlights on the mine at night and posted
a 24-hour guard around it. But the company didn't
give a hoot what the miners did off duty. The one
long and narrow street winding up the canyon was
lined with a concentration of "houses" bent on ex-

tracting everything a miner had earned or stolen.
Such activities weren't always painless, many a man
rolled or even killed for his wages.

One of the largest honky tonks stood just above
the National mine. It boasted a second story with
a hall down the middle between the cubicles where
the girls took their customers. Downstairs a grand
piano tinkled out its tunes, a long bar at the right
sported large plate glass mirrors and mahogany
fixtures. Out in back were two tall, narrow structures separated slightly, one "his" and one "hers."
Now the house of pleasure has fallen flat and all of
its fixtures have decayed away except the frame
and wires of the piano. Still standing are the two
little "Chick Sales."

Old fort buildings at Fort Churchill, Nevada.

NELSON, NEVADA

Nelson had once been called Eldorado, a name full of Spanish romance and suggestive of riches beyond counting, and indeed Spaniards had made the original discoveries of gold in this spot which now bears the name, Eldorado Canyon.

That was in 1775, but nothing much happened for a hundred years, when things got going under gringo ownership. The main operation became the notorious Techatticup Mine; notorious because wanton killings became so frequent there as to be almost commonplace. These were the results of disagreements over ownership, management or labor disputes, and the canyon with the romantic beginning became as sinister as the black rocks forming its walls.

Even so, the mine and its satellites produced several millions in gold, silver, copper and lead, before lowered values caused general cessation. The row of huge cyanide vats still form an imposing ruin.

HUGE VATS USED FOR PROCESSING GOLD ORE by cyanide treatment stand rotting in blistering heat of Eldorado Canyon. Vats are near cave where Indian "Public Enemy No. 1" named Quejo was discovered dead after 10 years of terrorizing area. His excuse for his crimes always was that he had been ordered by authorities to track down and slay his killer brother and to bring back the head as proof.

PARADISE VALLEY, NEVADA

If Lieut. John Lafferty agreed with scouts who said the only good Indian was a dead one, he had a sound right to his opinion. He spent so much time chasing live Shoshones and Paiutes off settlers' ranches in Paradise Valley, and counting the dead ones, he had little time to go fishing.

And when he did he still had Indian trouble. There was the time in August, 1867, when he went fishing up Cottonwood Creek with Hon. J. A. Banks and Rev. Temple of New York. Banks was a delegate to the Nevada State Constitutional Convention and Speaker of the House at the second legislature. From these labors he took a vacation trip to the fine fishing streams flowing into Paradise Valley from the Santa Rosa Range. Lt. Lafferty, com-

mander of Fort Scott nearby, agreed to go with Banks and the minister.

The three found good fishing but Banks wanted it better. He went on up the creek saying he would return when he had all the trout he wanted. When he failed to return, the lieutenant and Rev. Temple went after him and found his mutilated body in a gully. Lt. Lafferty was enraged, swore vengeance on all Indians and took a party of soldiers after them. They killed several but did not find the murderers of Hon. J. A. Banks.

This was only one incidence in the almost continual strife between whites and Indians in the early days of the town of Paradise Valley. It lay in the grassy, fertile area partly encircled by the Santa

PICTURESQUE BUILDINGS on main street of Paradise Valley. Sun has emerged after hard downpour, fails to reach north—facing side. Structures are among few in West to retain genuine, unspoiled atmosphere of early days. At left is post office established after first was destroyed in fire; next to it tiny shop, meat market at one time—bacon, when available, $1 a pound; next, gambling hall with rooms for girls upstairs, becoming more respectable rooming house later; next, notorious Mecca Saloon, whiskey at 50c a shot, "less for regular customers." Sign is partly discernible behind tree branches.

Rosas. Called Yamoposo by the Indians for its half-moon shape, it earned its English name when in 1863 prospector W. H. Huff climbed to a pass near the top of Santa Rosa Peak, looked out over the land below and exclaimed: "What a Paradise!"

One of Huff's companions was W. C. Gregg. More farmer than miner, the verdant valley so impressed him agriculturally that he brought in a herd of cattle and machinery for cutting and baling hay, thereby setting the pattern for Paradise Valley's future in spite of the hordes of hungry prospectors and miners who swarmed the Santa Rosas over the ensuing years. While some miners did settle in Paradise Valley, and many bought their outfits and provisions there, the real mining towns were Queen City, Spring City, Hardscrabble and the rough and tough Gouge Eye. Spring City was twelve miles away, a typical mining camp spawned in the boom days of the Santa Rosas and boasting of a brewery, seven saloons and a book store.

Gregg, for whom the green of grass was brighter than the glimmer of gold, drew other farmers into the valley. The Santa Rosas handsomely rewarded many with gold but many claims proved shallow or entirely sterile and many miners stayed to grow

hay for the nearby camps, to be used as fodder for riding and work horses.

Richard Bentley and Charles A. Nichols plowed the first furrows for the planting of wheat in the spring of 1864. The settlers put up sod houses and shacks of willow brush, planted large vegetable gardens and cut down the nut pine trees for fuel. And the original inhabitants — Paiutes, Shoshones and Bannocks — watched from the hills. They saw the pastures where game had fed being plowed up and saw the burning of trees which had borne one of their major food supplies, the pine nuts. They watched the sparkling clear streams being dammed, diverted and muddied in sluices and other mining operations.

Then they struck. Small forays grew to mass raids in depredations that lasted for years. The first was an attack on three prospectors just north of the town of Paradise Valley. Dr. H. Smeathman, W. F. White and Frank Thompson were riding out of town when an Indian bullet knocked the doctor off his horse. The other two ignored his cries for help, spurred their mounts on to Rabbit Hole and safety. About two months later a party of four was ambushed near the Santa Rosas, G. W. Dodge slain

STORE AND ORIGINAL POST OFFICE were housed in this structure built around 1870, store established by Charles Kemler, first man to freight supplies into Paradise Valley. Upper floor was dance hall, later boasted hardwood floor mounted on springs, novelty in this sparsely settled section of Nevada. Structure burned in spectacular fire of 1919.

and another man wounded. The next spring, in 1865, Paiute Chief Black Rock Tom organized his tribesmen against the whites, the first casualty being Lucius Arcularius, station keeper on one road and two other whites at another way station. Then came reports the Indians were gathering a war party on the Humboldt. W. H. Haviland of Paradise Valley went to Star City, a thriving mining camp north of Unionville, to ask for help to protect his town from expected attacks.

About the same time two friendly Indians arrived at Aaron Denio's cabin on Martin Creek to warn against an attack intended to slaughter every inhabitant and drive away all stock. Denio spread the alarm and organized plans for complete evacuation.

The fleeing families attempted to reach Willow Point down the Little Humboldt but had difficulty getting their heavily loaded wagons across Cottonwood and Martin Creeks which were running to the banks in spring freshets. Some got the ox-drawn wagons to Hamblin's corral but several stragglers were forced to spend the night in a wayside cabin and awoke to find it surrounded by a party of twenty-two Indians. By a ruse they succeeded in getting away, joining the others at the corral. Then short-

ly this refuge was under attack, the mounted Indians circling and yelling.

The besieged group consisted of ten men, one of whom was Aaron Denio, his 12-year old son Robert, three women and four children. They were armed with three rifles, a musket, two double-barreled shotguns and six revolvers. Everyone seemed agreed that Denio was in command and also that someone would have to go for help.

Whether young Thomas Byrnes was selected or volunteered, there is no doubt of his heroism. He managed to get to the barn without being hit, mounted the fastest horse and headed straight through the lines of screeching Paiutes. Possibly the element of surprise had something to do with the feat but the boy got through, even evading the braves who pursued him, firing as they rode. Thompson and West in their HISTORY OF NEVADA recorded: "It was a race for life. If overtaken by a stray bullet, or the mounted savages, all the lives at the corral would have paid the penalty, and seemingly inspired with the terrible emergency, the noble animal flew like a winged Pegasus out of sight from his pursuers."

The youth must almost have flown as he reached Willow Point at three that afternoon, finding thir-

OLD RED BARN, built by Alphonso Pasquale, early Italian farmer, lover of fine horses and fancy dress, is one of many relics remaining on streets of Paradise Valley. Wagons loaded high with hay were driven directly under projecting balcony, fodder pitched directly into loft. Pasquale built several other buildings along street.

teen men ready and anxious to help. There were only twelve horses and the oldest man named Givens was to be left behind. But as the party started, Givens grabbed one of the saddle pommels and according to the referred to HISTORY: ". . . kept pace with the relief party over the thirteen miles . . . every so often shouting "Heave ahead, boys, heave ahead! The women and children must be saved!', and this while carrying a rifle in his free hand."

The beleaguered group at Hamblin's corral was rescued without a shot being fired. It was just before dark when the Willow Creek party arrived, Given still hanging on. Not sure just how many men comprised the rescuers, the Indians fled. Settlers and deliverers headed for Willow Creek and safety, arriving at three a.m. to find Lt. Joseph Wolverton with a troop of twenty-five men who had responded to Haviland's plea at Star City. Under their protection the Paradise Valley settlers returned to their homes, resuming work in the fields under armed guards.

These and many other Indian incidents resulted in the establishment of two forts in the area — Fort McDermitt at the Oregon border and Fort Winfield Scott a short distance from Paradise Valley. Sporadic Indian fighting continued, with incidents like the fishing party murder of J. A. Banks. It was not until after the winter of 1869 that Indian attacks ceased and Paradise Valley farmers could till their fields without fear.

The protective influence of Fort Winfield Scott encouraged the development of farms and the group of buildings near the fort increased, was in 1866 officially known as Paradise Valley. Charles Kemler who freighted goods into the valley built and operated a store here with a hotel in connection.

The winter of 1867-68 was unusually cold far into spring. Supplies failed to come in and settlers were forced to live on wheat ground in coffee grinders. The next summer A. C. Adams erected his Silver State Flour Mill, putting an end to this. The following year saw the end of the Indian trouble and the start of long, peaceful progress of the agricultural area.

PINE GROVE, NEVADA

The best-preserved building in Pine Grove was apparently once a business headquarters, for a rusty safe lay just outside. A ruined picket fence surrounded the house, covered with withered hop vines. One of the vines still showed life, a forlorn sprig in the dead town. At one side of the door was a faded typewritten notice. "You are welcome to live here but please do not tear down."

Another building, the cookhouse, had several layers of paper on its walls, tattered and peeling off. The first layer was of newspapers, mainly the *San Francisco Chronicle* and *World Report*. These carried the dates from 1891 to 1897. Over this was fancy imported wallpaper. Later newpapers covered the torn elegance and the latest of these were dated in the early 30's.

The original discovery of gold in the area was in 1866. Within a year, Pine Grove had 300 people. There were three mills shipping $10,000 in gold bullion every week. The population continued to expand, then dwindled, grew again and, about the time the fancy wallpaper was added, in the 1880's, was at its height. The last small flurry occurred when the latest newspapers were pasted on the walls to keep out the cold winter winds. With the 1930's went the last inhabitants and Pine Grove has become a true Ghost.

IMPRESSIVE STONE RUINS of once busy general store. Occupying central position in original location of Pinegrove, it suffered by later removal of business section half a mile up canyon where boardinghouse and school remain. Portal now stands alone, looking out on hills scarred and torn by mine operations.

NEVADA'S HAVEN FROM HEAVEN PIOCHE, NEVADA

Bartender Faddiman had been warned often enough. Friends told him, "Don't take that job at Pioche." . . . "You're as good as dead if you go to work in Pioche" . . . "No bartender ever lasted longer than a year there." Not one of Faddiman's well wishers wanted to see him go to certain disaster but his reason was simple, his need urgent. "I need a job and I don't care where it is. I can take care of myself". He did go to the most notorious camp in Nevada — and stayed there. In his second week a drunk ordered a drink. "You don't need an-other drink", Faddiman told him — and those were his last words. The customer objected to them, simple and straightforward as they were, took out his six shooter and Faddiman set up no more drinks.

The killer walked calmly behind the bar, stepped over the barkeep's body and stripped the till. Then he went next door to the butcher shop of buxom "Nigger Liza" and for variation, slit her throat with his knife. He emptied her till too but by this time the sheriff knew about the bartender's slaying and met the murderer at Liza's door with a

LONG ROWS OF GRAVES, barely discernible, makes up famous Murderer's Row at edge of Pioche's Boot Hill. Nearly 100 killers of all types lie here in area fenced off from more respectable occupants of cemetery. During heyday of large mining town, tramline was run over Row, ore buckets clanging constantly. They now hang immobile, except as they sway in often violent winds.

PIONEER BURIED HERE lies in anonymity like many others in Pioche cemetery. Headboard inscription has long since faded away, unusual condition since most painted lettering preserves wood to some extent, outlasting unpainted surface. Perhaps this one was carved, allowing moisture, abrasive sand to erode lettering or could inscription have been chiseled away for some reason? Note horizontal marks.

rattle of lead. And this was the way the single row of unmarked graves in Pioche's Boot Hill grew so long, so fast.

Piochee, pronounced Pee-oche with accent on the last syllable, was developed by Frenchman F. L. A. Pioche, although original deposits of lead-gold-silver ore were discovered by William Hamblin in 1863. Hambin had it easy. Instead of spending years at prospecting, his Paiute Indian friends led him to the highly colored ledges that were to produce $40 million in ore. Hamblin had little money for developing and later sold the claims to the French banker from San Francisco.

By 1870 the camp was considered the wildest in the West, the gun being the only law. The climate was fine enough to keep people from dying of natural causes, unnatural being most popular, the first 75 deaths being from "lead in the head" or

violence of some sort. Not only did bad men drift into town to bully and shoot residents but mine owners imported their own bad men at the rate of 20 a day to fight encroachments. Death rate of these assassins was high and they got the camp's Boot Hill off to a good start, with special sections for various categories.

In Murderers' Row are two desperadoes convicted of the wanton slaying of an old prospector for his money. The sheriff's deputy in charge of their execution was the tidy sort and not wishing to dirty his hands unnecessarily or cause extra work, forced the two hapless killers to stand at graves dug at the end of the row when he shot them.

In 1871 a young lawyer, William W. Bishop, came from Illinois to spend a few hours in Pioche. He later attained some fame by defending John Doyle Lee in the notorious Mountain Meadows Massacre. Bishop brought his bride with him and as they stepped down from the stage, a shot sounded from around the corner, another across the street. By the time they got to the hotel room, says the story, a deputy shot and killed three bad guys on three different corners and the newlyweds had had it, heading back to civilization.

Legend departs from tales of violence to relate that during the Independence Day celebration of

WILLIAM L. McKEE must have been one of the solid citizens judging by his grave in Pioche cemetery.

THE CATHEDRAL, standing majestically few miles below Pioche. That haphazard erosion in chalky clay could produce near perfect replica of European cathedral seems fantastic and could well have inspired composer of "The Cathedral", title song in album named Cathedral Gorge. Cathedral State Park contains many beautiful shapes like this, none as aptly shaped.

1876 the town bell was kept clanging constantly for hours by drunken miners. The people could stand it but not the bell, and it cracked. Dismayed, the townsmen declared another holiday to melt enough metal for a bell that could really take it. A melting pot was fired up at the smelter and a procession of citizens filed by, each contributing dollars or silver bars or jewelry until there was enough mass for a pour. It is said that the new bell had a sweeter tone than any other in the country but no mention is made of its fortitude.

Today Pioche is no longer wild. Many relics of the old days remain, such as the Lincoln County Courthouse. Built of brick in the late 1860s, it cost more than half a million, was condemned as unsafe in 1933, three years before it was paid for.

RAWHIDE, NEVADA

"Rawhide was named by an early prospector who mended his worn out clothes with a strip of that material" . . . "The town was called by that name because some of the first ore was hauled out in raw cowhides" . . . "The first mail box was put up along the trail with a sign that read 'All mail for this camp here'. The box was nailed to a post which had a hide on it, tail still attached."

"All a pack of lies," says Charles A. McLeod. "I went into what is now Rawhide on Feb. 12, 1907 with Albert J. Bovard and prospected around that section and on Feb. 12 I made my first location on what is known as Hooligan Hill. My first claim was named Happy Day and the second Happy Hooligan. My partner Bovard went southwest to Pilot Peak, about four miles from our camp, but did not find anything. Charles B. Holman and my brother Mason arrived at our camp just a few hours after I had made my locations. I had left word at Schurz for them to follow Bovard and myself.

"Charley Holman was very bitter about his recent experience at Buckskin, a new boom camp not far away. They had told him they didn't want any more prospectors making claims around there. He was fuming about this all through supper and finally he exploded. "By God!" he said. "They think they're so darn smart getting that name of Buckskin on the map! We'll go them one better and get a Rawhide on it!' We always called the camp Rawhide after that, and that's what it was after others came in."

The man who relates this incident and other vivid and colorful ones is Charles McLeod who at 86 still makes visits to scattered claims in Rawhide and elsewhere, but living more quietly now in Yerington, Nevada. He is Scotty to his friends which

HERE WAS MAIN STREET of town. In background is Regent Range, composed of rock materials so light colored as to appear snow covered. Derelict buildings are survivors of fire which all but leveled Rawhide at height of inflated prosperity. Vegetation is sparse—dry, hot climate in summer and cold in winter hostile to most plants. Among few ornamental shrubs cultivated was Tamarisk, surviving example at left of small building left of center, still sending out airy panicles of pinkish bloom in spring.

FADED, DESERTED BUILDINGS on street leading to Hooligan Hill are silent only in rare periods of calm weather. When wind blows old structures come to ghostly sort of life, galvanized metal of roofs clanking loudly, metal barrels rolling noisily, loose boards flapping against walls, weeds gyrating wildly.

means everyone privileged to meet him and has a remarkable memory and keen wit. His birthplace was the early day camp of Aurora, Nevada and/or California — the town belonging to two states at one time. A boyhood spent in the never-ending clamor of hundreds of stamp mills and constant talk of assays and values conditioned Scotty to a life closely associated with mines and mining. Even before his family's stay at Aurora, his father owned a ranch at Yerington, the one-time Pizen Switch.

Here at the cross roads of travel west to the Sierra and north to Oregon, an opportunist once set a board on two whiskey kegs and peddled the contents to dusty-throated travelers. Business was brisk and as the whiskey level got low the resourceful samaritan fired up the raw stuff with tobacco juice and what-have-you, adding water for bulk. So Pizen Switch the spot was, the place where the McLeods settled on the ranch. Other settlers rebelled at the name and called it Mason Valley and later the village took the name of Yerington which today is still a thriving farm center.

Aurora was fading fast when the McLeods left it but Charles had a boy's curiosity and touch of gold fever. Before he reached his majority he was prospecting around Mason Valley and at about twenty-five staked out the claims on Hooligan Hill a few hours before the camp was christened Rawhide.

That was in February, 1907. Ever restless, as soon as the claims were proved to be rich, he and Charley Holman sold out their joint properties of some nineteen claims to Van Doren and Dunning for $20,000 plus 10% of profits. They went prospecting elsewhere but by fall the magnet of the booming Rawhide proved so strong they returned to start working the several claims retained at the north end of Stingaree Gulch. In the meantime Van Doren and Dunning had sold out to the Nat C. Goodwin Co. for $400,000, with McLeod and Holman still getting their 10%. Goodwin was a famous New York comedian enamored of western mining, his company incorporated for $3 million.

The landscape around Rawhide was undoubtedly as stark and barren, yet as fascinating, then as now. A small amount of grass and sagebrush grows along the sides of Stingaree Gulch which bisects the camp but otherwise the mountains, rising sharply on all sides, each of a different color, seem utterly unclothed. But the early inhabitants were likely unaware of such harsh beauty, busy as they were working their claims or prospecting.

Miners on Grutt Hill thought dynamite was necessary to follow a promising vein of gold. The head powder man had imbibed a few too many and placed the blasting material with too lavish a hand — which he was lucky not to lose. The resulting explosion startled the town but nobody was hurt, and a few even helped. The hoped for vein of rich ore was where it was expected to be — until the blast scattered it to Rawhide's far sides. The owners recovered about $14,000 but much was pulverized and lost, much picked up and pocketed by grateful citizens.

Another and less spectacular blast at the Coalition mine sent a chunk of ore through the window of the First National Bank of Rawhide. A bank official, able to "assay" the rock, deducted the value of it from window repair costs and returned a balance of $8 to the owners.

Not all the Rawhide ore was valued for its gold alone. Some material assayed out eight ounces of gold to one of silver, the next batch showing the same values in reverse. Some of the best left indications in the report of $26,000 to the ton. "And it was shallow, easy to get at," says Scotty. "Our claims at the north edge of town produced almost all their good ore between 35 and 94 feet, which was at bedrock."

Rawhide had its sharpies, hangers-on who didn't enjoy working in mines but made their living supplying workers with expensive pleasures of

RAWHIDE HOOSEGOW—most substantial building in town, Roaring waters of flood in Stingaree Gulch threatened foundations but did not undermine them. Part of stone walls caved but cells still held prisoners, roaring days of Rawhide's short prosperity furnishing good supply.

the flesh or extracting even more gold by mine stock manipulation. Rawhide did not seem to care about a man's previous reputation, was not even curious about it, as in the case of one of its more prominent citizens, George Graham Rice. He had done a very good job at promoting the L. M. Sullivan Trust Co. in Goldfield, so good that $10 million had poured into its owner's pockets, almost none in the stockholders'. The whole enterprise collapsed when these stockholders ganged up on President "Shanghai Larry" Sullivan who was thoroughly bewildered to find his erstwhile aide gone with the wind and a considerable chunk of the funds. But Rice hadn't gone far, only to Rawhide where he lost no time in setting up another operation. This was so successful he contracted for a magazine series at three cents a word. With neither caution nor modesty he titled the stories, "My Adventure With Your Money". The series attracted much attention, in-

WONDER LUMBER CO. building is one of monuments to failure in town where many fortunes were made. Founder was soon called "Hard Luck Kenny" by sympathetic townsmen. Kenny had come fresh from fiasco in Portland, Oregon, where real estate venture failed. Scotty McLeod and Barker Butler staked him to have fling at mine which proved a dud. Unfortunate man met end on Black Desert when car broke down. Trying to repair engine, Kenny got gasoline on hands which ignited, burning him to death.

cluding that of federal investigators who eventually confined the activities of the promoter-author behind the discouraging bars of the federal penitentiary at Atlanta.

And there was Tex Rickard who also came over from Goldfield, attracted as others were away from the slightly frayed-at-edge camp to the new bonanza town whose star was blazing. Rickard had been operating his Goldfield Northern Saloon, in which he owned most of the stock, but liked excitement such as his fantastically successful promotion of the Joe Gans-Battling Nelson fight which brought some forty thousand people to Goldfield. His Northern Saloon had been built with money from the stake he made in the Klondike rush where he cut his teeth on the entertainment racket.

Now Goldfield was growing tiresome and Tex sold his interests to one Johnny Mays and staged a farewell party at the Northern. Feeling exuberant on his way to his Thomas Flyer he took cue chalk and scrawled on the door of an abandoned church— "This church closed. God has gone to Rawhide."

A better than average photographer, Scotty Mc-

Leod loved to record the scenes of his early mining days. One of his pictures shows the spot where he and his companions camped at what would later be Rawhide, their little white tent the only sign of habitation in the lonely desert landscape. When Rickard arrived about a year later he bought a lot next to this spot for his new Northern, paying $10,000.

At this time, the peak of prosperity in Rawhide's short but hectic life, the population was estimated at some five thousand. The camp had three banks which stayed open until midnight before there was an official post office. A large portion of a business block shows clearly in a 1909 photograph — the High Grade Bar, G and K Drug Store, Rawhide Clothing House, the Northern and Hermitage, another bar. Not shown are the other thirty-seven saloons and four churches. In addition the town boasted of a school, steam laundry, twenty-eight restaurants, the "Princess" theater, twelve hotels, telegraph and telephone lines. During the first year, it is reported, Sunday masses for Catholics were held in a saloon that closed just before dawn which gave the "church" time to clean up and carry in benches and a crude portable altar.

Then came Elinor Glyn. The lady had recently written the novel, "Three Weeks". Sufficient effort was made to suppress the sensational book to assure its popularity and Elinor G. was riding high. Rickard seized the moment to invite the lady to Rawhide to see how "the other side" lived. Mrs. Glyn accepted, possibly because Rickard had been clever enough to extend the invitation through Nat Goodwin, a friend of the now famous lady author and promoter in Rawhide. Perhaps Mrs. Glyn also saw a chance to gather some publicity while researching the seamy mining camp. She arrived by way of San Francisco with two friends, Sam Newhouse and Ray Baker. All were made welcome with every stunt the ingenious Rickard and Goodwin team could think of.

After several rounds of champagne in Rawhide's best hotel the party was escorted to a poker game in another room. The players were hired to ignore Mrs. Glyn and put on a good show for her, six shooters and all. An argument developed and the guns barked — at the ceiling. La Glyn and her friends beat a hasty retreat, tarrying outside long enough to listen for further gunfire. One horrified glance showed the "bodies" of two players being carried out.

Escorts of the Glyn Guided Tour paused only long enough to make sure she observed the stretcher bearers headed for the combination furniture-undertaker establishment, then proceeded down Stingaree Gulch. Most of the lower end of the Gulch bisecting the town was given over to cribs and the girls had been coached to make every effort to seduce Mrs. Glyn's friends.

At the far end of the street a shack was set afire, the blaze being soon extinquished by the Rawhide Volunteer Fire Department. The fire laddies made up in flashy uniforms and flourishes what the tiny pump cart and meager water supply lacked. That evening another fancy champagne dinner was served for the novelist and the next morning she and her friends left for the East properly impressed with the "innate aristocracy" of the miners of Nevada. Large bursts of publicity in national newspapers both for Mrs. Glyn and Rawhide, made everybody's efforts well worth while though many editors saw through the farce and said so.

On September first rumors came to the town of a rich strike at nearby Silver Lake and Scotty McLeod headed there with his cronies. He was gone just long enough to miss seeing the near total destruction of Rawhide. Three days after he left some-one opened a window in a back room of the Rawhide Drug Store, the resulting stream of air blowing a curtain across a gasoline stove on which lunch was being prepared. In moments the room was ablaze and before the R.V.F.D. could get there flames were shooting from several stores. Jerry-built, tinder dry frame structures, they went up like match sticks and flung blazing brands on neighboring buildings and in a few hours nine blocks of the business district were leveled. Tex Rickard watched the flames devour his Northern Saloon, rushed to the telegraph office to order building material for a new one.

The gesture was brave but futile. Rawhide was never the same. Many stores were replaced on their old sites but business failed to get its strength back. The truth, painful as it became evident, was that Rawhide had existed more on promotion, flamboyancy and stock juggling than on the bona fide production of gold and silver. Values in these metals were there but not in sufficient quantities to justify the old, extravagantly-touted Rawhide. Mining by then in Nevada had passed its peak of glamor and as once prosperous businesses failed, ghosts moved in.

Rawhide today displays a large number of picturesque old false-fronted buildings, mostly those which escaped the fire. The ghost town fan who is willing to drive long distances over gravel roads will find atmosphere in abundance in Rawhide, an outstanding example of fast boom and quick bust, of flagrant over-promotion which ballooned it beyond reason, out of all chance for a less flashy but more permanent success.

TYPICAL OF PERIOD is pressed metal sheathing for face of building. This and galvanized roofing saved these structures from disastrous fire. At left was combination store and post office, former owned by Mr. and Mrs. Leonard, wife being postmistress for over twenty years.

RHYOLITE, NEVADA

Towering concrete remnants, dazzling white in the sun, are what is left of a city that expanded almost beyond belief from the day in 1904, when Eddie Cross and the renowned "Shorty" Harris discovered their rich specimen of ore. It was a sample of what the "Bullfrog Mine" to-be would produce, until its collapse such a brief period later.

Here is a depot with no train or tracks, and the vestiges of a school built for an expected population explosion which fizzled. The first school had been ludicrously inadequate, falling far short of holding the juvenile element by the time it was finished. So the next was conceived and planned on a grandiose scale. It was used only a short time and was never filled.

The panic of 1907 shattered dreams that did not have time to become reality. Succeeding financial difficulties, foreclosures, withdrawals of public utilities and pinching out of veins battered at the city whose concrete buildings were newly finished.

By 1910 Rhyolite's 10,000 people had dwindled to a few hundred, then to a few dozen. For years only two buildings have been tenable; the depot and a unique structure made of bottles. These are occupied, and serve as museums. The city that was the "Gem of the Amargosa" is otherwise deserted.

MAIN STREET OF RHYOLITE leads past remains of one of the biggest booms in all history. The school, its future grossly overestimated, stands forlornly in ruins at lower end of street.

HOLES IN FALSE FRONT show where birds are nesting. Scraps of sheet metal have preserved building beyond life of others, warding off weather and sparks of neighboring fires.

ROCHESTER, NEVADA

Rochester is all "uphill," with the center of town occupying the only nearly level area. This is the "old town." A somewhat newer, less picturesque Rochester is first encountered at a lower level.

In what was the business section of upper Rochester only one building still stands erect. It is a typical false front of the day, once the Post Office combined with a store and living quarters.

The little sliding window for dispensing eagerly awaited mail opens from a room filled with debris. Here is an old brass bedstead, and on it a moldy mattress. For a cover it has a motheaten sheepskin coat. Also on the bed is a little booklet, tattered and stained, titled "How to Play the Zither."

All around this building are many foundations and basements giving support to the town's history of 1,500 people. That was at the height of the period between 1860 and 1913. Over all, some $10,000,000 worth of silver was produced. As usual, other metals were a by-product, sometimes paying for the cost of production.

Above the main part of town are extensive mine dumps and ruins of head-buildings. Here also are the remains of a large building, recently collapsed, that must have been a saloon and dance hall on the grand scale. Broken tables are overturned everywhere, as are chairs and carved counters. A prone stairway once led upstairs to pleasures other than gambling, an expected adjunct to any drinking place of that day.

ROCKLAND, NEVADA

Joseph Wilson had an exciting life on the ranches and in the mines of Nevada. He died at ninety-four, leaving voluminous notes and memoirs among them the story of the founding of Pine Grove and its newer, smaller neighbor, Rockland. "On September first of 1863," he wrote, "my father, David Wilson, and uncle William Wilson, bought the squatter's rights to the Wheeler farm, consisting of 4,000 acres, for $2,000."

This was unsurveyed land on which Pat Wheeler and his seven sons had squatted under Utah law in 1860, on the west fork of the Walker river in the extreme south end of Mason valley. The Wheelers had erected earth boundary mounds, three years being allowed to fence the land. Once on it, young

William Wilson was eager to go prospecting in the Pine Grove mountains, included in the ranch, but his older brother and family persuaded him to stay, help get part of the land under cultivation and start a herd of cattle. David, however, was just as anxious to find out about mineral wealth and allowed his young brother to saddle a horse once in a while and have a look around.

Of the Paiute Indians who came to the ranch begging food, most persistent was a family trio—Hog-or-Die Jim who sometimes chopped wood, his wife Hog-or-Die Mary who did the washing and their son "Bummer Charlie" who "never did anything useful". To this family, Hog-or-Die meant something like "eat high on the hog or starve."

MILL WAS ONCE much more extensive. Fire, bruising weight of snows, vandals and time have all taken toll. Stone walls date from earliest period, cement foundations coming later.

SUTRO, NEVADA

Sweet are the uses of adversity. Every time a man was killed in the building of the Sutro Tunnel in the 1870s, the other men used it as an excuse for a big time. After the funeral and burial at the cemetery in Virginia City, they hung on a big drinking party and then needed two more days to sober up.

The big hitch in this giddy round was Adolph Sutro. He wanted no delays in the building of this tunnel and did not see why the dead could not be buried right in the new town of Sutro at the mouth of the tunnel. He laid out a burial ground but the men quickly told him it wouldn't work. When a premature blast killed Kelly, they said the burial would be at Virginia City, same as usual: "Because Kelly will be lonely all by himself in that new ground."

Sutro had to swallow one more lay off but shortly a careless powder man left some loose blasting material near a battery. A spark caught it and the explosion killed two men. "Now," said Adolph Sutro in Prussian gutteral, we have the funeral here and start new cemetery." Aching for another bust, the men searched frantically for some next-of-kin to insist on carrying out the final rites on Mt. Davidson. Finding none they were forced to have the services at Sutro and get back to work the next morning.

The story of the ghost town of Sutro is the story of Adolph Sutro. It begins in Aachen (Aix-la-Chapelle) Prussia, when on April 29, 1830, Adolph Heinrich Joseph Sutro was born. One of eleven children whose father Emanuel, and uncle Simon, owned a large woollen factory. Young Adolph had many interests, in machines at the mill, exploring the heavens at night with his telescope and in botany through his many walks at the edge of town. Adolph loved books too and acquired a knowledge of general science far beyond that of his brothers which furnished a grounding for his later interest in California and Nevada mining that led to the building of the tunnel to the Comstock Lode.

In 1848 his father went on a business trip carrying a brace of pistols for protection against bandits. On the way home, not having occasion to use them, he discharged the loads in the air. The horses bolted, throwing him out of the carriage and Emanuel suffered a broken back which paralyzed him. During the year he lived, the family's funds were nearly exhausted and Adolph was compelled to leave school at sixteen.

In 1850 the young man made his big move to America. In New York he was almost immediately caught up in the California gold fever and in two weeks left for San Francisco. His crossing of the

THIS WAS CENTER OF SUTRO. At left is blacksmith shop, complete with forge, in front of it ore car on tracks which lead from mouth of tunnel at left, out of picture. At right is large warehouse. Townsite was surveyed in 1872 in neat gridiron pattern. Streets were 80 feet wide with exception of central one leading from tunnel, 200 feet wide and called Tunnel Avenue. Lots cost $500 up. Cottonwood trees may be descendants of those originally planted along avenue although Sutro preferred more exotic types some of which could not survive climate. Each lot purchaser was required to plant at least one tree and care for it.

Isthmus was the usual battle of mosquitoes, thieving natives in the guise of guides and narrow escapes from dysentery, cholera and smallpox. At Panama City he was lucky in being booked for passage to California in a week where others were held for many.

In San Francisco, where one day he would be its first citizen, he was just another foreigner. Almost starving by the time his trunks arrived, he started at once selling the German cloth and articles they contained. When he had enough money for a few meals and a ticket to Stockton where a cousin

lived, the two set up a store on the levee. He stayed with this a year or so, then returned to San Francisco with enough of a stake to start a tobacco shop and two stores. One was a supply house from which he shipped groceries and mining equipment to the Mother Lode by way of Stockton and to the Northern Mines through Sacramento. When the Trinity Mountain area was opened up at Weaverville and Shasta, Sutro shipped by water up the Sacramento River to Redding, thence to the mines by muleback, or up the Coast to Trinidad Bay where the goods were transferred to small boats on the Klam-

STRING OF ORE CARS still on tracks in middle of Tunnel Avenue. At first cars were drawn by mules, later by small electric engines.

ath River, then in turn to mules for the rest of the way along the Trinity River trail.

Then he made a false move. A year or two later when the gold rush to the Fraser River was in full swing, Adolph left his wife and two children to go north and start a cigar store in Victoria. But the first full migration was over and depression was setting in. He returned to San Francisco to hear of the new gold push to Washoe in Nevada.

He went there, to Mt. Davidson and worked out a new system of greater efficiency for recovery of gold and silver from quartz, not only from virgin ore but in old dump residue. So he settled down at Dayton, at the foot of the mountain, and organized a company, built mills with stamps and roasting ovens and was soon making $10,000 a month.

As soon as the mill was well established he sent for his brother Hugo to run it. For some time there had been a plan in Adolph's head, a plan which was to embrace every thought he had for many years. It was to build a tunnel, a horizontal bore several miles long to start at a level lower than the bottoms

of the deep shafts descending from Virginia City. Those mine shafts were suffering badly from poor ventilation, even with forced air. Temperatures in the depths were so high that water, in itself an ever increasing menace, turned to steam and the high humidity suffocated the already exhausted miners. Sutro reasoned that such an opening to the outside air would drain off the water, ventilate the mines and bring temperatures down. It would also provide a cheap exit for Comstock ores.

With Hugo to take care of things at the mills, Sutro traveled all over the area by horseback, seeking out a logical spot for starting such a tunnel. As a skilled amateur surveyor, he actually lined up the nearly nine-mile tunnel to connect with the bottom of the Savage mine shaft so accurately that 13 years later, when the last charge of powder was set off, it caved in a hole in the side of the shaft.

The hard part was raising the money. Adolph Sutro would never have imagined anyone would stand in the way of such a humanitarian project, one that would benefit everyone, but he proved to be less a logician than he was engineer. He pointed out that with the tunnel completed, the necessity for Virginia City would be eliminated, that all mills and operations would then move to his new town to be named Sutro, where all mining operations and ore refining could be carried out on a level with the present operations.

The interests controlling the wealth of Virginia City would listen to no talk of this kind. The most formidable foe of Sutro and his plan was the Bank of California. It had already foreclosed on a number of Comstock mines, where poor management and less-rich ores had forced insolvency, and it owned many huge mills not only at Virginia City but on down the grade at Silver City and Gold Hill. Furthermore it was planning to build a railway to the city on top of the mountain for prospective patrons of the banks, hotels and restaurants and to haul practically all equipment and supplies to the mines — a veritable monopoly with the wagon roads so steep and rough. If Sutro's tunnel was ever built it would certainly be against the interests of these enterprises.

While William Sharon and other powers of the bank sat at conference planning strategy, Sutro was making contracts with mine owners that he was sure would enable him to start digging. His proposition was simple. He would drain the pesky hot water from their mines and even haul out their ores to the string of mills he would build along the Carson River — all this for free. Then for only $1 per ton he would mill all ores assaying up to $35 per ton, over that $2. The bargain was accepted by many, reluctantly by some, and Sutro agreed to start work by August 1, 1867, spending not less than $400,000 each year to speed completion of the tunnel.

He delayed only long enough to secure additional equipment and mules but the delay was disastrous. Sharon and other big men in the Comstock went to the mine owners, pointing out what to do if they knew what was good for them. So when Sutro was ready to start work, he found there was no money available and there would not be any, that almost every contract was being ignored.

DURING TUNNEL DIGGING DAYS large numbers of mules were used at Sutro, housed in this barn. Drilling and blasting equipment was hauled into dark tunnel by docile animals, each carrying own "headlight". Small building at entrance to tunnel was stocked with collar torches and oil, crew of young boys placing lighted torch in mule's collar as it entered, removing beacon as it emerged. Animals were invaluable to project, were well cared for, had good pasture along Carson River.

SUTRO AS IT APPEARS TODAY from site of mansion. In foreground are fireplace bricks and fancy metal cap which topped chimney. Blacksmith shop and warehouse show at right center. Tunnel opens at point about 200 feet this side of small buildings at extreme right. In distance is Carson Valley, river marked by trees.

Rather than sue, Sutro went to Washington where he appealed in vain to Congress for a subsidy. Sharon had already telegraphed representatives of the Bank of California in the capitol to block any move Sutro might make. Sutro tried to interest financiers William Astor and Commodore Vanderbilt and others only to be snubbed. Back in Nevada he tried to persuade legislators to put up money to start work already ratified by them but again the Sharon shadow stood in his way. As if the Bank of California were not enough to block his efforts, Sutro found another obstacle forming. A group called the "Big Four", Mackey, Fair, Flood

and O'Brien, bonanza kings of the Comstock, was becoming ever more powerful. These men also threw their weight against Sutro, recognizing in the projected tunnel a menace to their whole empire.

Then on April 7, 1869, tragedy struck in the Yellowjacket mine — fire that took the lives of forty-five men. Some members of the crew were rescued by raising them in the open "cage" but others died in the same operation, being so weak they fell against the sides of the shaft and were crushed by the rising platform. The rest, except for three who were actually burned to death, died of suffocation below. The disaster caused great feeling in Virginia City and Sutro took advantage of it, believing firmly that the proposed tunnel would avert future disasters like this by providing a means of escape.

On September 20 he made an impassioned speech for his project at Piper's Opera House. The reaction to the miners was overwhelmingly in favor of the tunnel, some even volunteering to lynch Sharon and the "Big Four". The ENTERPRISE, heretofore reluctant to print anything favoring the tunnel, now broke the speech across the entire front page. Popular sentiment was on Sutro's side and his project now had some backing. The miners even pledged enough funds so construction of the tunnel could begin October 19, 1869.

But even thousands of dollars supplied by miners were only a drop in the bucket compared to the millions needed, and the big money still had its feet planted solidly in the way. Congress eventually sent a commission to investigate the mines and the claimed need to run a tunnel to them. Of course the bank and the four Irishmen saw to it the committee of stuffed shirts never saw the steaming depths, never breathed air made intolerably fetid by heat, humidity, explosive fumes and sweating men. The investigators returned to Washington with the report that there was no real need for a tunnel, especially since the Virginia City powers had finished their railroad. Blow that this was, Sutro held stubbornly to the remaining benefits that would accrue.

Then came the first real money, $2,500,000, from McClamont's Bank in London, where Sutro had applied. Now began the pattern of going broke, getting money again, a succession lasting to completion of the tunnel 13 long years and $5 million later.

Even after the bore itself, twelve feet wide and nine feet high, had broken through to the bottom of the first mine, connecting branches to other mines must be built and a three-foot square trough laid down the middle to carry off the hot water

TOWN OF SUTRO about 1880. At extreme left is Sutro's mansion, rectangle of water beside it called by him an "artificial lake", by scoffers "Sutro's Frog Pond". It was aptly named, Sutro having stocked it first with fish and ducks, then insisted on bullfrogs also. These proving unavailable, not being native to western states, he settled for largest he could get. True bullfrogs have since populated Carson River, having been introduced much later. Warehouse building at right (with four windows on end) still stands as do many others. Courtesy Nevada State Museum.

TUNNEL OPENING 94 years after start of construction. Scene marks head of Tunnel Avenue, 200-foot wide thoroughfare down which passed ore cars headed for mill at foot. Also coming out of opening was steaming stream of water drained from deep mines of Comstock Lode. Water still gushes forth but from spring 2,000 feet back.

as promised. The trough would handle in one year alone, 1880, more than two billion gallons of steaming water.

Completion of the big job dealt a severe blow to the town of Sutro which was started to house and feed workmen. With construction crews laid off away went the town's main support. There was only the mill for processing tunnel-brought ores and the barns for housing mules used to draw ore carts through the bore. And Sutro continued for a time to live in the mansion he had built just above the tunnel.

But the sad fact was, by the time the long delayed Sutro tunnel was completed, the Comstock day of glory was ending. Royalties on ore hauled through it did pay the cost of building but that was about all. Sutro himself soon got out from under, the incentive of struggle gone. He sold his stock in the company and went on to other conquests in the city that was to be his home for the rest of his life — San Francisco.

The only residents of Sutro now are Robin Larson and his family. He writes: "I first saw the Sutro Tunnel site in the spring of 1959 on an automobile trip east with my father. At that time there was a caretaker. In the spring of 1962 I traveled to Nevada to see the Sutro Tunnel again and found it deserted with signs to the effect that it was destined to become a state park. The place interested

MULE PULLS LITTLE TRAIN carrying work crew from tunnel mouth about 1890. During construction days several attempts were made to use other power than mules. Horses failed, proving flighty and not tolerating heat. Mules worked longer in high temperatures until suddenly dropping dead as if shot. Most mechanical contrivances failed because of lack of ventilation causing fatal fumes to accumulate. Courtesy Nevada Historical Society.

238

CONE OF NUT PINE Pinus Monophylla, showing several "nuts" still attached. Cones are formed during summer, remain as small prickly balls until following season when growth is rapid. Late in second summer green cone is solid, hard and dripping with sparkling, clear, fragrant pitch or resin. In September they begin to open and shed seeds. Nuts were once staple article of diet for Indians who beat limbs with sticks to bring cones down. Fire was built over heaps of cones which caused quick opening of scales and release of nuts. Heat also dissipated small quantity of turpentine which made unroasted nuts bitter and inedible.

me very much and it disturbed me to see that it was deserted. People were breaking and stealing things at such a rapid rate that there was a great change since I had seen it last. I decided to make a personal effort to protect it until it should become a park.

"With the cooperation of the Nevada State Park System and the Comstock Tunnel and Drainage Company (the owners) I took up residence at the tunnel portal and lived there for a year, protecting the place, cleaning it up and campaigning to make it into a state park. The state refused to accept Sutro and rather than see it destroyed and looted and because I had fallen in love with the place, the history and the country, I took up a lease and I intend to preserve the tunnel portal and the existing eighteen buildings as an historical monument. I don't want to restore, only to prevent any further decay."

When they came to the ranch one day, David had no wood to be chopped so brought out a chunk of gold ore showing definite flecks of the yellow metal. He asked Hog-or-Die Jim in a jumble of Paiute and sign language: "Do you know where there is any more rock like this?" The Indian indicated he did and pointed out a location in the hills above the ranch, three and a half miles south of Mt. Etna in the Pine Grove mountains.

David now turned William loose with abandon and after some diligent search he found a gold deposit. The Wilsons then gave their full attention to mining. From the time the find was made in 1866 to about 1871 Pine Grove developed to a population of over 1,000. The three original arrastras owned by Portuguese Joe grew to several power stamp mills using steam from boilers fired by nut pine wood. The ore was known as "free-milling", the easiest type of work, needed only to be washed and crushed in sluices. In later years a mill was built to rework some of the waste, but most of the gold had been recovered by the cruder method.

The town was a boisterous one. (Ed: this information differs sharply from that gathered earlier which declared the Wilsons to be "Blue Nose" meaning intolerant of drinking or gambling, that miners went to nearby Rockland for diversion). See Pine Grove, WESTERN GHOST TOWNS. Joseph Wilson relates that Pine Grove had two sections, that "there were five saloons in the upper part and three in the lower, with a dance hall in the middle". There were also three hotels, Wells Fargo office and a large general store. The barber shop and shoeshine parlor was operated by a colored man who charged fifty cents for a haircut, twenty-five for a shine. The post office charged three cents for sending a letter in competition with the express company which charged an exhorbitant five.

With so many people drawn to an area where a few years before there had been no one, the surrounding hills got a close examination for precious metals. And in 1869 a Pine Grove resident, a Mr. Keene, found a rich vein of silver and gold three and a half miles from his home. As quickly as he could he built a quartz mill in Bridgeport Canyon just below his mine. He called the lively little town that grew up around the mine and mill Rockland, presumably for the fantastic and beautiful red rock cliffs towering over the location.

Keene had trouble keeping his expenses below his money intake. His men were paid irregularly and when no money was forthcoming they set up a howl. One in particular, a Mr. Rhodes, trouble maker at best, threatened to get even and when Keene was away raising money for the payroll, Rhodes set fire to the mill. He was arrested, convicted of arson and sent to the state prison. Keene got deeper in debt, finally lost control of the mine and ex-Gov. Blaisedell tried his hand at operating it and also failed. Then C. D. Lane stepped in, got some ore out but he too was unsuccessful. The mine was deserted and Tom Flynn stayed on as watchman for years, at length buying an interest in the claim and running some ore through the mill.

During this period a boulder showing chunks of gold and weighing several hundred pounds was found nearby. It assayed $500 to the ton and created great excitement. The chunk was definitely a huge piece of float from some rich lode near the area. Hordes of prospectors tried to locate the source but all failed and Rockland settled back to doze again.

The LYON COUNTY TIMES of Nov. 24, 1894, reported this item: FATAL ACCIDENT AT PINE GROVE. Last Monday morning between 8 and 9, John Redding, who was working on the Wilson tailing dump in Pine Grove, was caved upon and buried under tons of dirt. As soon as the accident happened, a force of men began to dig for the unfortunate man. After several tons of dirt had been removed, the body was found but life had been crushed out of it. The deceased was a native of Missouri, aged 26 and came to Nevada about 5 years ago. He leaves a father, three sisters and two brothers. The funeral took place Thursday at the Grove and was largely attended."

By 1948 Tom Flynn was thoroughly discouraged over his property, cleaned his little cabin and headed his old car down the mountain grade to think things over in town — maybe raise money or abandon the pesky thing. Just as Flynn drove into the canyon where the road in the defile is extremely steep, rocky and narrow, a torrent of rain he later termed as a "water spout" struck the rocky walls. The deluge of muddy water took out all semblance of road and carried Flynn and the car down into the gulch. He spent fourteen hours, he said, in reaching the town. No mind searching was needed. The decision had been reached. Tom Flynn kept driving on to leave his now inaccessible perch in the Pine Grove mountains to the buzzards.

LITTLE ROCKLAND LODGING HOUSE, once painted bright red, is faded but still upright. In back is large sleeping porch, open to breezes which at this altitude are considerable and the snows which are deep and long lasting. Nut pines show needle arrangement and bark texture.

TONOPAH, NEVADA

The story of the Mizpah Mine and its discovery has been told in several forms, but the most likely version is the one in which William Hall tried to boot his partner, Jim Butler, out of his blankets one spring morning in 1900, and failed. They had started from Butler's ranch on a trip to Southern Klondyke, a small mining camp. Fifteen miles short of their objective they came to Tonapah Springs and camped there.

Next morning, the early-rising Hall unable to rouse Butler, went on alone disgusted. In his own good time Butler arose, only to find his burros had "vamoosed" over the ridge. After tracking them down, he was pretty much out of sorts and picked up a rock to heave at them, but held on to it, not out of consideration for his beasts, but because the stone was flecked with mineral.

After locating the vein's source, he caught his burros and hurried to overtake his partner. Nothing much was happening in Southern Klondyke, however, and the partners soon returned to Belmont, gathering a few more samples at Tonopah Springs on the way.

It was Butler's wife who really started the ball rolling. She enlisted expert help in the person of Tasker L. Oddie, who was to figure prominently in Tonopah's subsequent history. Oddie, for an interest in the stake, had assays run proving the value of the samples would run $350 per ton.

Mrs. Butler staked a claim near Oddie's, naming it the Mizpah. This was one of the richest producers in the entire area.

There followed the usual influx; the sudden boom. Streets were laid out by Walter Gayhart, who saw fit to make his money in real estate rather than the sweaty job of mining.

Tonopah's heyday was the period centered about 1905, when it wrested the County Seat from Belmont. By 1913 there were definite signs that things were not going too well, and before long the big days were finished, having seen the production of $250,000,000 in gold and silver.

Tonopah is not dead, however. Some mining still goes on. The main street, flanked by the five-story Mizpah Hotel and many clubs, stores and restaurants, is still busy. Features of the town are the high curbs on each side. They rise to the height of about three feet and preclude stepping up just anywhere. The purpose of these is to channel the flood waters of frequent "gulley-washers" that pour through town.

The area is a veritable gem field, full of petrified wood, jasper and other semi-precious material.

STORM BUILDS UP over Tonopah. Town is at base of Mt. O d d i e (right) whose sides a n d summit are eroded by diggings.

TUSCARORA, NEVADA

Nearing Tuscarora one first sees the cemetery, its white headstones and boards conspicuous against the gray-green sage and brown earth. Then comes the red brick smelter stack so noticeable on the hill above the town.

It is surprising to see a little stream of ice cold water running right across the road. How blessed was Tuscarora! Among Nevada mining camps few had an abundance of good water. Not that the miners cared much for the stuff for drinking. And Tuscarora had no wish to be unique, its population imbibing more whiskey than water. It was as wild and rip-roaring a camp as any, and worse than some. Its biggest decades were from 1870 to 1890 when several thousand whites and two thousand Chinese kept excitement going.

The Chinese came to build the Central Pacific Railroad and remained to dispense opium in a dark underground section of the town, concealed by an innocent looking China Town. For a time at least, they also ran most of the brothels and gambling joints. Some of these were behind and under laundries and others brazenly exposed, with red lights hanging at the doors of the cribs.

The town of the euphonius name and beautiful situation on Mount Blitzen produced $40,000,000, in silver mostly, so it must have buckled down to work daytimes.

VAULT SEEMS TO INDICATE ruins might have been bank. Under many respectable buildings in Tuscarora were opium dens, other houses of vice.

SHIMMERING GHOSTS OF THE DESERT

UNIONVILLE, NEVADA

Spence Davidson, one of the residents along the creek, allows he arrived in town "quite a while ago!" He gives some data on Unionville.

"Quite a while ago" turned out to be 1890. "Was the town busy then?" "No, it was really dead even then; it had an early start, about 1860." Unionville saw only about ten really good, boom years, and was almost finished by 1880. In this brief period the place had undergone sudden expansion, with 20 new people moving in every day at first. These new residents soon needed, first, nine saloons; then 10 stores, an express office, livery stables and, at the fringe, the inevitable red light district. The girls of the cribs at first did very well, but many families moved to Unionville which, with its water and shade, offered more comforts than starker camps. The proportion of single men shrank and so did the "houses."

But the schools grew, and today the best preserved building is the one on the hill, facing the town. Several ranchers in the valley had as many as six children and these kept the school going until a few years ago. The last teacher was Mrs. Hammersmark, a sister-in-law of Mr. Davidson. She passed away recently in Reno.

Unionville, by virtue of its quick expansion, in the early 70's had become the seat of the then Humboldt County. The Courthouse was in a rented saloon in its early years. During Unionville's period of activity, it had produced some $3,000,000, largely in silver. The Arizona mine above the town had been the big one, with more than a third of the total to its credit.

Close by are the ruins of a small mill, and close to them the opening of the gold mine. From this cavern bursts a torrent of air of about 50 degrees, startlingly luxurious in the noonday heat of the Humboldt Foothills.

The cemetery on the way to the main road is large, but with many headboards missing. Those remaining mostly bear dates in the 70's, when the population had reached its peak of some 2,000 to 3,000. Many graves are enclosed in the usual ornate wooden fences. There certainly is a much larger population here now than in Unionville itself.

BUENA VISTA SCHOOL has not sheltered pupils for years but is in good condition. Heating stove stands in center, surrounded by desks graduated in size for different grades. Map of Africa on wall was made in 1887.

SPOOKS OF THE SHIFTING SANDS

VIRGINIA CITY, NEVADA

Virginia City is among the best known of the old camps. The town is neither dead nor abandoned, but nevertheless it is popularly considered a ghost town.

It is situated almost on top of a mountain, offering spreading views of the Nevada terrain in several directions. It has larger buildings than most and more of them. It has as interesting history as any, and since it has never been completely abandoned, most of the past has been preserved in print. The delver into the story of Virginia City can spend days or weeks among relics, books and newspapers on display on the spot where it all happened.

MANY BUILDINGS in Virginia City retain charm of early days.

ORIGINAL ATMOSPHERE still exists away from "C" Street.

IMPRESSIVE RELIC is Fourth Ward School. Located near south end of town on "C" St., it once provided vantage point from which to view spectacular cave-in across street. Sizable area collapsed into cavern created by mines which honeycomb ground under city.

BRICK BUILDING IS often called John Mackay residence. Structure was actually union mine office. Mr. Mackay did stay here whenever he visited Virginia City on business.

RIDERS IN THE SKY

SUPPLY CENTER ON THE TRUCKEE

Wadsworth, Nevada

To those weary travelers plodding toward California's golden El Dorado, the stopping place on the green banks of a river called Truckee was heaven on earth. Many of those who spent searing weeks in crossing the sands of the Great Basin plunged their dehydrated bodies into the river's clear waters. Twenty years later this welcome oasis was the site of a settlement, Wadsworth.

The Truckee is only 105 miles long. Beginning as a clear mountain stream in the High Sierra, over 6,000 feet above sea level, fed by waters overflowing from Lake Tahoe, it ends decimated by irrigation usage as a thick, silt-laden dribble in brackish Pyramid Lake. Famed Chief Winnemucca was said to have a son named Truckee and called the river that in his honor. However the Spanish name for trout is *trucha*, and as the river was called the Salmon Trout by Capt. John Fremont, that may be the true derivation of the name.

The Truckee makes its last sharp turn a few miles south of its end. Just north of Wadsworth it enters Pyramid Lake Reservation, established by President Grant March 23, 1874, for benefit of the Paiute inhabitants of the region. They lived largely on fish, especially the enormous cutthroat trout teeming in the river and Pyramid Lake. What they could not eat they sold to immigrants and later settlers.

The place once called the "Big Bend" is about 2,000 feet below the point where the Truckee emerges from Lake Tahoe. It was here Fremont left the stream he paralleled while descending the steep slopes of the Sierra in January, 1844, and where the pioneers taking this route west stopped, rested and then forded at a point just below the bend, a shallow place they termed "Lower Crossing." Some without the courage to climb over the mountain barricade called High Sierra, stayed and built shanties, living on fish and game while their stock grew fat on luxuriously growing grass. No town or settlement of any size resulted however until the advent of the Central Pacific Railroad.

The spot was a strategic one for the railroad. For the push east across a vast expanse of desert there would be no more wood or water for the engines. So at first Wadsworth served as a supply depot in the building of the line, then in 1868 became a permanent and important station. Settlers there now made a comfortable living cutting and hauling wood from fringes of the timbered mountains and the tenuous town became solid. Stores were established, hotels, saloons and gambling places sprouted like mushrooms as railroad building and maintenance crews roistered. Car shops for the Truckee division, extending from Truckee to Winnemucca, were located at the river's bend. These with work shops steadily employed a large number of men, roundhouse containing twenty stalls.

As soon as the railroad was completed to this point it became the base for supplies to mines then active to the south in Churchill, Nye and Esmeralda Counties. An old *History of Nevada* reads, "The excellent roads leading to Ellsworth, Columbus, Belmont and other towns are lined with long freight teams conveying goods and supplies from Wadsworth. As long as those points are supplied by freight wagons, Wadsworth will get the bulk of the traffic, but as soon as one of the proposed railroads invades that region the freighting business will materially decline. At the present time the population of about 500 are busy and prosperous."

For two years Wadsworth was a bone of contention between Washoe and Lyon Counties because of boundary uncertainties. It had been assumed the line followed the "old emigrant road" but the people of Lyon County discovered traces of a "cut off" which they insisted was the main route. If conceded this would leave Wadsworth in Lyon County which they wanted. Jurisdiction over Wadsworth had always been exercised by Washoe authorities and with Lyon's brazen attempt to take over a rich source of tax money, they took the matter to court. The case was tried twice in Ormsby County without arriving at a solid decision. A third attempt in Humboldt County cleared the matter for Washoe in 1871.

For some reason the section of railroad in the vicinity of Wadsworth was accident prone. The most spectacular near-disaster from the point of casualties was on June 13, 1872. Passenger car No. 1 passed over a broken rail six miles west of town. The two rear coaches jumped the track but plunged on, held upright by the rocky walls of the cut, dragged along to the end of it where they leaped down and were demolished. Had they tipped the other way they would have rolled into the canyon of the Truckee with great loss of life. As it was no one was killed although many were seriously injured.

COLUMBUS HOTEL, long abandoned, and little church with tottering weather vane stand alone in what was busy part of town. It was founded by overland emigrants on their way to California gold fields, stimulated by coming of railroad, nurtured as supply center for booming camps just south of Wadsworth. Collapse came with inevitable failure of mining camps to survive.